# Trail of Snow
# River of Ice

## By Marte Franklin

TRAIL OF SNOW~RIVER OF ICE

Rivers and Trails Books
Published by E. Blok Press.

martejsb@netzero.net
M. Franklin
555 East Arrellaga Street, Suite 8
Santa Barbara, CA 93103

Printed in the United States by CreateSpace.

ISBN 978-0-615-96070-8

## DEDICATION

This book is dedicated to all those who enjoy our National Parks and Parks Canada. For it is there that the natural beauty of our countries, its trails and its rivers, its history and important events, bring peace to all who venture therein.

# ACKNOWLEDGEMENTS

My grateful thanks to:

My many friends who encouraged me to write this book—including Sally Wilcox who joined me to hike the Chilkoot Trail from Skagway, Alaska, to Lake Bennett in northwest Canada, and then canoed down the Yukon River from Whitehorse to Dawson City, Yukon, Canada. This book begins on the family farm of a childhood friend, Winifred Waite Bobolz. This farm in Clinton, Wisconsin, brings back happy memories of living Clinton, and even now years later, I can draw a picture of the big farm kitchen and the happy Sunday dinners we shared together.

Special thanks to Cristi Franklin, Jan Cibull, Mary Keogan, Barbara Little, Mary Anne Rounds, and Sylvia Morikawa who proofread the copies; my heartfelt appreciation to Judy Herrick and Laura Little for working with me as I tried to learn the intricacies of the computer; thanks to PIP Printing for my working copies. Two others who helped beyond all measure and who have since passed away are Sylvia Oleksak who, even though she lived across the country, read chapter after chapter and made many positive corrections; and Jack Schumacker who drew the maps. Thanks also to John Vanderheide, M. D., who advised me about the effects of hiking on women. Special thanks to Dana Petersen for the book cover design.

I am eternally grateful for the time I spent reading and researching at the Klondike Gold Rush National Historical Park in Skagway, Alaska, and the Yukon Archives in Whitehorse, Yukon, Canada.

# TRAIL OF SNOW ~
## RIVER OF ICE

## HISTORICAL PROLOGUE - GOLD!

In the far north of Canada, three men, George Washington Carmack and his two Indian friends, Skookum Jim and Tagish Charley, stopped for the night by a small stream. These men were prospectors searching for gold, finding little, but ever on the move, panning one stream after another, always seeking that elusive strike which would prove to be the grandest of all. At the end of a day spent panning and finding little color, the three men made camp for the night. After the cook fire was built, Carmack stretched out for a nap while Skookum Jim and Tagish Charley went down to Rabbit Creek for water. As they kneeled by the creek, they saw on the rocks and ledges gold beyond their wildest dreams. Waking Carmack, the three panned for only a few short minutes, recovering gold worth $4 a pan. Gold at 10 cents a pan was good prospecting. This, they knew, was the discovery of a lifetime, a discovery which would change that part of the world forever!

The day was August 16, 1896. The next day, August 17, G.W. Carmack staked his claim by writing a note, nailing it on a tree, giving the date, and signing his name. By law his was the Discovery Claim, and as such he could claim five hundred feet of land on each side of the creek.

Carmack then left for the town of Fortymile, 42 miles downriver to register his claim. As was the custom of the prospectors in the Yukon Valley of northwest Canada, he told many others of his strike as he went along. The one person he did not tell was his friend,

Robert Henderson, who had found small amounts of gold in a creek he named Gold Bottom and had shared that news with Carmack. But in derogatory words, Henderson had added that he did not want the Indians, Skookum Jim and Tagish Charley, to have any part of the gold. This angered Carmack, so much that he refused to go over the nearby hill to tell Henderson of his good fortune. By his own vengeful words, Henderson missed out on the greatest gold rush in history and died almost penniless within a few years.

At Fortymile, Carmack went to Bill McPhee's saloon to share his good news and set up drinks for all, another custom. As he talked of the gold strike, no one believed him, calling him "Lying George" behind his back. Carmack had a reputation of always stretching the truth. Nonetheless, the men crowded around to examine the gold Carmack spilled out on the bar from an empty rifle shell casing. After all, a gold discovery was good news, and this just might be something big, though many were skeptical of Carmack and his discovery.

It was a known fact that gold found in one creek differed in color, texture, and shape from gold found in another creek or valley. And this gold was different. It was not like gold found near Fortymile or in other creeks in the area. As whispers spread in the saloon, many thought maybe he'd gotten the gold from a miner in another district as they might expect "Lying George" to do. Yet, this tale might be true. Quickly, the men began to leave one by one or in small groups, headed for Rabbit Creek with a dream of a fortune to be found just for the taking. After Carmack legally filed his claim at the Police Post no one called him "Lying George" again.

Almost immediately Rabbit Creek became known as Bonanza Creek. Men staked claims as fast as they could get to Bonanza Creek and other streams in the area. Arguments broke out between friends, claim lines were changed by others - called claim jumping - and confusion reigned as men scrambled for the best piece of ground. Some men even staked claims on the top of a hill. Other men just shook their heads. "Gold is found in creeks, not on the top of a hill," they taunted the men. But these prospectors soon realized they had staked their claim on an ancient river bottom and had one of the richest claims. Word of the gold strike spread with lightning speed through the country. Before freeze-up in 1896 when the Yukon River and its tributaries froze for the winter, boats crowded the mouth of the Klondike River and lined the banks of the Yukon River.

Still, some who staked claims then began to question the word of the Indian lover, "Siwash" George. "Siwash" was a scornful term for Indians and those who liked them. Others staked claims but simply did not work them, and many even failed to file their claims legally. To many, the Klondike was not a valley of gold. "The valley was too broad." "The willows grew on the wrong side of the creek." "The area was nothing but a moose meadow." Many were the reasons for this not being a good discovery. The area just didn't "look" right.

By the end of August 1896, less than two weeks from the time Carmack filed his claim, Bonanza Creek and all adjacent creeks and rivers were fully staked. Few really believed that this small bit of the vast Yukon wilderness, in a land locked up by winter nine months of

Marte Franklin

the year, would become the ultimate destination of 90,000 to 100,000 men, women, and even children within the next two years. To those miners who staked claims and legally filed them, the hard work was just beginning.

By the summer of 1897 word of the gold strike had leaked out from the North Country, but no one could imagine the extent of the discovery. On July 15, 1897, the ship *Excelsior* docked in San Francisco. News of the old, rusted ship's pending arrival had brought thousands of San Franciscans to the docks to catch a glimpse of the new millionaires. As the ship approached, those waiting saw shabbily-dressed grizzled miners, old beyond their years, standing at the railing. Their worn trousers were still coated with Yukon mud. The flannel shirts and jackets were tattered or patched in the elbows. Rubber work boots were split or worn nearly through. But there was something about them that fascinated the onlookers.

As the men struggled down the gangplank carrying old suitcases and grips tied with ropes to hold them together, packing crates strapped with heavy leather bands, and bedrolls taking two men to lift, the crowd on the docks realized these men were carrying loads far beyond what a suitcase or a bedroll should weigh. They were carrying gold, lots of gold! Others carried gold in pickle jars, coffee cans, and even tied up in worn and dirty blankets.

Two days later, on the morning of July 17, exactly eleven months after Carmack registered his claim, the ship *Portland* steamed into Seattle at 6:30 in the morning. Awaiting her arrival were over five thousand men and women wanting to see for themselves what these miners carried. The same scene was played out again as the miners left the ship, struggling under the weight of the gold. The phrase "Ton of Gold" was instantly coined. To a country trying to recover from a depression, this was the greatest news ever. Newspaper reporters in San Francisco and Seattle raced to get out the news in banner headlines. The *Seattle Post-Intelligencer* had sent a small boat with reporters to intercept the *Portland* while she was still at sea so they could have the first headline:

**GOLD! GOLD! GOLD! GOLD!**
**68 Rich Men on**
**the Steamer *Portland***
**STACKS OF YELLOW METAL!**

The news spread across the country like wildfire as each new edition of any newspaper came off the press. Men quit their jobs, if they had them. Firemen and policemen walked away from work. The mayor of Seattle, in San Francisco attending a conference when the *Excelsior* docked, left immediately for the north, not even bothering to return to Seattle and resign. Butchers left meat cleavers beside the meat they were trimming, took off their aprons and headed for the docks. Doctors left patients. Lawyers closed their doors and walked away. Preachers left churches without leadership. Men from the farms, men from the coal mines of Kentucky and Pennsylvania, men from everywhere, went home to pack and head for the Yukon. Few had any idea where the Klondike was or how to get there.

Though few in number, women came as nurses and teachers knowing they would be needed. Others came for the adventure or as "women of the night" - anything for a chance at the gold. In Pittsburgh a man advertised for poor but respectable women to go north to attract wealthy husbands. A woman professor wanted young women to go to the Klondike to experience the wonders of nature in its finest. It seemed that everyone had gold fever, and the mad rush for a fortune in gold many believed was lying around just waiting to be shoveled up began with a shout, a hope, and a dream.

From Canada, the United States, England, Europe, and as far away as Australia and Africa, ships left for the gold fields. Ships of all kinds were pressed into service. Derelicts that had been condemned were hastily repaired. Barges, yachts, old schooners, and junks from China became part of the armada of ships heading to Alaska and the Klondike. Ticket prices doubled and tripled as men fought to get on the first ships north. Nothing could discourage them. The gold was north, and that was where the men and women were headed. Those who had stashed away a few gold coins under mattresses, in cookie jars, and in boxes on closet shelves got out their money and made ready to leave immediately.

The greatest gold rush in history began with a shout and a rush by thousands to get to the gold fields as soon as possible. For surely the first there would be the next ones who would return home millionaires!

# 1

THE JOURNAL OF MRS. WINNIFRED
("FREDDIE") STANTON
A NEW BEGINNING AND A NEW
DIRECTION – NORTH

April 14, 1898 - Sheep Camp – the Dream

The mental pictures of what tomorrow will bring keep running through my mind, and I can't sleep. I've listened to the men describe the climb up those 1500 icy steps to the top of the Chilkoot Pass, and I wonder if I can make even one trip to the top. Yet, the men have climbed up so many times during the past weeks, always with at least fifty pounds on their backs, and I will climb with only my satchel.

Each has made twenty or more trips up those steps, and I will go up only once! I should be asleep, but I keep thinking about everything we have been through since we first heard of the gold discovery in August last year. So much has happened since then. We've come so far, endured so much, and now it comes down to one terror filled day up to the summit.

I remember that awful ship ride up the coast from Seattle to Skagway, the smell of the horses and dogs tied on deck, and the hectic landing in Skagway where thugs and thieves tried to steal anything they could get their hands on. Then this snow covered trail, with the ever present threat of avalanches and the wind making it feel much colder than the 20 degrees it actually was now, have kept us on edge and robbed us of much needed energy. What about Malinda? Will she ever be able to find us once we're over the top?

Now, almost everything is at the summit, and the sledges are packed with the few remaining crates. Tomorrow we will climb the Pass for the last time, enter Canada and push on to the lakes where we must build a boat and wait for the ice to break on the Yukon River and the lakes before we can even begin the long 550 mile river trip to the gold fields of Dawson City. We've come so far, done so much and yet I can't help but think of all the work we still must do before we can begin to realize our dream of finding the gold.

I turn over, pressing my back against my husband, Leonard, for extra warmth, pull the blanket up tight around my neck, and close my eyes. Even now, the memory of that last morning in Wisconsin over two months ago brings back such warm feelings. I can almost smell the bread baking.

Tuesday, February 15, 1898 – Clinton, Wisconsin,
in the Big Farm Kitchen

The aroma of freshly baked bread filled the room as I sat in the cozy, warm kitchen watching Mom cook breakfast. I usually helped, but today she insisted I just sit and talk with her as she prepared breakfast for the family.

I was sitting in my favorite old chair, a dark oak pressed-back desk chair, worn with years of use at the old roll-top desk. My legs were drawn up and crossed at the ankles, my feet on the chair seat, and my chin rested on my knees. My warm flannel gown reached down over my legs and feet, hanging in folds along the front of the chair. With my arms clasped around my legs, I felt as though I was holding all the love I had close to me. I wanted to stay this way forever or at least not forget what good feelings were found in this marvelous kitchen.

I closed my eyes and took a deep breath hoping, actually praying, that I would not forget this warm and wonderful place and the smell of the fresh baked bread in the many months to come. So many memories, thoughts, and picture images I wanted to keep close to my heart and remember always.

This was our last day on the farm. In a few hours Leonard, his best friend Walt, and I would be leaving. Tears slid down my face as I thought of the love of my maiden Auntie Pete who raised me after both my parents died of influenza when I was only 7 years old. She was a most loving person, and I wish she were here now so I could tell her how much I loved her. I am also sure the tears were for Mom and Pops, my loving in-laws. I thought of the day we first heard of the gold strike and began to make our plans to go north. We were about to begin a journey that was almost impossible to imagine.

You see, it all started on August 19th last year, 1897. Leonard, Mom, and I were shopping in town for groceries and farm supplies when Leonard ran up to us holding a newspaper showing the big headline reading **Gold – Tons of Gold Found in the Yukon.** The article

3

in the paper told of the first men to return from the gold fields who were millionaires. The article said men found nuggets as big as plums in the rivers all for the picking. Now the country was going crazy with gold fever.

One man implored, "Why, young men go North! Git y'ur gold and in jest a few weeks you 'kin come home millionaires y'urselves! It ain't hard work, and the trip ain't so difficult that the little woman cain't go with ya!" The papers carried stories of old men and young who had struck it rich.

Leonard threw his hat in the air and hugged us both. He decided right then to go to the Yukon. On the way home he only talked about the Yukon and the gold. You would have thought he had already packed and was ready to leave. There seemed to be no stopping him. Mom finally said, "Enough of this talk. There's work to do on the farm right now, and you can't just up and leave it all to Pops and your brother."

That night at supper talk revolved around the farm work, almost as if Mom's words had changed his plans, but I knew there was something going on in Leonard's mind. Finally, when the hot, spicy apple pie was served, Leonard told of the article in the paper. He had his head bowed, and he started speaking very quietly, but his voice grew more excited as he went on.

"I'm going to the Yukon. And I'm gonna get the gold, enough gold to pay off the farm debts, buy the new farm equipment we really need, and build a house for Freddie and me. This will be my way to help the family. The men who've come back millionaires said it won't take more than a few months of work. So I won't be gone long. Give me this opportunity, please. Pops, you've worked hard all your life and insisted we kids finish school and then follow our dreams. Well, this is my dream, and I want to go. This is a way I can help, and I want this chance."

Mom and I just looked at each other. Could he really get enough gold to change our lives so much? Oh, and by the way, where was this Yukon where all the gold was supposed to be anyway?

Leonard got up from the table and went to his Mom, kneeled down beside her, took her hands in his and said, "Mom, you deserve this and so does Pops. I want to do this for the family and for Freddie and me. Mom! Pops! Freddie! The paper says thousands are heading north right now, and I want Freddie to go with me, too."

Me? Go? I hadn't even thought about that. The Yukon! We wouldn't be alone as there were many others going, but I had to start teaching in a few weeks. Could I leave my job when I knew the family counted on the money? Could I even make the journey? Were other women going? The newspaper had really only talked about the men going.

After supper that night, we pulled out some geography books and found the Yukon. It was a territory and a river in northwestern Canada. We couldn't find a town named Dawson City where the gold had been discovered but figured it had to be on the river somewhere. We could see no roads on the map leading there. We wondered how we would get there, and what we would need to take - warm clothes for sure were needed as it was much further north than our farm here in Clinton, Wisconsin.

We were both young; Leonard was 23 and I was 21 and both of us were able to do a lot of work, so the challenge of being physically fit was not in question. However, Leonard thought we would be better off if we had another man going with us to share the expenses and camping chores along the way. We both knew an extra pair of strong hands would be a great asset, but that would also mean making plans with someone else. Of course, we would share the gold equally when we found it. "Well," I told him, "cooking for one more won't be any more work so maybe it is a good idea to ask someone to go with us."

We knew there was really only one man we would ask, Walter Jackson. Walt and Leonard had been friends since first grade. Walt was a hard worker, and he treated me like a lady, was courteous, didn't use bad language, and most of all didn't smoke or drink as a lot of young men did.

After church the next Sunday, we drove the buggy over to the Jackson's to visit with Walt and to ask him to come with us. Boy, were we surprised when we arrived! We had not even mentioned the reason for our visit when Walt took us aside and told us of his hopes to go to the Yukon to get some of the gold so many were finding there. Leonard and I just laughed.

"What's wrong? Don't you think that I could do it?" Walt said indignantly.

"Of course you could do it, Walt. It's just that Freddie and I came to ask if you would like to go with us and make it a great threesome. How about it?" Leonard could hardly speak he was laughing so much.

And so it was settled. We will be the Stanton-Jackson party going north to find the gold, and we would be a good team. Walt had not told his folks about his idea, so we said he should do that first and come over to our house the following Sunday. We could then start making some definite plans. I'd have my file of newspaper clippings and a calendar ready, and he could bring any ideas he had.

The ride back home was quiet, but a wonderful sort of quiet. We had a good traveling friend to go with us, and it looked as though we could start putting our plans on paper. Leonard put his arm around me and hugged me close. It was as if our life together finally had a direction and that direction was north to the Yukon.

Now we earnestly began making our plans. Leonard read everything about the gold rush that appeared in the newspapers and the preparations others were making for the journey. We learned it was not going to be as easy as driving a couple of horses and a wagon down a country road to Dawson City. We weren't even sure at first how we would get into Canada, but we did learn we had to go across the country to Seattle, Tacoma, San Francisco, or Vancouver in Canada to start the trip north.

For weeks articles had appeared in the papers reporting that stores in San Francisco and Seattle were ready to help with the necessary food and best of all, they had the extra warm clothing we would need. There were even maps published showing the different routes to the Yukon. At least that's what the advertisements said.

It seemed as if it were meant to be. We decided to work as hard as we could to earn extra money, leaving some for the family and taking the rest with us. I did sewing for ladies in town and tutored students after school and on weekends. Leonard helped out on other farms with the Fall plowing and preparation for the coming Winter. Many nights we were so tired we could hardly eat, but we could see the results as money began to come in. When Christmas approached, ladies in town wanted holiday clothes, and I did even more sewing.

I kept the articles telling us what we would need, but when was the best time to go? Were the rivers up there really frozen until late May or even June? And which of the many routes would we take? It was now time to decide on a date to leave.

Then one Sunday afternoon in early January, with the sun shining brightly on the new-fallen snow and the sweet smell of crisp Fall apples baking in the oven, their cores filled with brown sugar, cinnamon, and raisins, the three of us sat at the kitchen table. Spread all over were articles and lists we had made, but first we had to set a date to leave.

"Let's look at the calendar and set a date to leave, or we may never go." I was actually surprised at myself for speaking up, but we had to start sometime, and we might as well do it now.

Leonard and Walt studied the calendar, turning the pages back and forth, neither saying anything. Finally, Walt pointed to the third week of February and said, "This looks like a good time. Spring should be coming by the time we get to the gold fields. It's as good as any date. Let's set this as the time we will leave." We all agreed that now is the time we need to make definite plans as to what we need to take.

* * *

Well, the date was set and the plans were made, and now here I am sitting in Mom's kitchen curled up warm and cozy as she gets ready to serve breakfast. Our trunk is packed with clothes, and there are several boxes of cook pots, small tools, and other things we might need. We leave shortly with Walt's parents who will take us to Sharon to catch the train. We could have gotten the train in Clinton, but Walt wanted to say goodbye to his aunt and uncle, Sheila and Lloyd Michaels, in Sharon, and all three of us want to say a very special "Thank you" for the gift of $300 they had given us for our adventure.

Mom turns from the stove, gives me a big hug and says, "Get dressed, child. It's time for breakfast." I came out of my dreaming to return the hug of this wonderful woman, and pray she and Pops will always be with us in spirit on this journey, and that the wonderful aromas found in this kitchen of love will be with me every day.

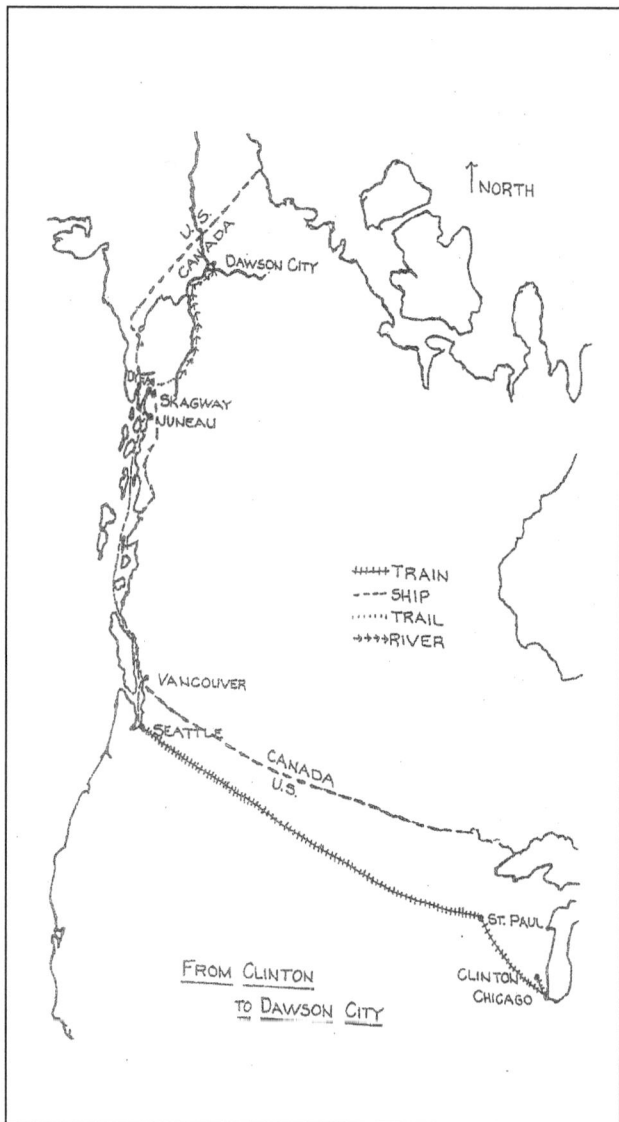

NORTH

DAWSON CITY

U.S.
CANADA

DEA
SKAGWAY
JUNEAU

++++ TRAIN
---- SHIP
...... TRAIL
→+++ RIVER

VANCOUVER

SEATTLE
CANADA
U.S.

ST. PAUL

FROM CLINTON
TO DAWSON CITY

CLINTON
CHICAGO

# 2

## TRAINS ACROSS THE COUNTRY

February 15 - Later that Morning in Sharon

Following a tearful good-bye to Mom, Pops, and the rest of the family, we left with the Jacksons. The weather was cold and windy, and even though we were wrapped in blankets, we were happy it wasn't snowing. The horses pulled the spring-board wagon with us and our trunk and boxes at a rather slow pace. It was mid-day when we arrived at the Michaels, who welcomed us with a delicious meal.

After eating, we sat around the fireplace in the parlor talking excitedly about the adventure we were just beginning. As I listened to Leonard and Walt talk, I realized what an undertaking this was going to be. We had talked about it for so long but usually we spoke only of one phase at a time. Now I was listening to the whole adventure come together. We would go by train to the west coast, then by ship north to a small town in Alaska named Skagway. The next part would be the hike over the mountains to a lake where we would board a boat for the ride down the Yukon River to Dawson City. It seemed such a long way just to get to the gold fields. We did know it was about 2500 miles to Vancouver in Canada where we hoped to get a ship north, but we had no idea how far north it was to Skagway, nor for that matter, how much further north from Skagway it was to Dawson City.

We talked for a long time, until finally Aunt Sheila and I fixed scrambled eggs and bacon with toast and hot chocolate for a late supper. It had been such a good afternoon, and I was so glad we had taken the time to visit with them before we left. I knew that I would always remember their generosity with a gift of $300 to help with our expenses. I was sure that both Leonard and Walt felt the same way.

## Wednesday - February 16 - Leaving by Train

This morning, after a good night's sleep, the Michaels and the Jacksons took us to the train station. Leonard and Walt got our tickets to Chicago, and the agent said he would telegraph ahead for the Chicago agent to have our tickets ready for the trip north to St. Paul and Minneapolis and then on to Winnipeg in Canada. From there we would go by the Canadian Pacific Railway to Vancouver on the West Coast.

As we boarded the train, Aunt Sheila handed me a box of food to eat on the train ride west. Of course, we didn't tell her Mom had already given us a similar box. With a trip this long, we would certainly need the food and were grateful for it. Though we tried, no words could adequately express our thanks to the Michaels for the generous gift of money. We promised to come see them when we returned and tell them all about our adventure. Saying goodbye was harder than I expected. I didn't know the Michaels very well at all, and yet I knew I would remember their kindness and generosity for a long time to come. Soon the train would leave, and I realized there would be no other people we knew to meet us anywhere along our way. We would be truly on our own. We would have to depend completely on each other.

We found our seats and pressed our hands against the cold window glass, wanting to touch the Michaels and the Jacksons just one more time. The conductor shouted "All Aboard!" and the train started moving. The Jacksons and the Michaels waved until we were out of sight, and we kept looking back toward them saying softly, almost to ourselves, "Goodbye, and thanks so much for everything."

The trip to Chicago via the Chicago and Northwestern Railway was pleasant enough though not too long. We were so excited finally to be on our way, and we talked so much that those around us began to take an interest in where we were going. I let Leonard and Walt do the talking while I arranged the few boxes we carried on. We had put our trunk, and the other boxes along with some of Walt's things in the baggage car.

Arriving in Chicago, Leonard and I went to get our next tickets while Walt went to get our remaining things from the baggage car. The agent said we would not be able to make our connection in Canada as there was a time change in the schedule on the Canadian Pacific line. He said our best bet was to take the Chicago, St. Paul and Pacific Railway to St. Paul, then the Great Northern Railway to Everett, Washington, which is about twenty miles or so north of Seattle. We could then continue on to Vancouver, Canada if we wanted to start from there.

This seemed fine to us, and we got the tickets to St. Paul for $2.85 each. We decided to get a tourist sleeper for the three of us from St. Paul as we would be several nights on the train. The sleeper would be quieter than the regular coach, and we would have more space in which to put our things. The train from Chicago did not leave for St. Paul until evening, so we found a place and settled down until time to leave.

With our trunk, boxes, and parcels around us, I opened the boxes of food to see what we had to eat. Mom had fixed fried chicken, a jar of cooked carrots and peas, three loaves of the bread she had baked our last day at home, one already spread with her special home-churned butter sweetened with just a bit of honey. Aunt Sheila had packed thick ham sandwiches, a jar of pickles, and chocolate cake. We decided to save the sandwiches until tomorrow. And oh how good the chicken and vegetables tasted. Leonard even found a box of candy tucked inside the carton. Showing it to us, he said softly, "It's Mom's. She must have saved this from that she made at Christmas. What a special treat."

After boarding the train for St. Paul, we took seats near the rear of the coach, and because the coach wasn't filled, we just put all our things in with us this time. We tried to sleep, but the benches were hard and sleep did not come easily, though I am sure at some time in the future I would give anything to be inside a heated place like this train and at least be warm and dry.

We arrived in St. Paul shortly before noon and had about four hours before we would leave on the Great

Northern. We were able to put the trunk and some boxes in the baggage car and the rest of our things in our tourist sleeper right away, and then we took a short walk around the business district.

Now underway about an hour, we are settled in our sleeper compartment and on our way to Seattle. The compartment is rather simple but suits our purposes just fine. It has two seats which face each other during the day where we can sit and look out the window. At night the porter changes the seats to form a bed for two below, and part of what I thought to be the ceiling comes down and rests in wooden brackets on the side walls forming the third bed above. The porter put on sheets and blankets, even giving us small pillows. With the beds in place we still have plenty of room to sit on the double bed and talk until time to go to sleep.

Right now Leonard and Walt are trying to find the list of things we will need to purchase before we board a ship north. We have a list somewhere that was printed in the newspaper, and I recall it is a rather long list.

Leonard has decided to grow a beard to go with his mustache, and his cheeks and chin are all stubble. I like his mustache but am not too sure about a beard. As he searches for the purchase list, his head is down and his dark brown hair has fallen across his forehead. He is sitting cross-legged on the bed, and his six-foot four-inch body seems to take up most of the room, leaving little for Walt. Finding the list he straightens up revealing his dark brown eyes. His eyes always seem to be smiling, and I like that about him. He is such a contrast to Walt.

I think there must be a bit of Scandinavian blood in Walt. He is shorter than Leonard by maybe three inches but is built stronger. He probably outweighs Leonard by twenty pounds, but then Leonard only weighs 185 pounds, making him tall but lean. Walt's hair is very light blond and straight as can be. His eyes are the color of the brightest blue sky in Summer and seem to sparkle even with the limited light in the sleeper. He, too, intends to grow a beard and mustache. I wonder what each will look like in the coming months. For that matter I wonder what I will look like.

I took a short walk down the sleeper car before going to bed. Opening the dark red curtains separating our sleeper from the hallway, I noticed it was dimly lit by small lamps, their chimneys musty and dirty, spaced about fifteen feet apart along the aisle providing a subdued light. Most everyone seemed to be asleep or at least quiet in their own compartments. I wondered if others might be going to the Yukon. I suppose we will find some who are, and maybe we'll even share ideas of our plans with them. I returned to finish my writing before I go to bed. I am so glad Mom suggested I keep a journal of our adventure, and I appreciated the three tablets of blank paper she gave me.

The only sound I hear is the clickity-click of the wheels on the tracks. It is a rhythmical sound, not annoying in any way. Rather it is a peaceful sound, one which could easily lull me to sleep. Walt and Leonard are already in bed. The small lamp above my head gives our room a warm glow. While thinking about the months to come, I get the small looking glass from my bag. I am not sure I really want to see what I look like now as it has been three days since I have brushed my hair well. One of the things I remember from years ago was my own mother brushing my long dark auburn hair every night. Then later Auntie Pete also brushed my hair, and it was our special time to talk about the day's activities. How I wish one of them were here to brush my hair now so I could share the events of this day. Maybe I should have cut my hair shorter, but it has always been down to the middle of my back, and I think I would feel so different without it long.

Looking in the glass, I see dark circles beneath my eyes, from lack of sleep I suppose. As I think about the journey, I know I will do whatever I can to help the men. Besides cooking, I am to be in charge of the money and our expense records. Leonard and Walt both think the money would be safer with me because unscrupulous men would not question a lady or threaten her with harm as they might a man. Before we left home, Mom and I made a pouch with buttons and ties for me to wear around my waist under my petticoat. I call it my "hope belt" - hope we strike it rich and find the gold.

The sound of the train wheels makes me really sleepy. I slip under the covers next to Leonard and pray that God will be with us as we go to the Yukon and with our families back home. I don't know what the future will bring, but I pray for strength and courage for all three of us. Good night, dear Mom and Pops. I wish I could give you the usual hug before going to bed, but in my heart you are hugged and loved. I smile to myself thinking of Sis, Leonard's sweet 14-year-old sister, knowing I will bring back a special gold nugget just for her.

Friday, February 18 - On the Way West

The porter just came by and changed our beds back into seats. Outside the plains seem to go on forever, flat, only broken here and there with trees surrounding farm houses. It is really beautiful with the sunlight sparkling on the snow covered fields untouched by footprints, and snow-capped fence posts marching in straight lines like soldiers across the fields.

We ate some of Mom's bread and a few of the apples we had bought in St. Paul for five cents. Walt and Leonard divided the last piece of fried chicken. A lady from the other end of the car stopped by to chat and gave us some caramel rolls she had brought along. She is on her way to Portland to meet her new grandson, born a month ago. She said Portland is warmer but much wetter than Minneapolis where she lives. The men told her where we were going and her only reaction was to put her fingers to her lips and say, "Oh, my!" I wonder if many others think the same thing. We have thought about this and planed our trip well, so I am confident we can achieve our dream.

Later in the day –

Aunt Sheila's ham sandwiches and the chocolate cake were delicious though the cake was a bit smashed by the time we ate it. We appreciated all the food the folks sent with us as we have spent money only for apples. Pretty good, we think! We still have two more loaves of bread Mom made and some cookies we found she had also given us.

When I got my journal from my bag this morning, I noticed Mom had tucked in my small Bible. I meant to bring it but couldn't find it at the last minute. I guess she had already put it in. I wrote in my journal for only a short time when I started nodding my head. I remember leaning my head against the window, feeling the swaying of the train and listening to the clicking of the train wheels. Leonard must have covered me with a blanket when I drifted off to sleep.

Later, when Walt noticed I had wakened, he mentioned that the conductor had come by to say we were running late. I'm not sure what that might mean to us as we plan to go straight through to Everett, but it may mean a lot to others.

I noticed that the scenery has changed, and we can now see the Rocky Mountains in the distance. They look quite massive and are covered with snow. We even saw Indians on horseback on the plains of Dakota and Montana. It looks very cold outside as the dark shadows of night approach.

Sunday, February 20 - In Seattle

Well, we finally got to Seattle. Because our train was late and we couldn't make our connection to Vancouver, Leonard convinced the conductor to exchange that portion of our tickets so we could go to Seattle. However, by being late we were able to see the beautiful Cascade Mountains in Washington. They were spectacular and very high with deep valleys. There was plenty of snow in the mountains and on the many trees, their branches drooping from the weight of the snow.

The conductor said there were three engines pulling the train with a rotary snowplow in the front clearing the tracks. A number of snow sheds have been built to keep the snow from covering the tracks. He also commented that there was over eighty feet of snow this Winter but several days of rain had caused a lot of it to melt or compress down.

The most interesting part was the switchbacks the train had to make going up the mountains. The conductor showed with his hands how the mountains went up quite high and the train went in a zigzag way up the mountain until it reached a point where it was finally able to cross to the other side. A couple of times we could see the engines at the front and the caboose at the back end at the same time as the train rounded a valley.

Once over the mountains, the country opened up into beautiful green farmlands with sparkling rivers flowing full from the rains. Most of the trees here were shades of new green, reminding me of Springtime in Wisconsin though the farms are bigger and the rivers faster.

In Seattle, Walt left us in the station with all our things and went to find us a hotel room nearby. We'll be here for a few days until we can buy our "outfits" and book passage to Alaska. We have finished the first part of our journey. The train trip is behind us, and adventure is before us. But we are not alone. It seems as if there are thousands here all doing the same thing: getting gear together and booking passage.

We hope to leave in a day or two. The weather is nice right now, actually quite sunny today with no rain in sight, but I understand this will not last. Seattle is supposed to be quite cool and damp during the Winter months with rain almost every day. We have been quite fortunate to have had such nice weather, and for that I am most grateful. I hope the good weather stays as we have much to do before we leave.

So as I finish my writing for the day, I pray for a safe journey and ask God to keep watch over the three of us and our families back home in Wisconsin. I know I would miss my daily conversations with Mom, and I knew that Leonard would always wonder how work was going on the farm. And we would both miss his brother's family and the two little girls.

# 3

## SAILING NORTH BY STEAMER

### February 24 - North of Vancouver

For several days we were so busy getting our "outfits" and boat tickets that I neglected my writing. Now I will bring my journal up to date.

While Walt went to find a place for us, Leonard and I stayed in the area near the train station. Hundreds and hundreds of men and a few women appeared to be milling around as if trying to decide what to do. Store owners have hired men to tell why we should buy from them and not some other store. Some even offer to take our picture in the new outfits so we can send it back home. Every store is selling something to do with the Klondyke or Klondike as most spell it. I am not sure where the name comes from, but I am sure I will soon learn.

Walt found a nice place for us in a private home about four blocks from the train station. The lady was tending her flowers when Walt mentioned he was looking for a room for Leonard and me and one for himself. He asked if she might have rooms to rent or if she might know someone who did. She thought a bit then said she had two rooms she could rent for a few nights since her husband and two sons had just left to go north. The cost was $1.50 a night for each room, and that price includes meals! What a bargain!

Hotels and boarding houses bulged at the seams as hundreds arrived daily to head north. Restaurants fed hungry men as quickly as they could shuffle the men from the table and out the door to let others in. Men with "outfits" crowded and shoved their way toward the docks. Anyone going to the Klondike was treated like royalty, even given free drinks and food. Some dressed in the Klondike clothes which were heavy boots, wool trousers, flannel shirts and heavy jackets, and the so familiar wide brimmed miner's hat just to get the free drinks. Con artists and confidence men were everywhere selling such things as mechanical gold rockers, boats with wheels which could be used to carry gear over the trail and later used as boats on the river, and one even said he had gophers trained to dig for the gold! Another had Klondike bicycles for sale. There was a ski in front, and the back tire had what looked like little nails sticking out to grip in ice and snow.

We were fortunate to have found such a nice place. Mrs. Palmerston, the home owner, was most helpful. I guess even though she had not been to the Klondike, she had heard enough to give me some good advice, the first bit of which was to get rid of our trunk. She heard the hike over the mountains would be hard enough without taking along a heavy trunk. She suggested I leave most of my clothes, taking only a few very serviceable ones, and I should put these clothes in flour sacks, which would be much easier to handle. After all, she said, I would be able to buy anything I needed once we reached Dawson City.

So while Leonard and Walt were busy getting tickets and buying our "outfits," I went to the grocery store, and with Mrs. Palmerston's help, got some flour sacks. The grocery man knew what I needed them for and also suggested I wrap the flour sacks in oilcloths to keep them dry. Tied with rope they would be easier to carry.

I spent the rest of the day sorting our things into smaller piles and packing back into the trunk much of what we had brought. Mrs. Palmerston offered to store our trunk in her basement until we returned since we hoped to be home by early Fall.

Leonard and Walt found most of the faster boats were filled and only the smaller, older ones had spaces available. They also heard tales of some boats so over-crowded they floundered in the high seas and sank. One ship, carrying dynamite and passengers, which was against the law, had blown up, killing everyone on board. The men finally purchased three tickets for $35 each on an old, decrepit looking boat which they were told was seaworthy, though they had their doubts. The ticket agent commented that the price was not nearly as high as it had been last Fall. I guess that's one thing in our favor.

The men returned later looking very discouraged. It seems each "outfit" must contain 2000 pounds of food and supplies. This is what is required for one person to live for a year at the gold fields. But we don't plan to live there for a year. We're sure we will return by Fall. But we must still abide by the rules in order to cross into Canada. Store owners said we each needed a full outfit even though some of the items would be duplicated such as the Yukon stove, cook pots and utensils, tent, and tools. Leonard and Walt even doubted we needed some of the things. At least they had our tickets, and we knew we had little over a day to purchase the rest and prepare to leave.

After a delicious supper of pot roast, mashed potatoes, green beans, and a fresh tomato salad, yes, that's right, fresh tomatoes in February, the men looked over what I had done. Each then went through the other things, leaving behind anything they felt wasn't needed. With the job done, the trunk filled and stored in the basement, we went looking for "outfits." Mrs. Palmerston suggested we bargain with the store owners as some might come down in price rather than let us buy from a competitor.

The streets of Seattle were very crowded with people pushing into stores, dealing with shopkeepers, and all talking about the Klondike. Stampeders, as we are now called, are required by the Canadian government to have one year's supply of food plus heavy Winter clothing, and all the tools we might need during that time. We saw store after store selling full "outfits," but we wanted to take less since we were traveling as a group. We finally found one store whose owner would help us, and you should see us now. We really look spiffy in our clothes! We saved about $150 not having to buy three of such things as a stove or a tent for our group. We still spent about $200 each. The list of supplies that we needed to purchase for the trip to the gold fields was quite long, and we wondered how we would ever be able to carry it all over the mountains. We began to see that this was going to take us much longer to cross the mountains than we had anticipated. Here is a partial list of some of the food items we have:

20 cans evaporated milk
10 lbs. tea
25 lbs. evaporated potatoes
30 lbs. rice
10 lbs. evaporated onions
50 lbs. sugar
100 lbs. white beans
20 lbs. coffee
10 lbs. baking powder
12 lbs. salt
10 lbs. laundry soap
5 lbs. butter
1 lb. ground pepper
1 lb. mustard
50 lbs. dried beef
15 lbs. candles
75 lbs. dried fruit
10 lbs. oatmeal
1 tin of matches
300 lbs. flour
2 lbs. baking soda
15 lbs. cornmeal
5 lbs. hand soap
10 lbs. split peas

This is just a partial list of the required food for *one* person, then add to that the different pots and pans, baking tins, tools, patching supplies like oakum and pitch. Boxes, more boxes, and crates of things, but we did save by not buying three of a lot of things. We got a tent for three that is nine by ten feet, with side walls about four and a half feet high before the roof slopes up to six feet high at the tallest point. Leonard and Walt will have to lean over inside, but the next larger size cost a lot more and was much heavier. "This one will be cozy," I said, and the men just laughed.

After two nights in Seattle, we boarded the ship *Thistle* on Tuesday evening. As we left, the weather was stormy and the sea rough, causing the ship to toss around more than I wished. Once the ship was sheltered between Vancouver Island and the mainland, the sea calmed, and now as the sun sets, beautiful streaks of red and gold paint the sky and the water.

We three share a room with three other men, all sleeping in bunk beds, and we have to use our own blankets. It is very cramped, has no place to hang up coats or such, and it's dirty, smoky and smells musty. Every cabin is crowded, and many men even sleep on the floor in the common room. There are dogs of all kinds and sizes tied on the deck. I guess they are going to be used to pull sleds along the trails, but they do not look like the sled dogs I've seen in pictures. There are even some goats, a few sheep, and four pigs. They will most likely be used for food along the way. There are crates of chickens and a number of horses. The deck smells awful from the animal waste!

The boat furnishes us with meals, but we have to wait in line for almost two hours, and then the food is not really good. Breakfast is hot oatmeal, thick and sticky, and probably cooked about an hour before and served with no milk or sugar, a slice of bread, and a cup of coffee. Supper last night was beef stew, but none of us could find any meat, only beef gravy and vegetables. The trip to Skagway should take about nine to ten days, but a lot will depend on the weather. On our first full day on board we bundled up in some of our new clothes and stood on the deck. Many of the passengers were outside trying to get away from the crowded, miserable conditions below deck. In spite of the problems though, I am enjoying it. The scenery is spectacular! It took us a day and a half to pass Vancouver Island, and then we were in the open ocean and again the sea was rather rough.

We have seen many ducks, seals, and even killer whales but usually only their tall back fins. Their black-and-white colors are really striking. The trees start at the top of the mountains of British Columbia and go all the way to the ocean. Small streams skip in and out of the trees and finally splash into the sea. Waterfalls are everywhere, some short but many plunging from very high points. Walt pointed out the many bald eagles flying around, tilting their heads one way and then another, trying to sight a fish. Then they dive down, grab the fish in their talons, and fly off to eat.

There are folks here from everywhere with so many different tales of why they are going to the Yukon. We have talked with many who, like us, are hoping to find enough gold to send home to their families. I learned the name Klondike is the name of a large stream which empties into the Yukon. The gold was actually discovered on a small creek off the Klondike now named Bonanza Creek. So we are stampeders off to the

Klondike, and the slogan **Klondike or Bust** is on every advertisement we have seen.

There have been several lighthouses on the islands or the coast line. Each looks lonely sitting on a piece of jumbled rock or the tip of a very small island. Sometimes we can see a clothesline with washed laundry drying in the wind, but we have not seen any people. Most on the ship don't seem to be too interested in the scenery, though Leonard and Walt appreciate it when I point out something to see. We passed an Indian village named Bella Bella this afternoon. It's a mission community, but I am not sure what denomination runs the mission there. It was quite a small settlement, and the ship didn't stop. This country is really very peaceful and beautiful, but it also seems like a lonely place. I have seen only two small cabins other than the settlement of Bella Bella and the lighthouses. It would be a hard life here, but the splendor of the mountains, trees, and sea animals would all make it a very special place.

It is now getting dark as the sun has set, and the sky has turned very cloudy. I hope we are not in for a storm. The three of us lingered just a bit longer enjoying the fresh air before going to our room. Others have drifted off to bed though there seems to be a good number of men in the small dining room playing cards.

As I write, the boat rocks gently, and the sound of the engine muffles the snores of the other men in our room. I am in a lower bunk, and it does feel good to lie down and rest. I just wish I didn't feel like I am getting sick. My stomach seems to be upset, and I suppose it is the rocking of the ship that makes it so. I heard some

29

ladies on board commenting that they, too, were nauseated though they thought it was sea sickness. Walt and Leonard appear to be fine, and I pray I will feel better soon, but right now I just want to get a good night's sleep.

Next morning, February 25 - At Sea

We have been at sea more than 40 hours now. The weather is very pleasant and the sea smooth as we sail between many small islands and the coastline of British Columbia. The islands offer protection from the rough open ocean.

We passed a school of dolphins, or maybe I should say they just passed us. They were leaping and diving along the front and the side of the boat. Someone said the dolphins were supposed to bring good luck. The country around us gets more spectacular each day. Running close to the coastline, we can see no snow at this level or on the tops of the nearby mountains, but we can see plenty of snow in the higher mountains beyond the coast. It is cold, and we do find the new clothes very comfortable.

Two men in our cabin are very nice; actually the third one is, too, but he seems to be traveling with another group who are split up in several cabins. We are beginning to feel it might be better to travel with others for safety and to discourage the swindlers and confidence men we hear are everywhere in the towns and on the trails. Leonard and Walt asked the two cabin mates to join us, and they were most happy to be asked. They are from California and were laborers in the orange orchards outside of Los Angeles. They are looking for a better life, and, like us, are willing to work hard at honest work to attain that goal. I'm glad Mark Hendricks and Tony Kimble, our cabin mates, will be new partners on the trail and the river.

Mark and Tony bought larger outfits than we did. They have two sledges to use pulling gear on the trail over the mountains. In talking with them we have learned a great deal. One trail starts at the community of Dyea (pronounced Dy-ee), and is 33 miles long, ending at lakes on the Canadian side. The other is up a valley leading from Skagway, and though longer, it is not as steep. Both trails are covered with snow and follow a river valley up the mountains. After reaching the lakes, we will have to build our own boat to go down the river. This was something we did not know, though we should have surmised it since we had not heard of any boats available on the lakes. Now we know why we had to buy such things as saws, nails, oakum, and pitch. The man who sold us the outfits did not tell us much. So we are all the more grateful to have men like Tony and Mark joining us.

The trip down the river is over 550 miles long, and Mark did not know how long it would take to get to Dawson City. I guess the weather will play a big part and also how soon we can get across the mountains and build our boat. Then again we have to wait for the ice to melt on the river.

I'll try to sketch some word pictures of this country through which we travel. Seals and ducks abound. Dolphins leap happily from the dark blue water. Bald eagles, with white heads and tails, fish every day right beside the boat as though we were not here. Streams dance and sparkle in the sunlight as they race to the waiting ocean. It is not always sunny. In fact, we've had some drizzle and fog, but it is still a beautiful, peaceful country through which we are traveling. I think it would be difficult to live in this place since the only way to go from one place to another is by boat, and the distance between the few villages is quite far.

This boat is a different story, however. Leonard thinks it is safe enough, but the smell of so many people and all the animals on deck is terrible. Men just spit tobacco juice anywhere on the floor. The dining room is always crowded, and the dishes are not really clean. The food is definitely not Mom's cooking. Oh, how I remember the aroma of Mom's bread baking that last day at home.

We often spend time outside with Tony and Mark. Mark helped build a ranch house in southern California so I think that will be a big help when we build our boat. He did say, however, that one experience does not mean he can do the other, but at least he has the necessary skills to build a boat. Mark is very quiet but seems well educated though he left school after the fifth grade. He loves to read and has brought a few of his favorite books with him. Tony is more outgoing and seems to be one who thinks ahead on any plans to be made. This makes them both valuable additions to our group. And the best part is that Leonard and Walt like them and feel comfortable with them, and I enjoy having them around and I really think five of us will make a congenial group going north to the gold fields in the area of Dawson City. I do wonder what we will find when we get to Dawson City, though Leonard did say I would just have to wait and see what it will be.

February 27 - Sunday Evening - At Sea

For the past two days big storms with steady rain have now washed the deck clean. Walt soon located some of our things on deck and covered them with the canvas tent to keep them as dry as possible. We don't get the big crashing waves that the outer part of the islands get, but our ship rolls constantly. A number of us have been sick and not able to keep food down. I actually did not even try to eat this morning as my stomach was so upset. I spent most of the last two days in the cabin feeling very nauseated.

Leonard insisted I come on deck this afternoon. He said staying closed up in the cabin was probably making me sicker, and he was right, of course. It has stopped raining now though it is very foggy out. The clouds are so low they make me feel as if they are pressing down on my head and shoulders. It is a tiring feeling, and I want to duck down to take the weight off me. Sometimes it is actually hard to tell where the sea ends and the sky begins. The slate-gray sea just merges with the cold gray sky. Even so, the air is clean and crisp, and it smells so good after the rain.

As we stood on deck, the steamer *Danube* passed us. This ship left Vancouver after we did and even made a stop along the way and is now ahead of us. Both Walt and Leonard said they knew our ship was slow but feel it is very seaworthy. Besides the folks on the *Danube* can't get to the gold much before us anyway since we all have to cross the mountains, build our boats and wait for the ice to melt on the river.

One of the ship's officers stopped by to talk and said we should reach the town of Wrangell in Alaska later today. I doubt I will be able to tell where Canadian water ends and Alaskan water begins unless someone tells me. We would have time to get off and walk around the town as the crew loads on supplies, but later seeing the crowds in Wrangell, we decided to remain on board. We are now over half way to Skagway. The officer also suggested we stay on deck after we left Wrangell so we could see how narrow the route is through the Wrangell Narrows. And it really was narrow! The steamer had to make very short and quick turns first one way and then another, and all the time I felt we could almost reach out and touch the shorelines. As we slid quietly by, the waves gently washed up on the nearby rocks. I held my breath in a few places. It was very quiet going through the Narrows, and even though many were on deck, no one spoke. It was almost as if we felt we couldn't make any noise in order to pass through undamaged. It took over an hour before we were again in wider passageways.

Before I stop writing tonight, I want to add a bit more about Mark and Tony. Mark is about as tall and thin as Leonard. He has broad shoulders and a straight back. He doesn't stoop as so many tall people do. His brown hair is very straight and seems to have a mind of its own, sticking out in this place and that. His eyes are dark brown, and he always seems to be deep in thought. I wrote earlier that he left school after the fifth grade to work in the orange orchards earning money to help his father care for his ailing mother and a younger brother and sister. He is 28 years old and has a girlfriend back in California. He said if he had known I was coming, he would have brought her. I laughed at his remark reminding him that he didn't know he would meet up with us. He showed me her picture which he carries in his shirt pocket. Her name is Marie, and she looks like a sweet young lady.

Tony is about the same size as Walt. He has straight black hair, cut short now, but he says he'll let it grow. Already he has let his beard start growing. His mother's family came to America from Mexico when she was only three. She married an American man which is why his last name is not Spanish. Tony is the oldest, with two younger sisters. His father was killed one night when vigilantes tried to mistreat his mother. Tony was eleven at the time. He left school at fourteen to work in the orange orchards. He loves anything to do with nature, and is thrilled to see the dolphins, eagles, and the two otters we saw this afternoon. He hopes to get enough gold to buy some land for himself. He has a good singing voice and treated us to a song from his Mexican heritage, sung in Spanish. I have no idea what the words meant, but his voice was very nice.

March 3 - Skagway

We reached Skagway early this morning after a rough run up the Lynn Canal. It was bitterly cold with the wind coming right off the glacier up the canyon beyond town. We had made a quick stop in Juneau to let some passengers off and picked up a few more. Seems some are going to work in the Juneau gold mines, while others left those mines to try their luck in the Yukon.

From Juneau to Skagway, we ran straight into the wind. This made for very rough seas, and a lot of us were sick. I am really glad we are now on solid ground even if it is windy, and the wind is cold! We appreciate our nice new, warm clothes. This place is worse than Seattle with men milling around. Most don't seem to have any idea of what to do next. We have been warned that thugs are everywhere so we are wary of everyone.

On shore all is chaos with boxes, bags, suitcases, crates, cages, and everything else just heaped in huge piles. Leonard and Walt were happy they took extra time in Seattle to paint all of our boxes and crates with the first letters of our last names, S-J, plus a number and a big black X. This way we can more easily identify our things and tell if we have everything by making sure we have numbers 1 through 61. As they look for our things I stand guard keeping track of the numbers. Mark and Tony have added their things to the pile which is now growing quite large.

Finally, with everything in one place, Leonard and Tony set out to find a place to stay until we decide which trail we'll take. The two sledges will be a big help from now on. Tony returned and saying there's a rooming house on the edge of town, though it is very crowded. Now I must stop writing and give them some help. I will write more later when we decide which trail we will take, the White Pass or the Chilkoot.

Two parts of our adventure are over: the train to the west coast and the steamer to Skagway. It has taken us sixteen days to get this far, and this is the easy part. I wonder how long it will take us to cross the mountains and get to the lakes? This is something to think about as I go to sleep tonight.

# 4

## SCANDALOUS SKAGWAY

Friday, March 4 - Skagway

I need to add to the description of the chaos here when any ship ties up to the pier. All boxes, crates, and baggage are tossed on shore. A lot of the crates and baggage are simply thrown in the water, some creaking open, exposing the contents to the salt water, and no one seems to care except the owners. It took almost three hours for Leonard and Walt to get our things together, and by that time both men were wet up past their knees from wading in the frigid water. Fortunately none of our crates had broken open when tossed overboard. Mark and Tony had a harder time as they had not marked their crates with any special marking other than their last names. Then the men had to put on dry trousers and boots, as the water was so cold they were freezing.

Piles of gear are everywhere, with only small walkways around each pile. Some use carts like wheel barrows to move gear; others use two wheeled pull-carts. Most use their own backs to carry or push their crates. It is like an ant hill with everyone searching for their things, than moving them from one place to another.

When Tony returned with news of the boarding house, we got busy loading things on the sledges which are about six feet long, heavily constructed on runners somewhat closer to the ground than the sleds of Leonard's nieces. There is snow on the ground, but it is quite rutted, and in many areas the snow has melted from all the foot traffic making it quite slushy mud. We could not load the sledges too heavily or the men could not have pulled them. Since Skagway has such a bad reputation, we decided one person would stay with the gear on the beach while the others pulled the sledges to the boarding house area. I would go with the first trip and stay there while the men moved the remaining gear from the beach, and Mark said he'd stay at the beach area.

Off we went. Pulling the sledges was really hard work, and we are just beginning to realize what it will be like to pull things uphill on the trail. We were greatly discouraged at the condition of the "boarding house." It was just a big tent! Leonard went in and found there were only canvas partitions between the "rooms", which could be reached only by going through the saloon. Plank tables were set up to serve meals at $2.00 each. Leonard said the food was only beans with bacon and a slab of bread. The cost of a bed was $1.00 each and this with no privacy even for women. Each "room" would sleep as many as could be squeezed in on the floor between two plank beds. There was no window or any door covering of any kind.

After hearing this news, Tony and Leonard went looking for a place large enough to set up two tents: ours and the one Tony and Mark have. About 20 minutes later Tony returned with news of an area with room large enough for the tents and away from the town near the river, which, of course, is frozen. So off we went again.

This area is cleaner, though it too is crowded. The sledges were quickly unloaded, and Tony and Leonard left with them to bring more gear. Walt looked among the things we had brought, trying to find our tent. We had not taken the time in Seattle to set up the tent, and you should have seen the two of us trying to figure it out. It looked really simple, but the tent did not include the poles that form the framework, and we tried to find things nearby which might work. Finally, we just sat down and laughed. I'm not sure if it was really funny or if we were so tired it was better to laugh than to cry. I've known Walt for some time, but I've never heard him laugh so much. In fact, both of us laughed so hard we ended up crying. People around us just stared, but we couldn't stop. Here we are thousands of miles from home, getting ready to start a long hike across the mountains and then must go down an unknown river, and we couldn't figure out how to use the most important piece of equipment we had - the tent.

Well, a couple of nice, middle-aged Scotsmen came to our rescue. They went off, found some suitable tree poles and helped put up the tent. Once up, Walt saw how to do it and said it would be easier the next time. I certainly hope so. But it was funny.

The Scotsmen even offered to help bring the rest of our things from the beach. They are really nice but a bit hard to understand, and even though they speak English, you have to listen very carefully.

It took several hours for the men to bring everything to the area. Certainly, we could not have done it that quickly without the Scotsmen. I would like to say that while they were bringing the gear, I was supposed to cook supper, but I had not the slightest idea where the cook pots were or for that matter which crates or boxes contained the food. I felt rather useless except I told myself I was protecting our things. When the last of the gear was finally brought from the beach area, the two Scotsmen invited us to share tea with them. It was very good, and the company of these two men felt really pleasant.

Then it was time for supper, and we were really hungry because we had not eaten since early morning. Our new friends asked us to share the stew they had simmering though they did say we might want to add anything we had as they hadn't cooked enough for seven people. We searched through our things, coming up with some bread, apples and some oranges Mark and Tony had brought from California. It was a delicious though meager meal, the company was great, and we laughed again as we told of Walt and me trying to put up the tent.

Discussion revolved about which trail to take - the Chilkoot Trail, known as the poor man's trail, from Dyea, or the White Pass Trail from here in Skagway. The Scotsmen had joined up with four other Scotsmen to go over the White Pass but added they would rather go by way of the Chilkoot. The rest of their party had voted for the White Pass and so majority ruled. As we listened to them, we felt the Chilkoot was the better way to go and even though it is 750 feet higher, it is shorter. But to use that trail we will have to find someone with a boat to take our things to Dyea, a few miles up the coast.

After finding our bedrolls, the three of us crawled into the tent for the first time. "It's cozy," Walt said with a sigh, but we were too tired to make any further comments.

This morning, we found the Scotsmen packing up. They will leave a lot of their things here, making a number of trips as they move gear part of the way up the trail, then return for more. We bid them farewell saying we would have supper waiting for them tonight. Walt and Mark set off for the beach to find a way to transport our things to Dyea, while Leonard, Tony and I sorted through our things and labeled the boxes and crates with what each contained. This was not as bad as I thought as some of the cases and crates were already labeled.

Skagway is situated by mountains close in on one side and the frozen river on the other side. Beyond the river, there is a flat area and then another range of mountains. A rather long, narrow valley leads north. There are some trees throughout the area though most have been cut down to make room for the hundreds of tents the stampeders have put up. The streets, if you can call them such, are nothing more than areas of frozen or partially frozen mud between the tents. Closer to the business area of town some streets are straight though many still go around trees or tree stumps.

There are many saloons and dance halls, all noisy, and filled with some very unsavory looking men. Skagway has a terrible reputation. We've heard thugs and confidence men are everywhere. The most notorious is a man named Soapy Smith, who runs a saloon and is the leader of a group of con-artists, thieves, cheats, and maybe even murderers. These men are out to cheat anyone they can. Stories abound of men who have lost everything – all their money and even their outfits to these criminals.

The town is never quiet. All day and night men lug gear over oozing mud at low tide or from the water at high tide, trying to get everything above the high water line before their crates and boxes are soaked in salt water. Add to this the men circulating among them trying to steal their money, and you can see what a mess this place is.

There are very few women here except the ones who work in the dance halls or saloons, and Leonard said a lot of them were probably prostitutes. I think of that each time I see a woman and wonder "Is she or isn't she?" The Scotsmen think women are seldom preyed upon by the confidence men, but they could not say exactly why and cautioned me to watch out for myself.

Once while Leonard and I were in town and did see Soapy Smith though someone had to point him out. He is a rather short man, about five-nine or ten inches tall and slightly built. He has a large and bushy black beard. He talked with people nearby, didn't appear to be a thug, and in fact seemed most cordial and friendly. Of course, we were just listening to the conversations as we passed by. Leonard left me near the telegraph office so he could try to find someone to take us to Dyea. A very nice man came up to me and started talking, asking where I was from.

"I'm from Wisconsin, here with my husband and our friend." I politely replied.

"Have you been gone from home long? And which way are you going over the mountains? There are several ways, you know, and you must choose carefully.

A young lady like you needs to be wary of the unsavory characters around here. This town seems to have more than its share of such people," the gentleman said, often looking over his shoulder as if to spot some confidence men nearby and point them out.

"We've been gone almost three weeks, but things are going pretty well right now. We are going up the Chilkoot Pass as soon as we can find a way to Dyea." He was such a nice man, I thought, and clearly concerned about my welfare. I was happy to think there was someone here who cared.

"I see you here in front of the telegraph office. Have you sent a telegram home to let your family know you are OK? It would bring such peace to them to know you were here and well. You know there have been some ship wrecks and word gets out that people have drowned; it would be a comfort to family back home to hear from you. I think it only costs $5.00 to send the message, and that seems a small price for peace of mind. And if you wish a reply, it usually comes in an hour or so." He certainly seemed concerned for me. We chatted on, and he even pointed out some unsavory men that I should avoid.

Soon, Leonard came up and put his hand on my elbow. He smiled at my new friend, and cordially shook hands with him, introducing himself as my husband.

"Come on, honey, it's time we join the rest of our group. We must find someone to take us to Dyca, and we've got things to do." Leonard eased me away, but I felt bad realizing I hadn't taken time to thank the gentlemen for his kind attention and concern.

When we were a bit away, Leonard stopped and looked sternly at me.

"Honey, do you know who that was?"

"A very nice man who suggested I send a telegram home telling the folks we were here and all was well. I thought it a very fine suggestion."

"Freddie, turn around and look at the telegraph office. See the wire going from the office to the big tree nearby? The one directly back of the building?"

"Yes, but a telegraph office would have a line running from it."

"Honey, look again. The line stops there. It doesn't go any further. That man is one of Soapy Smith's con-men, out to get you to send a telegram for a few dollars, but the telegram would never go anywhere. It's all a sham." Then he put his arm around me as we walked back toward our camping area.

"Don't feel bad, honey. I wouldn't have known it either if I hadn't run into a man who warned me. He had sent a telegram home which started by saying 'Dear Ones' and asked how the kids were doing. It seems about an hour later he got a reply saying the kids were sick and could he please send money by wire as quickly as possible for some medicine. It was signed 'Your loving wife.' He knew he had been cheated because his wife had died last year and his parents were caring for his children."

I felt so ashamed and naïve. I thought I was more aware of what was going on, but I realized I could also have been so easily cheated. I do hope the trail is not full of men like him. I don't want to wonder if everyone I meet and talk with is trying to steal from us.

I think of my life in Wisconsin and how safe and secure it felt, and now I have to grow up very quickly to the ways of the world. I am not too sure I like what I am learning.

On our way to the tents, we saw a man selling chickens and bought a couple to cook for supper. We also found a tent store selling potatoes and carrots and bought some of each. Arriving back at the tents, we found our Scotsmen friends with a fire going and hot water for tea. They told a tale of woe. It seemed their party of six started on the White Pass Trail but turned back after they saw so many dead horses. Others on the trail told of men who beat their horses unmercifully wanting to make them go faster. Some beat them until the animals actually died in their tracks. They just left them to rot there on the trail. Some said there were dead horses all along the trail. The Scotsmen said the White Pass Trail is quickly becoming known as the Trail of Dead Horses.

"We couldn't stand it so we come back here to start a'gin by the Chilkoot this time."

As I cooked supper, Leonard and Walt talked with them. It seems they have a problem going either trail since they bought their outfits in Vancouver, Canada, after crossing the country by train. Now they need to find someone to go with them and convoy their gear through the American territory and pay them $10 a day to do it. Their things are now sealed and bonded until they reach Canada. A member of the party can act as the convoy if he bought his outfit in America. They wondered if they and their friends could travel with us, meaning we would be their convoy. They even wanted to pay us.

"Of course, we'll do it, and we won't accept pay. We'll use our food until we get into Canada, and then we'll use yours until we get to Lake Bennett" And Leonard wouldn't even argue the point with them.

They quickly left to talk with their friends who were camped nearby, and all of them returned very happy with the idea. Walt and Leonard quickly jumped up and shook their hands in agreement. We were still talking excitedly about the solution to their problem when Tony and Mark returned with news that they had arranged for two Indians with a large canoe to take us to Dyea tomorrow. So now our group of three from Wisconsin, two added from southern California, and six from Scotland has grown to an international group of eleven, and it will take many trips to get us to Dyea.

Supper was unusual as I had stewed the chicken and vegetables, and the four other Scotsmen had made a moose meat stew. We enjoyed both and cleaned up everything. Afterwards, while enjoying more tea, we wondered when we would again get fresh meat and vegetables.

Mark and Tony said the canoe would be near the dock before noon tomorrow, and we needed to take our things there. With such an expanded group, we knew we would have to make many trips to Dyea. The cost of the canoe would be $15 for our original five, and the Scotsmen said they would agree to a reasonable rate for all their things.

The men stayed up talking, but I went to bed. Tomorrow will be a very busy day for us. Skagway will be behind us and the trail before us, but Skagway has been interesting. Again tonight, I think of the family back home. I must write them soon the let them know we are here and safe, and soon we will be starting the long hike up the Chilkoot Trail and then into Canada.

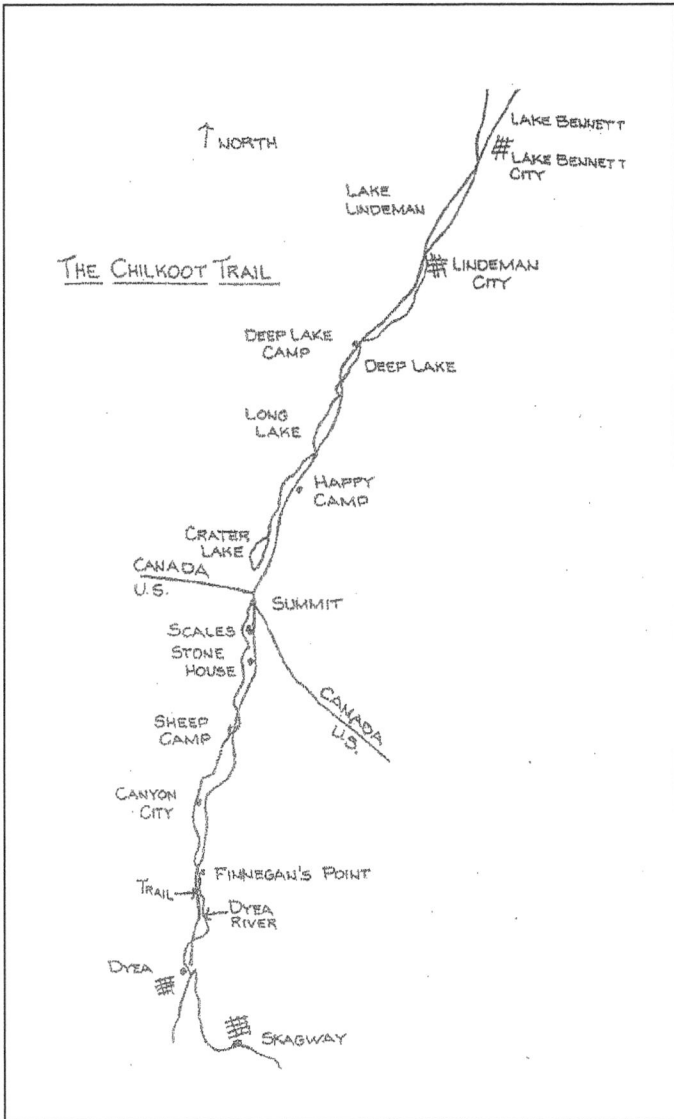

THE CHILKOOT TRAIL

↑ NORTH

LAKE BENNETT
LAKE BENNETT CITY

LAKE LINDEMAN

LINDEMAN CITY

DEEP LAKE CAMP

DEEP LAKE

LONG LAKE

HAPPY CAMP

CRATER LAKE

CANADA
U.S.

SUMMIT

SCALES
STONE HOUSE

CANADA
U.S.

SHEEP CAMP

CANYON CITY

FINNEGAN'S POINT

TRAIL

DYEA RIVER

DYEA

SKAGWAY

# 5

## DYEA - THE BEGINNING OF THE TRAIL

### Saturday, March 5 - To Dyea

We were up very early this morning to find the Scotsmen had a fire going, making hotcakes. The men call them flapjacks, but I've always called them hotcakes. They even made coffee knowing we Americans really liked coffee especially with breakfast. What good men! I don't think I mentioned their names. They are Ian McTavich and Liam McDougal, both in their forties with families in Scotland. Ian has red hair and a nicely trimmed beard. He is a slim man, about five feet eight inches tall (about two inches taller than me), loves a good story, and likes to tell tales of life in Scotland. He dearly misses his family, especially his twin sons who were both recently married. His wife, Molly, is at home, probably worrying about him.

Liam is a stocky fellow, six feet tall, and I'm sure he enjoys eating as he has an abundant middle. His wavy hair is dark brown, on the longish side, being almost to his shoulders. He's a widower, with two daughters, one married and the other staying with his sister while he is gone. Both men love being outside. I seem to remember them talking about crops, so they must be farmers or maybe sheep herders.

While enjoying coffee and getting ready to make our first trip to the beach area, Ian said there'd been another change in plans. Immediately, I thought that we would not be able to act as their convoy. But it was much different. The other four Scotsmen decided to go by the White Pass, with three other Americans who will act as their convoy, while Ian and Liam will go with us. Since the White Pass Trail is twelve miles longer, and the Chilkoot shorter but steeper, they think both groups should reach Lake Bennett about the same time. The first ones to arrive would try to find an area large enough for both groups when we finally meet. This would also mean fewer trips for the Indians taking us to Dyea. We are more than ready to get started. I know, though, that we have just arrived at the point where the hard work will begin.

After the delicious breakfast, the sledges were loaded with as much as possible, and the men started to the beach area. I packed up our eating utensils, bedrolls, and leather boots, since we will now use our rubber boots. Leonard and Tony took down the tent and put it away, tying it up for easier transport.

The sledges returned in about thirty minutes and were quickly re-loaded. I went to the beach with the second trip and will stay there while the rest bring the remaining gear. The sun was just coming up over the mountains when we left on the second trip. The mountains are so close by, that while it is light about twelve hours a day, the sun doesn't reach the beach area until later in the morning. Someone said in December and January there are less than seven hours of daylight.

The further north we go the more daylight we will have as the days are getting longer now that Spring is coming.

At mid-morning, Mark saw the two Indians rowing to shore and showed them where we had our things. Not much seems to have changed here on the beach. It is still just as hectic with ships unloading new arrivals and equipment constantly. Today the tide is out so everything will have to be hauled over the mud flats. We had our things piled off to the side by a shallow area of the bay and away from where the ships land. The Indians greeted Tony and Mark, who quickly paid them the $15 agreed price. Ian and Liam settled for a price of $10 for transporting their things.

The Peterborough canoe, really a type of scow, is used by Indians and white men for heavy duty transportation especially on large rivers or the ocean. The canoe was loaded quickly and left for the first trip. Tony and Leonard went with them. I was really surprised at how much the canoe could carry. While they were gone, many more trips were made to bring the remaining gear. The piles were even larger now with the gear of the Scotsmen added. By the time the Indians returned for the second trip, all the rest of our gear was waiting and ready to be transported to Dyea.

Ian went with the second trip. The Indians seemed to think it would take at least a half dozen or more trips to Dyea before the job was finished. And they might not finish today. They knew of another man with a boat, a bit smaller, who could help, but it would cost us another $10. We agreed this was a good investment. We wanted to get to Dyea to start making preparations for the trail.

When the second trip left, Walt and I sat on the crates and looked around at those now landing here from arriving ships. Soon a man, Frank Reid, stopped and greeted us warmly. I was a bit on edge, but Walt felt this man was not a member of Soapy's gang. Mr. Reid spoke softly, warning us about Soapy and assuring us he was not one of them. His home is in Skagway, and he felt there would be a future for the town. He said the town had been homesteaded by an old sea captain, Captain Moore, in 1887. He built the first log cabin here, laid out the town with long straight streets. He had learned of small gold strikes in earlier years and foresaw a larger gold rush to come. Since Skagway has a nice, deep harbor, a large beach, and the valley leads directly to the lower pass through the mountains, Captain Moore felt this would be an ideal place for prospectors to use. He even laid out home sites for cabins and tents he hoped to sell. He thought later it might be possible to build a railroad across the mountains from here. The idea sounded good, but when the gold rush began, the prospectors ignored Captain Moore. He was a farsighted man but didn't anticipate such hordes of men.

With the arrival of Soapy Smith's gang, the town fell prey to his wicked ways. Mr. Reid assured us there were many honest, hardworking town folks who wanted to be rid Soapy and his gang, and he felt at some point they would either drive him out or kill him. I wonder what will actually happen. It seemed impossible to think someone like Soapy Smith could cause such problems, but easy money drives men to do terrible things. Now Skagway is in the grip of this terrible gang, and it seems the judges and policemen in town can do little about it at present. I do hope somehow Soapy Smith will be run out of town. I don't care to stay in Skagway any longer then we have to.

March 5 - Late Evening After Supper in Dyea

We made it here and are all together, the seven of us, in an area not too far from the frozen river, the beginning point of the trail. Leonard had met some men leaving on their final trip up the trail to their first relay point, and before they finished loading the last of their things, Leonard began putting our crates in their spot. It took six trips to bring our things from Skagway, and that included four trips with the two canoes.

Once again, we set up the tent, much easier this time. We think we'll be two days here arranging everything into loads easier to move, making sure the tents and other essentials go on the first trip. This way camp can be established quickly after the first trip, and I can get supper started. As cold and windy as it is, the men will need hot food at the end of the day. No one has any idea how many trips it will take to move our things from one camp to the next. Much will depend on the trail, how steep it is, and of course, what the weather is like.

We learned from others that there are boarding houses or hotels at several places along the trail which serve hot meals. Since we have planned to save as much money as we can, we agreed to camp and cook our own meals.

The Indians who brought us here are interesting men. They are Tlingit Indians, and many of them are being hired to pack outfits up the trail. I asked one of them how Skagway got its name, and he said the Indians called the town "Skagus," meaning North Wind. I agreed they certainly named it correctly, because the wind really did blow from the north, and it felt like an ice box. The Indian nodded his head saying "ice box" was a good description, and it certainly was cold since the wind blew right off the snow and the icy glaciers, some of which remained all year. I wonder how deep the snow will be when we reach the summit. I suppose we will have more snow falling before we reach that point, and I wonder just how many days and how many trips the men will have to make to get that far.

March 7 - Early – The Beginning of the Trail

The men have left now with the first of the boxes and crates. The plan was for me to go on the first trip, but the men wanted to see what the trail was like before I went.

I've written a bit about the Indians who transported our goods. Well, the first evening here, as we were enjoying some tea, the two Indians walked into camp. One of them had made a comment about my auburn hair while I was in the canoe coming from Skagway. It seemed he had not seen auburn hair before. They really didn't talk to us much while transporting our things but did answer questions we asked, so I was surprised when he commented on my hair.

Well, he apparently told his wife about the woman with dark, red hair, and she didn't believe him, saying she wanted a snippet. I was ashamed of the way

55

my hair looked as I have not brushed it much at all, but he stood before me looking so serious I said sure, he could have a small bit. He took out his knife and cut about two inches of a small section from under the back. He nodded thanks to me, then turned and left without another word. His friend spoke not a single word during the entire time they were here. After they left, we just stood there around the fire wondering why his wife would want a bit of my hair.

About mid-morning yesterday (Sunday), the Indian returned with his wife. She showed me a small flower she had made from my hair. It was absolutely lovely. In the center she had put a small white seashell, looking almost like a pearl. To this point she had said not a word, just stood there with this flower in her open hand. I was not sure if she wanted to give it to me or what, but I didn't take it. Her husband then indicated his wife wondered if I would give her more of my hair. She wanted to make more flowers to decorate boots and slippers which she makes to sell to stampeders for themselves or their wives back home. She pointed to her fur lined, soft leather, calf-high boots. They had lovely bead work on them and looked very warm.

Well, with everyone watching, I let her cut off about eight inches of my hair. She did a nice job, meaning it was straight across the bottom. Leonard and Walt stood there shaking their heads, but they approved of my new look. And I am delighted since it won't be so hard to care for now.

The story does not end there, however. Just as the men were packing the sledges for the first trip, the Indian and his wife returned. I thought surely they wanted more hair, and I was ready to say enough is enough. Instead, his wife presented me with a most beautiful pair of fur lined leather boots. The beadwork contains two flowers made of my hair. I almost cried. They spoke very little but wanted to make sure "the lady with the lovely hair" was warm on the trail. I tried on the boots, and they fit perfectly. And they were so warm! I wanted to give her a hug, but as quickly as they arrived, they turned and left. All the men admired the boots, and I think, wished they had a pair.

We spent a good part of yesterday sorting things to take on the first trip. The first loads were packed and roped onto the sledges, each to be pulled by two men. The other two men would carry things on their backs. Leonard had seen a man with a pack frame to which bundles were tied and carried on his back using straps over the shoulders. He then proceeded to make his version of such a frame. He and Walt both tried it after putting on small bundles, and found it worked very well. So they made another. Now, each man not pulling a sledge will use a frame, thus carrying more things each trip.

Late in the afternoon, five of us - Ian and Liam wanted to stay by the fire - decided to see what Dyea had to offer. We were pleasantly surprised. Since the first of the stampeders arrived late last Fall, a real town has developed here. The streets are laid out in squares and along a number of the streets trees have even been planted which will grow to offer shade during the Summer in years to come. Main Street is very broad and looks north toward the Chilkoot Pass, but we can't actually see the Pass itself. Two-story buildings are found on both sides of the street, interspersed with small hardware and mercantile stores. The area appears to be larger than Skagway with an even longer sloping beach that, like Skagway, oozes deep with mud when the tide is out. There is a large log warehouse, many false front saloons, small cafes, retail stores, and a fairly large number of log cabins. We even saw signs for a doctor's office, three lawyers' offices, a dressmaker, and several bakers. Between the saloons, cafes, warehouses, and all, hundreds of tents are crammed into any available spot. We even found a real estate office and wondered how many lots for permanent homes had been sold. I like Dyea much better than Skagway.

The same confusion on the beach and near the warehouse is present here as in Skagway. Piles and piles of boxes and crates are stacked everywhere with no apparent order to anything. We saw a couple of men arguing over some gear, with one of them finally brandishing a gun. Almost immediately another man took the gun away from him before real trouble could begin. Tempers are short, and nerves are thin.

We continued on, thinking about the argument, when we met a constable who lamented that indeed some of Soapy's gang had been here and warned us to be very careful. We asked about the Indians who lived in the area, relating our experience with the two Indians. The constable expressed surprise saying the Indians are usually quite reserved or even ill tempered. It seems this particular area is usually the Summer camp of the Tlingit tribes who have used the Chilkoot Trail for probably hundreds of years as a trade route to the Stick Indians of the interior. So, long before the gold rush, the Chilkoot

Trail has been a well-established route to the interior. The Tlingits fiercely defended the area and the mountain pass from other tribes who wanted to get to the interior. The constable commented that a lot of the Indians, both men and women, were hiring themselves out as packers. They would often bargain at great lengths for the highest wages possible. He also made an interesting comment, saying these Indians had been taught Christian ways by Presbyterian missionaries, and because of this they refused to pack any gear on Sundays.

Returning to our tent, Leonard, Walt, and I walked along the beach area, thankful for having our things all together and knowing tomorrow they would make their first trip up the trail. Mark and Tony went back to their tent, wanting to check the sledges one more time. With the incoming tide, new arriving men were scrambling everywhere moving goods from the beach to higher ground. Leonard and Walt stopped to help a couple of men trying to push a big crate in the mud. Then I leaned over to pick up a smaller bundle when disaster struck. I fell flat on my face in the sticky mud. I was covered from head to toe. Leonard and Walt helped me up, and I looked them straight in the face with a dead serious expression and dared them to laugh. Well, they kept straight faces for probably ten seconds and then burst out laughing. And I have to admit, so did I. We laughed all the way back to the tent. The others did pretty well keeping straight faces for about ten seconds, and then they, too, burst out laughing.

There was plenty of hot water so I washed my face, hands, and even my hair. What a luxury! Ian even graciously loaned me an extra pair of his wool trousers, and a wool shirt. I changed standing between the piles of gear and really didn't care if anyone saw me or not. Tony washed as much mud from my coat as he could and loaned me a coat he wasn't wearing. My dress and undergarments were put over the piles of gear to dry or probably freeze first, but even if they froze, I knew they would eventually dry though not quick enough for me to wear now. So now I look like one of the men, and I don't care what others may think.

Sleep was most welcomed, knowing dawn would come much too early. The men left quickly after breakfast. Ian and Liam pulled one sledge, Tony and Walt another, and Leonard and Mark used the pack frames. I watched them as they left noticing how strong and straight Leonard carried himself, his broad shoulders giving him a look of pride and dignity in what he was doing. I was proud of them, silently wishing them, "Hurry back!"

# 6

## THE TRAIL - DYEA TO SHEEP CAMP

March 7 - Mid-Afternoon

After the men left, I realized I was truly alone for the first time. I stood for a few minutes watching the activity on the beach as ships disgorged more men and equipment. How well I understood what these men must have felt and thought. Here was the beginning of the trail, what do we do first? How long would it take to move things up the trail? Some questions have been answered, but others are part of a great unknown.

I added more wood to the fire and was thankful the men had left a nice stack for me, then I put on water for tea. It's cold and windy, and cooking over an open fire is a dirty, messy job, but at least I stay fairly warm. While enjoying a cup of tea, soothing to body and mind, I noticed a good sized group of about 15 ladies. They must have landed several hours ago and have already carried a good bit of gear from the beach to a tent area across the frozen river from us. It was a rather small area, and they were really crowded together. I wondered who they were, and if they would hire Indian packers or try to move everything themselves? Most were about my age though several were older ladies, maybe in their late thirties or forties. I thought they might be teachers, nurses, or maybe shop keepers, maybe even the wives of men who had gone earlier, and now they were going to join their men folk.

After having some bread and tea about mid-day, I stirred the beans I had started soaking and then took a short walk. I stopped to talk with two middle-aged couples traveling together. They were from Michigan, having arrived here yesterday. Now they were preparing to leave tomorrow on their first trip up the trail. I wished them good luck on the trail and continued on my way.

As I returned to our area, I went a longer way so I would pass the group of newly arrived ladies. Of course, I really wanted to go by them in the first place. They were a chatty group, talking about the trail, and wondering how far it was to Dawson City. I started to speak to them but hesitated when one of the older women gruffly shouted for them to "Stick together, and don't mingle with the riffraff." I didn't consider myself riffraff, but knew I should move on.

Back at the tents, I checked on the beans. They were fine, nice and plump, so I added bacon, a tin of tomatoes, salt and pepper, and a large onion chopped fine like Mom always did. I wanted to use some of the syrup the Scotsmen had for breakfast the other day but hadn't asked, so I hesitated. Then I realized the syrup was now in our supplies since Liam gave it to us because their goods were sealed in bond.

I'm getting pretty good at making biscuits, but they are not exactly like those I make at home. After mixing the flour, a bit of salt, some lard, baking powder, and water, I form them into balls with my hands, then flatten them somewhat before dropping them in a Dutch oven to fry in plenty of grease. More like fried bread than oven baked biscuits, but they are plenty good. Usually there are none left so the men must like them, and I make quite a large batch. I would like to bake some bread but haven't been able to figure how to make the dough rise in this cold weather. So fried biscuits will have to do for now anyway.

Though the sun was shining, it wasn't warm. The men put the tents up with very little space between them. Our larger tent is placed with its back wall to the wind, and the other tents are on each side forming a half circle. Near the tents it wasn't really much colder than our Winters in Wisconsin, but it is the wind that is so cold. And the wind seems to blow all the time.

While cooking, I realized I was really warm now. The woolen trousers, tucked into my new Indian boots, keep my legs quite warm. No more cold coming from the snow beneath my skirt. With the flannel shirt tucked into the trousers, my nice warm jacket, wool hat and gloves, I'm doing just fine.

I was wondering how the men were doing on the trail when a man came through the area asking if anyone knew of a lady named "Freddie." I acknowledged that I was "Freddie," and he said he had a message from "my men folk." They were doing fine when he met them near Finnegan's Point, five miles up the trail. That was about an hour ago. They were planning to stop there, making it their first relay point.

"How's the trail across the mountains to the lakes?" I asked, adding, "Maybe I should just ask 'how's the trail to Finnegan's Point?'"

"Well, the trail's not bad to Finnegan's Point, rather nice, in fact. It follows an Indian road over the meadows and frozen marshes by the river, often crossing and re-crossing the river. It does present some rather difficult points where the water's frozen over what would be rapids in Summer. Pulling a sledge over the ice covered rocks is really hard work. Beyond Finnegan's Point the trail climbs up a gentle grade into Canyon City."

He accepted the tea I offered and sat down a minute. "The men are doing fine. Don't worry about them. It'll be a couple of hours yet before they return, but they seemed pleased with their first trip. And I thought they were doing rather well myself."

He was returning to Dyea from Sheep Camp for supplies. Some of his things had gotten wet in the ocean and had been ruined, but he didn't know it until he opened a crate up the trail. Then someone stole his whipsaw and a keg of nails. He was furious, "I know it was Soapy's men. They're all along the trail with their shell games, and the sneakin' thieves will steal anything, generally causing as much trouble as they can. There's very little law on the American side, but the Canadian officials at the summit keep 'em out of Canada, so I guess that part of the trail's pretty safe."

Seeing the distressed look on my face, he added, "But don't worry, young lady. They don't seem to bother the women on the trail though I've seen only a few. So far I haven't heard of anyone being killed, though losing gear at this stage of the trip could actually be life threatening if food or warm clothing is stolen." As we chatted, I began to feel really sorry for him, though he only seemed upset having to come so far back to replace his things. I invited him to have supper with us on his way back up the trail. Surely the men will have returned by then.

"Thanks, I'd appreciate that. I'm tired of my own cooking." He gave me his empty cup, adding, "You're a lucky young lady to be traveling with six strong men," as he left for the general store.

By then it was getting late, and the sun was starting to slip below the mountains on the other side of the bay. It remains light for some time after the sun goes down because the snow reflects any light there is, but I sure wished the men were back. I wanted to hear about their day on the trail.

The beans were done and tasty, too. I made the biscuits, wrapped them in several pieces of cloth and put them on top of the Dutch oven to keep warm. A pot of coffee is made just waiting for them when they return. I even have hot water for tea as the Scotsmen do like their tea. And I'm enjoying it, too.

The sun had been down about an hour, though it was still fairly light, when the men finally came back. They were tired but happy with the results of the day. They found a place at Finnegan's Point for our tents and stacked things in that area.

Soon, the man returned from the general store, greeted the men, asking about the rest of their day. I gave him a plate of food and some coffee while the men thanked him for stopping by to see me.

The men spoke about their day with Liam speaking first. "The trail's not too bad. I was actually surprised 'cause I thought it'd be much worse. Sure am glad we had them sledges, though. They worked out well."

As Leonard took another helping of beans, he said "Really, Freddie, it's not bad. 'Course this is only the first day and the first trip, but it shouldn't take more than several days to move everything there. I think tomorrow we'll take the stoves and tents so we won't have the long trip back before we eat."

Tony and Mark stumbled over each other's words trying to be the next to speak. Tony won. "But the best part of the day was coming home. We found we could come down part of the river riding on the sledges! Felt almost like a kid again."

"Yeah, until you steered us right into that pile of rocks and over we went!" Mark wasn't going to let him forget that. But everyone must have enjoyed the sight because they shook their heads in agreement.

We talked a while longer but the men were tired, and we all needed sleep. Walt and our new friend, Mr. Hale, washed the dishes, and then bragged about having the cleanest hands in the group. Mr. Hale stayed sharing Tony and Mark's tent, saying he'd help us the next day if he could put his new purchases on our sledges.

March 11 - Finnegan's Point

It took longer than anticipated to get our things to Finnegan's Point. I did come with the second day's trip, and realized the men were right. The trail was not bad. Ice on the river was covered in places with a thin layer of fresh snow though mostly it was blown bare and slippery. I fell only twice.

That morning I cooked oatmeal with sugar while the men loaded the two sledges. Moving seven people with a so-called "ton of gear" each is a long process. When I came with the second trip, I insisted on carrying something and ended up carrying only one bedroll. Walt said it wouldn't be any heavier to put it on the sledges, but he gave in to my wishes. I must admit though, when we got to Finnegan's Point, I was tired, and I don't think I'll argue the point next time.

We bid farewell to Mr. Hale and thanked him for the help. He said he'd watch out for us when we get to the lakes. It was really nice to have the extra help he gave us.

The trail was certainly busy with people, a steady line of men, a number of dog sleds, two-wheeled pull carts, Indians packing gear, and even horses. And the line never stopped. We'd stop to rest, but the line moved on. Then we would pass others resting. So many men looked worn and haggard, their eyes sad, their faces coated with campfire smoke. For some this may be the last trip to Finnegan's Point or wherever they were going. Many could have been like Mr. Hale, returning to Dyea, needing to replace lost or stolen goods or to replenish dwindling food supplies.

The day I came was cloudy, though it didn't snow as I thought it might. But the wind really blew down the canyon along the river channel. It was good to reach camp though it took a long time to set up the tents and get a fire going. While I started supper - with the Scotsmen's help, we had hotcakes - Leonard and Walt put our Yukon stove in the tent with the stove pipe sections fitted together going through a hole in the sloping tent roof top. Now we can stay warmer at night by using the stove. Someone said it was usually below zero at night, and I almost believe them.

The men left early the next morning going back to Dyea hoping to make two trips. For the last four days the men have trudged back and forth I don't know how many times. On two days they did make two trips, but they didn't get back until well after dark. Now that we are on the trail, the dark of night seems to come quicker in among the trees.

The first day here, I wrote to Mom and Pops, sending the letter with Leonard to be mailed in Dyea. I realized I hadn't written since before we left Seattle. While I was writing, a couple of men stopped by with arms loaded with freshly cut spruce boughs and told me something very important. If we put fresh spruce boughs on the snow inside the tent, then put our sleeping blankets on top of them, we would stay much warmer. I thanked them, and they even gave me some of their boughs to try.

Finnegan's Point is actually a small town. There are a few log cabins, a saloon, restaurant, and even a blacksmith's shop for the few horses which are used as pack animals. Across the river, a frozen waterfall looks about one hundred feet high. It comes right from the foot of the glacier tucked up in the canyon high in the mountains. If it were sunny, the glacier would sparkle, but, alas, the clouds hung low most of the time.

The trail is so well traveled that it would be hard to get lost. In places it is actually muddy from the many feet trudging by every day. And the trail is never quiet. Dogs bark, men yell orders to dogs, horses snort, and the constant sound of feet moving, crunching in the snow, or sloshing through the muddy areas adds to the cacophony of noise. The tree cover reflects the sounds, though they diminish somewhat at night.

As the going gets harder, men begin to throw things away. Weight seems to be the deciding factor for what they don't need. I have seen parts of cast iron stoves, a rocking chair, which I am sure by now has been used for fire wood, and trunks by the score. Mrs. Palmerston was sure right telling us not to bring ours! Men have even discarded clothes, boots, and carts they thought at one time might be helpful. I am sure there are many more things beneath the snow. A person could almost re-supply part of an outfit from the cast-offs found here.

Tomorrow the men will make the first trip to Canyon City, about three miles away. Leonard said the tents will go on the second trip, giving them time to locate a place for them on the first trip.

Right now, we're all enjoying coffee or tea around the fire before going to bed. Tomorrow will be another transfer point. From what others have said Canyon City is supposed to be a larger area with an established town. I wonder what it will really be like. I would like to see if there was a store there where I could get some more tea as I think we are drinking more that we really planned on.

I wish Sis, Leonard's little sister, could be here with us. I'm sure she would find this exciting in spite of the cold. She has always seemed to be one with a spirit of adventure, and this is certainly an adventure. I think of our families back home knowing they are thinking about us and I wish I could tell them about our new friends. I'm sure they would like to hear any news from us.

March 16 - Morning at Canyon City

By mid-afternoon yesterday, all our gear was here, and we enjoyed part of a day of rest. Five men just left on the first trip to Sheep Camp. Mark stayed here, not feeling well. He took a rather nasty fall yesterday, tripping over something buried beneath the snow. He hit his head pretty hard, leaving a big lump on the side, a black eye, and a splitting headache. He felt dizzy when he stood up quickly, so we thought he should rest today. Actually, it was nice having someone around even if he slept off and on.

The trail from Finnegan's Point to here was steadily uphill. Again it was mostly under tall trees, with very straight trunks and their first branches rather high up. There are some smaller bushes and such, but since they have no leaves I don't know what they are.

The farther up the trail we go, the more discarded things we see. I saw a beautiful picture frame with a portrait of a man, his wife and three children. Maybe that extra bit of weight was just too much to carry. Rubber boots are the most frequently discarded item. We kept ours for use on the river, though I am sure if the men were packing everything on their backs, our boots might well be discarded. We now wear our leather boots which we lace tightly giving us good support so we don't twist or break an ankle if we were to fall. A really bad fall could really slow us down. I'm just thankful Mark's fall was not that bad.

Mark awoke a while ago and had a cup of tea. We sorted through some things trying to find our hot cocoa but couldn't locate it. His head must still be hurting as he winced and closed his eyes a couple times while leaning over.

The ladies from Dyea just arrived here. They are using Indian packers though each of them is carrying something, several even pulled small sleds. They don't look as sprightly as they did in Dyea. In fact they looked rather grumpy. One of them must have recognized me from Dyea because she waved.

Canyon City is a thriving community. It's located on the western side of the river in a good-sized clearing with restaurants, a post office, hotels, outfitting stores, and even a barber shop. The town is laid out with property lot lines, and a number of log cabins. Most people just move through, but it seems there is a spirit of community here.

Leonard and Walt were glad to have the first load at Sheep Camp. Tomorrow they'll load the sledges differently as the first part of the trail was definitely a hard pull, but from there on to Sheep Camp they said the trail was a lot easier. But it will still take time to move our things there. I sometimes feel as though I'm not doing much, but I know Leonard is glad we have hot meals

Mark was feeling much better today. This incident reminded us to be very careful. Tomorrow Mark and I will join the rest going to Sheep Camp. As I drifted off to sleep, I asked God to care for us on this difficult portion of the trail. Getting hurt up here could really be a disaster.

## March 21 - Sheep Camp at Last

It took a day longer than we hoped to get everything here. The first part of the trail was really difficult, but then it leveled off to Sheep Camp. The two carrying the pack frames actually took their loads to the top of the hard part, left them, returning to give a third hand pulling the sledges.

The area is crowded with people, dogs, horses, and crates. Beyond here horses can't be used as the trail is too difficult. For now, we've decided to take a day off to sort things out and get some much needed rest. Then the men will start up the trail to the border where our things will be left until we are ready to cross into Canada.

The weather has turned very bad. Clouds hang low and winds, blowing off the mountain tops, drive the snow almost horizontally. Trees are much smaller and are quickly being cut for firewood. Just up the trail is the tree line where the trees stop altogether. It's about four miles to the summit from Sheep Camp, and the trail is quite steep. The wind is supposedly awful near the summit, and though I know I will only have to make one trip, I am not looking forward to it at all. The men will have to make many trips in those dreadful conditions, while I sit by a nice warm fire. I think of what Mr. Hale said in Dyea. I am so fortunate to be with such good, hard working men.

# 7

## SHEEP CAMP - A PLEA FOR HELP

March 23 - Sheep Camp - Early Morning

The weather is bad, snowing right now, and the sky is steel gray. The men just left for the first trip to the summit, assuring me they would be careful. Reports from other men returning from the summit say the trail is very difficult. The struggle up is terrible, and men here are filthy dirty, smelling unwashed, their hair matted, their clothes very worn and crusted with ice and snow. They are the picture of total exhaustion. Icicles hang from beards and matted hair, many with frost bitten cheeks.

The men were dressed in the warmest clothes they had, even tying wool scarves around their faces and tucking them into their coats. Only their eyes showed. Each took extra gloves tucked into pockets. Fingers would freeze quickly in wet gloves.

There must be well over a thousand people here in Sheep Camp. This place is hemmed in a small bowl between the mountains with the frozen river cutting the area into two sections. Tents are crowded so closely together there is hardly any walking room between them and the trail.

Horses can't be used beyond here, and many have been turned loose to fend for themselves. Now they wandered through the camp looking half dead, and indeed some are. Some have sores on their backs caused by wet blankets rubbing beneath the loads they carried. They have been pushed beyond the limits of endurance, and with no place to go, they really make a nuisance of themselves. I did see some Indian packers yesterday leading several of them down the trail.

Alas, it seems hopes and dreams are also thrown away. Yesterday we saw a man just throw down his gear and exclaim in anger that he could not continue. Then he dropped the load he was carrying and headed off back down the trail. The boxes broke open revealing canned foods, eating utensils, even a new shirt. Poor man. I wonder if he was trying to make this trip by himself? Just as quickly as he left, others began to search through his discarded things for something which might feed them a little better or at least longer. The shirt was quickly snatched up by a man who looked as if he really needed it. This may be the trail to gold, but it is also a trail of broken hearts and dreams.

We heard the story of some men who were caught stealing here at Sheep Camp sometime last month. One man killed himself rather than face a trial by other men. A second man was tried, convicted, and sentenced to a whipping, and then sent down the trail and told not to return. But there are not many such events. The hardship is the trail itself, and it is a stern taskmaster.

Sheep Camp has few amenities. There are some hotels offering sleeping space at night and serving meals. Most are nothing more than a large tent. The Palmer House is a large log cabin structure which boasts of having running water – only in the Summer though. It seems the owners built one corner over a small stream which is frozen now. Over forty people are crammed in on the small wooden floor at night.

Late yesterday, Leonard, Tony, and I took advantage of some sunlight and looked around the area. At the Palmer House, we saw a line of men waiting to get inside for a meal. The hotel seemed to be huddled against a forest of tents in a shaft of light, like a cat curled up in a ray of sunshine coming through a window. The log structure appeared to be a bit smaller toward the top than it was at the bottom, but this could have been just the way the light was shining. Anyway, it sort of reminded me of an old man with his shoulders hunched over trying to stay warm. Perhaps it was trying to do just that. Then the sunlight disappeared and with it the image of the old man.

The steady diet of hotcakes or oatmeal for breakfast and beans and bread for supper has not agreed with me. I have had an upset stomach for the past three days. I manage to keep food down though I certainly don't feel like eating anything. I hope none of the men feel as I do as their jobs would be much more difficult. I am thankful that after a cup of tea at mid-day, I feel better. I do know I have lost weight as my clothes are looser, and I've taken the belt in a notch on the trousers Ian loaned me.

While diligently searching through the food crates for something different for supper tonight, and feeling that nothing sounded good, I failed to hear someone approach until I heard a soft voice whisper, "Hi."

Startled, I looked up and saw a nun. She was dressed in the warmest of clothes, but I could see her black and white head covering beneath the wool scarf pulled tightly around her head.

I stood up quickly, too quickly, and I almost fainted. I managed to return her greeting, and asked her to have a seat and some tea. I always have the pot of hot water near the fire. She sat on one of the crates and graciously accepted the tea.

"I've watched you and the men you are traveling with since you've arrived here a few days ago. I take it the tall dark haired fellow is your husband." She cupped her gloved hands around the hot tea, and looking down, spoke almost to the tea rather than to me.

"Leonard. Yes, he's my husband. We came with another friend, Walt." I fixed myself some tea and huddled closer to the fire. "There are two Scotsmen who joined us in Skagway. We're acting as their convoy over the Pass and into Canada. The other two we met on the ship to Skagway. They are from California." Trying to be friendly, I asked, "Are you traveling by yourself?"

"Oh no, dearie. This would be much too hard for me alone. I am here waiting for three to return from Dyea where they went to mail letters and re-supply some of our food. We've had Indian packers this far, but soon must re-negotiate the fee for the remainder of the journey. We are three nuns and a priest going down the Yukon River to a smaller river, which I think is named the Pelly. From there we go up river to an Indian village to help in the clinic there. The priest is also a doctor, and we three are nurses. My name is Sister Margaret Mary. And you are?"

"My name is Freddie. Really Winifred, but everyone calls me Freddie. I didn't think you were with the large group of young ladies."

"No. No. You're so right I'm not. They are in a completely different line of work."

Well, that got my attention. "What do you mean?" I questioned.

Quietly she replied, "Why, they're on their way to get the gold, too, but from the men after they finish their work and want a little company for the evening."

She put it about as delicately as she could, but I must have been surprised as I gasped, "Prostitutes?"

"Yes. They were recruited on the East Coast by the three older women in their group. It seems they were promised an adventure with some work but lots of rewards. Only since they have been on the trail have they realized the true purpose of their so-called 'adventure.' They each paid $400 for their transportation to San Francisco and with anything left over they had to buy their outfits. That's the reason I'm here." She reached over to refill her tea cup, stirring in a teaspoon of sugar, too.

I didn't reply as I couldn't think of anything to say. I just remembered seeing them in Dyea and thinking they were teachers or nurses. How wrong I was!

"You see, one of the young ladies is terribly upset because she was led to believe they would be doing honorable work. She came to me last night after most in her group had gone to sleep. She is not Catholic, but she recognized my clothing and hoped I could help her. She wants out, as she put it. She can't afford to go back to the East Coast as she has no money left, but she asked if I knew someone who might take her in so she can get away from the others. And that is why I am here to see you."

I was quiet. I thought about the young girl and how she must be really troubled by her position. What could she possibly tell her family, and why did Sister Margaret Mary come to me? Finally I asked, "How can I help?"

"That's just it, I'm not sure, but I thought, if the young lady could just come by this evening and talk with your group, maybe a solution could be found. I would come, too. In fact, I would drop by earlier. Could we do that at least? For her?"

"Sure, but I'm not certain when the men will be back."

"I'll see them when they come in as I can see your fire easily." She pointed over toward the frozen river about twenty feet from where we were.

"Alright. We'll see you tonight. Should I mention something to the men before you come?" I didn't want to upset her plans.

"That would be a help." She stood up, straightened her back as if it hurt from leaning over, and handed me her cup. As she turned to leave, she stopped and looked over her shoulder saying, "It's nice to see your men folk don't get mixed up in all the drinking and gambling around here."

I didn't tell her the Scotsmen and the two from California did put a bit of something in their tea after supper occasionally but never very much. The rest of the day I thought of the young lady's plight. I really wondered what, if anything, we could do.

I made a different supper for tonight, hoping I would feel better. Using some of our evaporated potatoes, onions, one tin of beef, and some of the sun-dried tomatoes and green beans the two from California had to share, I made a hearty soup. I had never heard of sun-dried tomatoes or green beans, and I must ask if they have to do anything special or just dry them in the sun as the name indicates.

The men returned earlier than I expected. It was about mid-afternoon when I saw them coming, and wondered if something might have happened, but all was fine. They left their loads at a place called Stone House, so named, they thought, because of a huge rock about as big as a house. From there they could see the men climbing up the pass. Just below the pass, was an area known as the Scales. This is place where the Indian packers again weigh all the things they must carry up the Pass and now charge $1 or more per pound, thus its name, the Scales. After seeing all the piles of outfits there, they decided to make their relay point at Stone House, which is not quite as crowded.

"It's possible to take a load from here to the summit in one day, but you can only make one trip a day. By relaying just to the Stone House, maybe we can make two trips each day, and then put all our effort into moving everything up the steepest part of the trail to the Canadian border. A lot will depend on the weather though." Walt did the talking but everyone was in agreement.

Tony quickly added, "There's no wood between just a bit up the trail from here until we are well into Canada. So the tents will have to go on the last trip, and that trip will be from here over the top to the next relay point, about five miles or so into Canada. That day will be very long."

Everyone appreciated the soup and was most glad not to have beans again. As we ate, I told them of Sister Margaret Mary's visit and the meeting later this evening with both the Sister and the young lady. All agreed we should try to help, but wondered if she had her own food and gear. That might make a difference.

We didn't have to wait long to find out. Sister Margaret Mary arrived as Ian and Liam were doing dishes. She sat on a crate and accepted some tea just as a young lady appeared and said "Hello." She was supposedly on her way to find some wood, she said.

"I'm Malinda Price from Vermont. I think the Sister has talked with the lady here and told her of my problem. I hope you can help me. I don't know what to do. I'm not going to do what the leaders say is our job." She was almost in tears as she spoke.

"Come on and sit down. Have some tea, and let's talk about this. There must be a way to help." Walt offered her his crate to sit on, and I gave her some tea.

Well, we talked for some time. The hardest problem to solve was how to get her across the border since everything she had, except her clothes was part of the group things. If she left, she would have no food, shelter, or any other part of the things required by the Canadians for entry into Canada. Also, the leaders had threatened anyone who wouldn't "work" or wanted to

80

leave. If such a situation arose, the young girls would be sent back down the trail with nothing but their clothes, and that was unthinkable in this climate.

We could find shelter for her, but the food and other equipment remained the problem. Once in Canada, things would be different, so we urged her to stay with her group until they had crossed the border. The men told her to have courage, and they would do whatever they could to help. As Malinda left, she thanked us and said she'd keep us informed as to their plans for the final trip over the Pass.

Sister Margaret Mary stood to leave, put her hand on Liam's shoulder, saying, "Thank you. I will pray for you and Malinda. She's doing the right thing and so are you. We leave tomorrow, but I'll keep a look out for you along the way. God bless you all."

Even though it was cold and the hour was late, we stayed around the fire talking about this new development. Only time would tell if she could get away and join us. And what if they insisted she "work" before then? We had to find some way to help her. As I settled beneath our warm blankets, Leonard softly spoke, "She is such a lovely young lady. I just hate to think of her in that situation for even one night longer."

"And what if they get their things to the top before we do? What's going to happen then? They might even reach the lakes before we do." Walt's comments were low, muffled by the blankets he had pulled almost over his head.

"I don't know. Shelter would not be a problem as she could sleep in the tent with us even though four would make this one cozy!" Leonard never tired of ribbing me about the cozy tent, but actually we had plenty of room even with the stove inside.

I said good night to both men and curled up against Leonard's warm back. I remembered Malinda as the young lady who waved to me at Canyon City. Now, it is time for sleep, and so as I say my prayers tonight, I will put the problem in God's hand, knowing that is where a solution will be found.

# 8

## SHEEP CAMP - BLIZZARD CONDITIONS AND A WARNING

March 26 - Saturday

Yesterday we bid farewell to Sister Margaret Mary and her three companions as they headed up the trail. Their Indian packers had taken almost everything to the summit, and now they were ready to make the climb and get across the border. Sister Margaret Mary stopped by to say she'd look for us at the lakes. They plan to go to Lake Bennett City and wait there for the ice to break so then they could go down river.

Malinda has stopped by several times when she was getting firewood. Once when she came, the men had just left for another trip to Stone House, and I was in the tent resting, trying to get my stomach to settle down. I still do not feel well but think I'm getting a little better. As she stepped into the tent, she indicated for me to be quiet. Then she sat down and whispered, "I told them I'd look for some wood." She seemed quite nervous.

She carried something under her heavy coat which she quickly pulled out. "Can you keep this here for me? It's some of my clothes. I'll try to bring some food when I can. I'm getting panicked because I heard the leaders say that with the delay caused by all the snow, maybe we could earn a little money before we get to Dawson. And I just can't."

I took the bundle and put it in the corner of the tent, then proceeded to tell her we had talked and the only plan we could come up with was to have her bring her things to us, as she just did, and then when her group was ready to cross into Canada, she should go with them and then find a time to slip away to join us. There was no other way we could think of to get her into Canada without all the required items.

She looked very scared, and my heart ached for her. She understood but hoped something might change between now and then. Smiling as best she could, she thanked me and slipped out to go find wood.

The day seemed very long. I got supper ready - beans again - and waited for the men to return. Since we arrived here a week ago, the weather has been very bad. It has snowed every day, but it's not really cold. The new snow is wet and heavy, however. I brushed some snow from the tents because they sagged so much from the weight.

Leonard said the trail was hard packed and always up. The cloud cover stayed, and the snow got deeper and deeper the further up they went. They have begun taking things up to the border. Often Leonard just shook his head saying he wondered if it was easier to pull fifty to a hundred pounds of goods on a sledge or to make the trip with fifty pounds on his back. It is hard both ways. In fact, I think his words were something like, "At the rate we're moving things, it will take all Summer just to get to the lakes."

Tony said the final half mile up to the summit was so steep that it was even hard to climb carrying nothing on the awful steps cut into the ice and snow. Men stood in line for a long time just to start up the stairs, and if they stepped out of line to rest, their place was quickly taken by others. Then they might wait a long time before there would be a break in the line, and they could start up the stairs again. Walt quickly added that coming down was much easier - they slid down on the seat of their pants.

After supper, we huddled around the fire trying to think of some other way to help Malinda. She seemed so scared and though we wanted to help, we really didn't know what else we could do. Ian and Liam, with daughters and daughters-in-law, could not imagine what heartaches she was having. As we finally went to bed, we agreed something must happen and happen soon.

March 30 - Late Afternoon

The men returned with more tales of the ever deepening snow, with blizzard conditions, and tempers short among so many on the trail. Then suddenly there was a terrible commotion not too far away. Men were shouting, even women were getting into the argument. Walt and Mark went to investigate, hoping Malinda's plan of leaving had not been discovered.

It turned out to be related to those women but not to Malinda directly, and Leonard said it might be good news. It seems the Indian packers will not pack the ladies' gear unless they are paid $1.25 a pound. About half their things are at the summit, but the Indians complained about the amount of gear and would not continue without a raise. The older ladies were arguing, and the shouting match began.

"How can that be good news for Malinda?" I asked.

"If the Indians won't work for a few days and we can get more things to the summit, then maybe we could cross the Pass at the same time." Walt hoped this would work.

"The Indians left saying they would return tomorrow to see if the women agreed to their higher price, or they said the women could carry their own things." Mark smiled, and none of us could picture these women carrying boxes or crates.

As of now, Malinda has brought over most of her clothes and a bit of food, mainly a couple tins of beef, some dried fruits, coffee and tea. How she manages to get these things without others knowing, I do not ask.

After supper, we crowded close to the fire while the men made plans to take more things to the top. Ian said he'd rather have everything buried in one place - the top - than in several places.

Liam actually felt once our things now at Stone House were at the top, it would take about a week to ten days of hard work to move everything else from here to the summit. The last trip would be with the tents, then across the top and on to the next relay point. But if the snow continues, it might take longer. Liam talked with the Canadian officials at the summit who said the snow is already seventy to seventy-five feet deep at the summit, the most they've seen in years. The summit has had much more snow than we've had here in Sheep Camp.

And so to bed again. In two weeks we should be over the worst part of the trail and into Canada. I don't know what to expect once we are in Canada, but it will be good to have this part of the trail behind us. Once over the top we'll have only fourteen miles or so to the lakes. And that is downhill! Joy!

I stop writing tonight still thinking of Malinda. Somehow we'll find a solution to her problem. In this short time, I have grown to like her very much, and we both enjoyed the few times we have been able to talk together.

## April 2 - Saturday, Still at Sheep Camp

Thursday, March 31, the men left very early, taking with them fried biscuits, dried fruit, and some hard candy Liam had found in his coat pocket. Today four would climb the Pass with crates already at the Scales, while the other two would use the sledges to bring more things from Stone House to the Scales. They said not to expect them until late because they wanted this part of the job finished.

Indeed, it was late when they got back, very tired and cold. The snow was so deep at Stone House it took a long time to uncover all our belongings.

April 1st, they left immediately after breakfast, pulling the sledges piled high and more boxes strapped on the pack frames, planning to go all the way to the top. It would be a long, hard haul, almost four miles in near blizzard conditions.

Malinda came by to say the older ladies had agreed to pay the packers price, but the Indians will only pack the gear to the summit. The women leaders said they would find others to take their things down to the lakes. She thought it would be more than a week before they could cross the border. I thought their new schedule might just coincide with ours, so maybe things would work out after all.

When the men returned very late, Mark said they had only moved things to the Scales. It was too late for them to start up the Pass as that took about four hours or more, the pace being set by the slowest climber in the line.

Ian and Liam were upset about something, but they didn't seem to be too anxious to talk about it. Finally, Tony urged them to tell us what the problem was if it might affect us in any way.

Ian hung his head and assured us it had nothing to do with us, but it seems they ran into some of Soapy's men while relaying gear from Stone House to the Scales. As they struggled to pull a sledge, a couple other men carrying gear offered to help them pull it if they could put their packs on top.

"So they puts their loads on the sledge and starts to pull the ropes. After a short time, the other men threw down their ropes and said they couldn't go no further. The sledges were just too heavy, and they needed to rest. We wanted to go on, so they took their loads from the sledge and also a couple of our boxes. We said they'd taken some of our things, and they argued accusing us of lying. Well, it turned into a big argument until finally Liam took one of their packs and tossed it aside." Ian seemed embarrassed to admit that he actually had lost his temper.

"Ya, but when I tossed that pack, I realized that it didn't weigh nothin'. It was as light as a feather. So I asked 'im what he was carrying as it certainly didn't weigh much. And he says it ain't none of my business. But he says he wants his crate, or he's gonna tell people we stole his things." I could tell Liam was really angry.

"Just then, a couple other men who had heard the argument grabbed the arms of them men. They asks us to verify that them crates was ours, and I said we could. I shows them the S-J 21 and S-J 14 that was painted on those two crates. I tells him those markings are the initials and numbers of two of the men we's traveling with."

"Lucky for us those was the two things they tried to steal, and they was marked clear as can be. Then I told them about the light packs of those men. Well, then one man he checks out their packs, and they's filled with straw. Them men was some of Soapy's gang, and we got tricked by them. It'll be good to get into Canada, 'cause the Canadians check everyone and won't let Soapy's men cross the border."

"Well, what happened to those men, Ian?" Leonard asked.

"One man he told 'em to get on down the trail to Skagway, and if he saw them again anywhere on the trail, he'd personally march them down the trail and give them a "blue ticket" home. That means he'd make sure they got on the first ship south and out of the area." Ian was not happy to have been tricked.

"Well, thank goodness nothing worse happened, and they chose the wrong boxes to steal. Guess that extra work of painting the initials and numbers on the crates in Seattle has paid off again." Walt was pleased with the outcome and thankful for those men who stepped in to help.

"I guess we was just tired of all the work and tried to help a couple of supposedly honest men, but I sure don't like being tricked like that." Liam is a good man, as is Ian, and I knew they felt bad about the incident.

"Say, Freddie, that stewed fruit sure tasted good tonight. We should have it more often. It goes down real nice." Tony, always the one to cheer us up, made sure the conversation turned to something more pleasant.

"Thanks. Actually, it's some of the dried fruit Malinda brought to us. She stopped by this afternoon with a few more tins of meat and the fruit. She thinks they will be another week at least before they cross the Pass."

April 2nd was another day not to be forgotten. It was Saturday, and again the men left early headed for the Scales and then the Pass. But it was snowing something terrible at the Scales, actually blizzard conditions. Some other men who had made a trip to the top said over five feet of new very wet snow had fallen on this one day alone. So, the men came home rather discouraged at not having made the climb up.

As we were eating supper, Leonard jumped up excitedly when he recognized our Indian friend from Dyea, whose wife had made my fur lined boots. It was so good to see him again, and we insisted he share our meal.

"How you do with your things?" he asked while eating some beans and biscuits.

"Things are slow in this terrible weather, but we'll be across in a week. It'll be good to have this part of the trail behind us." Leonard filled him in on our progress.

Shaking his head, the Indian warned, "Big storm, bad on the top. Don't work tomorrow or few days. I not pack, no way. Trouble. Bad trouble."

Walt quickly answered, "But you don't pack on Sunday anyway. You Indians always rest that day, and we want to get this over with. We don't want to take a day off."

"No! Rest! You tired. Bad! No work! Please, friends, no work!"

With that, he bid us goodbye saying he would see us in a couple days, and again urged the men to take a few days off until the storm was well over.

After he left, the men talked about it, and finally decided he was probably right. They were all terribly tired, and the blizzard conditions made any work doubly hard. But they agreed to only one day off.

So with the prospect of a day off, everyone had another cup of coffee before retiring. Yes, everyone! We've even gotten the Scotsmen drinking coffee once in a while now!

Inside the tent Leonard and Walt agreed a day off would be nice. The snow was very deep at the summit, and more was falling all the time, but like so many terrors on the trail, the biggest fear seems to be the fear of the hard work and of the unknown conditions. But it seemed once the sledges have been loaded and the men picked up the ropes, they are ready for the job. I'm rather glad they agreed to take the day off. They all look extremely exhausted, and a day off would replenish their spirits, and a good night's sleep will do them a world of good.

# 9

## SHEEP CAMP - AVALANCHE!

April 4 - The Day After

I must be careful to explain what happened yesterday, and I must get everything down as accurately as possible so I will remember the events of the dreadful day. I am most thankful we took the day off and will always remember the warning of our Indian friend.

With the prospect of a day of rest, we looked forward to a good night's sleep, but the fierce winds and driving snow kept us awake a good portion of the night. Twice Walt got up to brush the snow from the tent. It's snowed here almost every day for over two weeks now, and though the men have made a trip to the Scales each day, the work has been brutal.

That's why we were all looking forward to Sunday off using the time to dry out clothes, rest, and renew energy to begin again today, Monday. But it was not to be.

Very early Sunday, April 3 - actually Palm Sunday, if my calendar is right - two men came running into camp, banging on the hotel door, shouting there'd been an avalanche up the trail, and a number of men were buried. That got everyone's attention, and soon others who had been on the trail stumbled into camp, winded from running, saying those who had been caught in the avalanche were being freed. So we actually felt a relief that it wasn't worse.

Just before noon, however, thundering from 2500 feet above the trail, a monstrous wall of snow gave way about two miles above Sheep Camp. It roared down the mountainside covering the trail and an area about ten acres in size to a depth of twenty to thirty feet. Immediately the call went out for help.

Hundreds raced from Sheep Camp with shovels. All six of the men went. A man from the hotel came by asking me and the other women in camp - few though we were aside from the ladies group - if we would make coffee and have it ready when men came back for they would surely be tired, cold, and in need of something hot to drink. He said he'd started cooking lots of hot food for them, but he would appreciate our help with coffee. Of course, I was ready to do what I could, but I feared for everyone.

The first ones to come back told of the snow on the mountain still groaning and sounding as if another avalanche would come down any minute, but it held. All day men came back and forth with stories of snow so densely packed it was almost impossible to dig even when they could hear someone buried beneath calling for help.

By mid-afternoon, the first of the bodies was brought down. Then the scene played out like a bad dream. Other bodies were brought down. Men came into camp for something hot to drink and immediately went back. I kept looking for Leonard, Walt, or maybe some of the other men.

The longer I waited the more worried I became about the others.

Finally, Tony and Mark came in. Their faces, beards, hair, even their eyebrows, were encrusted in icy snow, and when they took off their gloves, their hands were red and almost raw. Their wool gloves were soaked. Tony said the rest would be in soon, but they just needed to continue digging a while longer.

It was almost an hour later before the rest finally came in. By now all daylight was gone and around the whole area, fires were lit showing the way back. There was a hush over Sheep Camp never before present. Even the dogs were quiet. It was almost eerie, and a chill went up my spine.

As the men huddled near the fire, holding hot coffee cups, drinking to warm themselves inside and their hands outside, they told of hearing voices below the snow, some cursing one minute and praying the next. As quickly as they could, men would start digging near the sound of the voices only to hear the voices grow weaker and weaker until finally no sound came. Then bodies would be dug out.

According to Ian small air holes would sometimes appear in the avalanche field which they knew were caused by the breath of those buried alive, but too soon, those holes would no longer grow. All agreed that by far the worst was hearing voices calling for help and not being able to dig quickly enough to rescue the trapped men.

Several were dug out alive and rushed into camp where they were covered in blankets and warmed in the hotel. All evening, men came to camp for a rest, to warm up, and go back out. Even late at night, more bodies were brought down. My heart went out to those who lost a son, a brother, a father, or a husband.

Liam heard of a woman who was dug out alive. She had been turned upside down on her head by the avalanche and was found just that way, cursing and shouting for help. As he came back for some supper, men were busy digging out another man, whose legs were still encased in snow so hard the rescuers were using picks to break the tightly packed bond of snow holding him.

I let the men talk as I finished fixing supper, beans with bacon tonight was about all I could manage and lots of hot coffee and tea. As they drank, they continued to talk amongst themselves, almost as if I wasn't there. I listened but stayed out of the conversation. I knew they just needed to talk. As cups emptied, I filled them again. The men were cold and tired, and soon would need to sleep.

I even had a big pot of hot water by the fire and encouraged each man to wash his face and hands in hot water, even though this was not always done as we tried to use the wood mainly for cooking, but tonight they agreed to clean up - maybe more like trying to wash away the awful sights they had witnessed today.

Then slowly, they relaxed, their heads slumped over, and finally hunching their shoulders forward to relieve the tension in their backs, they bid all good night and crawled into bed. It would be a restless sleep, but sleep was what everyone needed.

Very early this morning, Monday, other men began taking the bodies down to Dyea. Coffins had been quickly made from the lumber of crates, and into each coffin was put a bottle or some such container with a paper giving what little information was known about the victim - maybe his name, if someone knew him, or maybe the town or city where he had told others he lived - anything that might help in notifying relatives.

Someone stopped by a while ago and said over a thousand men were up at the site yesterday digging and trying to save anyone they could. So far about fifty bodies have been taken down, but they fear there are more still buried.

News just came that the trail would be officially closed for several days as the rescue work continued, but now only the dead would be found. Leonard and Walt got ready to go back out to help as did the others. They had to. They couldn't let anyone remain entombed in the ice.

After breakfast, with dry gloves, warm wool hats pulled down over their ears, and wearing their heavy coats, they picked up their shovels and joined the many others going back to the avalanche area. They were quiet as they left, and I had to turn away from them. I prayed for those who died. What awful news would be forthcoming for those families.

I must write to our families to let them know we are safe. I'll ask them to share the news with the Jacksons, as everyone will surely hear this news long before my letter arrives, and they certainly will be worried. It is always bad news that travels the fastest.

I closed my eyes briefly, asking God to be with the families of the men who died. The families would not know of their loss until much later when those men could be identified.

## Late in the Afternoon

After writing my letter, I started supper. My fried biscuits are finished and staying warm on top of the big pot of beef and vegetable stew. I even made more of the stewed fruit. Maybe I'm using more food than I should, but the men have worked so very hard and need a good meal at night. I'm not sure how they do it. Sometimes I don't know if I can keep cooking and getting them to dry their gloves, hats, and especially socks each night. They now each wear two pair of wool socks to keep their feet warm. I've heard stories of rotted feet from wet socks, and I don't want it to happen to them.

In contrast to the last few weeks, the sun actually came out today, and it was pleasant in the sun, though not warm enough to melt any snow, just enough to feel good on my face. I shook out the blankets we used each night and hung them on the tent roof poles to air. I did the same for the others, too.

The men dragged in after sunset but while the sky was still somewhat light. Reports from up the trail are that there have been at least fifty men and one woman killed. The sun was even shining up there making this tragedy even worse. Just as the terrible storms ended and the sun began to shine, that's when the avalanche happened. But the storms dumped so much heavy, wet snow on the top, as much as six feet in one day, and that weight was just a bit too much and down it came.

Both Canadian constables and American officials are coordinating the rescue work, and while that is going on, no one would be allowed to cross the border. All outfits piled up at the Scales are now under six feet of new snow and would have to be dug out before the anything could be taken to the border when the trail re-opens. And no one had any idea of when that might be.

I wondered when we would finally cross. It seemed so close a few days ago; now it seems so far away. We remembered the warning from our Indian friend about not working on Sunday. I'm sure the warning saved our lives, and I hoped other Indians might have made those dire warnings to those along the trail and in camp. But almost no one takes Sunday off. What a tragedy to happen at any time but especially when so many men were on the trail.

April 8 - Mid-Morning

The trail has finally opened again, and now that the snows have stopped, the men were anxious to get an early start today. They had been around camp for a couple of days while final attempts were made to find any other bodies. The official count of those killed will not be known for some time - maybe not until after the snow melts in Spring – but last reports of bodies recovered is less than forty, not fifty as first reported.

One unusual story coming from the recovery teams was that of an ox found two days after the avalanche in sort of a snow cave. He had stomped around enough to give him standing room, and he was found contentedly chewing his cud. It must have been quite a sight when the rescuers finally broke through the ice packed snow to find that scene.

Tony and Leonard had taken my letter down to Dyea to mail during the time the trail was closed. They could have mailed it here, but they wanted to get some more tools. They feel a couple of extra shovels will come in handy, and maybe some extra gloves as the ones they now have are beginning to wear thin. We have heard there are only a few stores at Lake Bennett City, more than twelve miles from the border.

Returning along the trail, they looked through a number of piles of discarded items to see if there was anything which we might use. They found some extra eating utensils and a plate which might come in handy when Malinda can join us. They even brought me something. They found a pair of wool trousers which with a bit of hitching up around the waist will fit me. I can now give Ian back his trousers that I've been wearing since Dyea.

They also found big a piece of canvas about four feet wide by ten feet long. I wasn't sure what use it would be, but Leonard and Tony with Mark's help rigged it between the tents as a wind break. The weather may be sunny during the days, but the temperature was still at freezing most of the time and below zero every night.

This morning as the men were ready to start up the trail, our Indian friend quietly came into camp. He was as glad to see us as we were to see him. We thanked him for his dire warning knowing it saved our lives and promised always to look to the sky for signs of storms from now on. He couldn't stay long as he had to start packing up the trail again, but he left us a package wrapped in some old newspapers. Inside was dried salmon. He said this would be especially good to eat while on the trail, giving the men strength for the day. We graciously accepted his gift, and the men left at the same time, but this time with pockets filled with dried salmon. What a special gift!

How fortunate to have met this man so long ago in Skagway, and how special he has treated us. Tales of the taciturn Indians who drive hard bargains, even throwing down packs and refusing to pick them up again until they are paid more, have not been our dealings with this friend. We have been most fortunate indeed. I hope we will see him again before we make our final trip to the top. I wish I could think of something to give him for his wife as a token of how we feel about him.

When the men left, I turned to my daily routine. I have been so busy and worried during this avalanche time I hadn't really noticed how much better I feel. My stomach was still somewhat upset but not as much. I also realized I haven't seen Malinda or even heard from her for several days. As I looked around I saw only a few ladies in their camp but did not see Malinda. Maybe later I would go chat with them about the terrible avalanche and find out where the others were.

I pulled a crate closer to the fire, made a cup of tea, and sat down to read the old newspaper in which the salmon had been wrapped. Even old news is welcomed as we've not heard anything from the Outside, a term meaning anywhere but here, for many weeks now. The paper was one from Skagway so the news pertained mostly to there with only a little from Outside. One article caught my eye. It seemed Skagway was really fed up with Soapy Smith and his gang. Men were robbed as they come off the ships still landing in Skagway, and now murder was added to the list of crimes. Men coming back over the Pass from Dawson City to Skagway and then to a ship heading south were being robbed of the gold they had worked so hard to get. I thought of Frank Reid and his words, hoping someday those in Skagway would drive Soapy out or kill him.

Finally, I decided to walk over to talk with the group of ladies. I remember the rebuff about "riff-raff" made in Dyea but realized times were different now. All of us have been conditioned by the difficulties of the trail and the disaster of the avalanche, and now maybe the leaders would not be so brusque. With a cup of tea in hand, I bravely, yet with a bit of trepidation, walked over to their camp.

"Hi, how are things going for you folks. I certainly hope none of you or your things were caught in that avalanche." I tried to be sympathetic to their situation.

One of the younger women looked up from the fire and seemed pleased to have someone to talk to. Even one of the older ladies smiled in response to my remarks.

"Actually, we were fortunate. Our packers, of course, refused to work that Sunday, so we were here. We were able to help out by making coffee. Wasn't that awful though? I'm glad we weren't going up the trail. Come sit a while.

"But we are far behind schedule, and now some have started hauling things to the top. Our packers thought that was pretty funny as the ladies couldn't carry much, but two did manage to leave with our small sleds tied up with things. Others were carrying what they could." I think she was very happy she had not gone or maybe she didn't volunteer to go.

"Well, I just noticed your group was smaller and thought maybe some had gone down to Dyea for some reason." I tried to make my comments casual rather than questioning.

The leader quickly expressed the thoughts of all of them, I think. "Never! Once up this trail is enough. I just want to get over the top now and get on with this trip or whatever it is you want to call this miserable hike we're making. I'll be so glad to get a hot bath at Lake Bennett City I don't know what to do!"

We all agreed and laughed, at the same time knowing it would be a number of days yet before we got to that point. I stayed a few more minutes, still not seeing Malinda but at least now thinking she was probably one of those hauling boxes to the top.

I actually took a nap in front of the tent this afternoon near the fire with the warmth of the sun on my face. I hoped this meant Spring was really on the way, but I knew that while Spring may be coming at home, Winter was far from over here.

This evening after supper, the men reported good work at the Scales. They dug out our things and then made a trip to the top. There, even though everything was buried, they recognized the long handled shovel with the painted black handle they had put in the snow by our things to mark the spot.

But they also have experienced a new danger. With the sun shining on the snow, their faces were getting sun burned, and their eyes were stinging something fierce. They were told this could cause snow blindness, and they should blacken their faces with ashes especially around the eyes. Better yet, they should wear snow goggles.

Well, we didn't have any snow goggles, and now wished they had gotten some in Dyea. Walt and Liam went to check the stores here after supper, returning later with snow goggles for all. They also looked a bit sheepish. Walt mumbled something about stopping to speak to some men they'd seen on the trail, and they had enjoyed some hot coffee with cocoa in it. That sounded so good! Too bad we didn't all go looking for glasses!

Tomorrow would come soon enough, and as we got ready for bed, Walt quietly commented, "Thanks, Freddie, for all your hard work. I know you were worried when we were gone so long after the avalanche, and we appreciated the hot coffee very much when we returned."

Leonard hugged me tightly and whispered softly, "Thanks from me for coming to this frozen land, but most of all thanks for being my wife and my best friend."

I felt warm indeed, and sleep came quicker than I expected.

# 10

## SHEEP CAMP - ON THE TRAIL TO THE SCALES

April 10 - Sunday, Sheep Camp

I finally got a chance to talk with Malinda. She has been making trips to the Scales at least every other day and said the climb was hard but not as hard as she expected, but then she admitted she wasn't carrying the fifty to sixty pounds the men carried. She hastened to add, too, that when she first looked up at the final 1000 feet to the top, she was certain she would never be able to make that awful climb. I wonder about me, but after more talk about the conditions we have been through, we both felt there was nothing we couldn't do if we just put our minds to it and took one step at a time.

There are still many boxes, crates, and bags to take up, and Leonard thinks it will be five more days before we cross the border. I told Malinda this and asked how they were doing. She had no idea, but their piles of things don't ever seem to get much smaller.

Malinda has brought almost all of her clothes to us, and we have packed them inside some canvas bags the men found on the piles of discarded things. She has only one dress to wear now and hopes the others don't notice she always wears the same thing. We both laughed realizing we wear the same clothes all the time. It's been too cold to change clothes anyway.

Ian and Liam can hardly wait to get over the Pass so their goods will no longer be sealed by the bond imposed in Skagway. Liam said they had a surprise to share with us. They won't give us any kind of hint except to say they were very sure we would be excited about it. Those two are really hard workers, and I'm so glad they came with us over the Chilkoot Pass. We talked about where the other Scotsmen might be. They went over the White Pass Trail, so if there has been no trouble on the trail, they should be at the lakes by now. Ian and Liam seem anxious to meet up with them again.

Today, with a very early start, they were each able to make a trip to the top. Then after supper, they re-stacked the remaining boxes. When the sorting was finished, Leonard and Ian thought that if they continue as they did today, but leave even earlier, they might be able to make two summit trips each day. This would mean we could possibly go over on Friday of this week!

That means only five more nights here! It's hard even thinking about that when for weeks and weeks we have been so focused on getting from one relay point to the next, and now our thoughts actually are on the final few days until we can go up and over the Pass! I wondered how much earlier they would leave each day and how long after dark it would be before they came in. Then Tony remarked that with all the work, none of us have realized the days are actually getting longer.

"I have my father's pocket watch with me though I don't carry it during the day. I don't want to lose it. But I've checked the last several days before we left and when we came back, and we now have about thirteen to fourteen hours of daylight every day. That's much better than we had in Skagway."

This really surprised us, but maybe it explains why we are so tired. Since we didn't take notice of the longer days, the men just worked until it was almost dark before coming back. So with better weather and spirits lifted, the men want to work as long each day as they can. Just knowing the days are longer seemed to boost their energies. Sometimes all it takes is something small to revitalize us, like longer days and sunshine! With an end in sight for this very hard part of the trail, we go to bed in a much happier mood. I pray the snows do not come again or at least not the heavy wet snows as our plans certainly would change once again. We are so close to getting this terrible part of the trail behind us, I really don't want anything to alter our plans. And I only hope that Malinda's group plans will coordinate closely with ours.

April 14 - After Supper

There are only a few boxes left here now. Tomorrow we will get up early, pack the tents, bedrolls, Yukon stoves, pots, and utensils. Then we will begin our final trip. I will get to see what the trail looks like for myself instead of imagining it from what the men have said. I have great trepidation about what tomorrow will bring, but as I told Malinda on Sunday, "I only have to take it one step at a time." And I will only have to go to the top once. I wonder how many trips the men have made. Leonard guessed the number at over two hundred for all six them so far!

Malinda came by, distressed to see the sledges empty, knowing tomorrow would be our last day here. The ladies will still be here several days before they are ready to cross the Pass. What does she do now? How will she ever find us once we're across?

Liam put his arm around her, and told her not to worry. We plan to stop at the far end of a small lake named Deep Lake. And she could meet us there. Most people go all the way to Lindeman City or Lake Bennett which is five to eight miles further. If her group was delayed for some reason, we would be at Lake Bennett, starting to build our boats.

Ian got up and went in his tent, coming out with a big bright red plaid scarf. "No need ta worry that you can't find us. Jest look 'til ya sees this bright flag a flyin' from our tent pole. And thar we'll be, ready ta take ya in. We'll be alookin fa ya, young lady, so don't ya worry none."

Malinda cried happy tears knowing we had made plans, and we'd be looking out for her. Walt said she'd better wash her face before going back or the others might wonder why she was crying. Later, Walt and Malinda took a walk, careful to go away from the ladies' group, so she could compose herself before she returned to her campsite.

We didn't stay up for another cup of coffee or tea. This is something that we usually did, but I was almost too excited to sleep, knowing that tomorrow at this time the worst of the trail would be over! I just hope that I will be able to keep up with them men and do my share of carrying something. And I hope I will not have to rest on the steep part of the trail.

April 15 - Up to the Scales!

I awoke with a start. Where was I? The dream – it was so real. It was as if I had repeated our entire trip. And it was as clear in my dream as it had been when it happened. I shook my head to clear my mind and orient myself to where I was. Propping myself up on my elbow, I could see Leonard and Walt still asleep, and it was still dark outside. I snuggled back under the blanket and pressed against Leonard's back, maybe to reassure myself that I'd do fine going up the Pass today because I had a good husband to look after me and good friends like Walt, the two Scotsmen and the two from southern California. I closed my eyes and drifted off to sleep again, this time without the dreams.

I got up just before sunrise when I smelled coffee brewing. What a joy! Ian and Mark had gotten up, made coffee, hotcakes, and bacon! And I even felt like eating! I wanted to tell everyone about my dream, but there was so much excitement about our final day on this side of the Pass, that it slipped my mind. Maybe I'll tell Leonard tonight when the Pass is behind us, and we are on the downhill side of the mountains.

No one really sat down to eat, but rather stood around eating a bite and then taking down a tent, rolling it up and putting it on the sledges. No one wants me carry anything, but I want to carry my canvas satchel with some of my personal items in it.

As the men were tying down the last of the items, I walked over to the ladies' area and said goodbye to them. I saw Malinda but she neither spoke nor acknowledged me by any other obvious indication that she knew me other than a wink when no one was looking. I told the ladies we would look for them somewhere over the top.

Then it was time to leave. Two men carried the pack frames with the bedrolls, while the tents, stoves, cook pots and eating utensils and the last of the boxes were put on the sledges. Leaving Sheep Camp I felt as if I were leaving a safe haven. Cold and stormy though it was, Sheep Camp did seem more like a community. Maybe it was because we'd been here so long. Maybe it was all of us working together at the time of the avalanche. We got to meet some fine folks, and even though Soapy's gang filtered in with their shell games, we pretty much ignored them.

North of Sheep Camp we began to climb, not a hard climb but a steady one. The trees became shorter and further apart until suddenly I realized there were no more trees. Looking up toward the mountains there was nothing but snow covered fields with big rocks sticking out from under the dirty blanket of snow.

Up, up, up! I really didn't get tired. The trail got steeper, and then again it leveled out somewhat. But mainly it was up. Always up. Leonard finally pointed out a very large rock up ahead saying it was Stone House. I asked where the avalanche occurred, and he said we have been walking over it for a while now. Looking up, he pointed to where the ledge of snow had broken away. Once Leonard pointed it out, I could see it clearly, but on my own I probably would never had noticed it.

It was a rather steep climb to the Stone House area but then the trail leveled off for a while, then it went up again. We were certainly never alone. As far as we could see in front there were men, some pulling sleds or the larger sledges, most with boxes and crates strapped on their backs. If I turned to look back, it was the same scene. I can't even imagine how many were on the trail today, and this is only one day. It must have been like this each day for weeks now. So many trips to the top for each person. It never seemed to come to an end for those going day after day, until one day they, like us, realized this was the final day to the summit.

Even though we wore our snow goggles and had put charcoal on our faces, I could feel the reflection of the sun off the snow on my face. I'm so glad we got the goggles.

Walt pointed to an area stacked with goods indicating it was the Scales. This had only been a point they talked about, but now I could see it myself. As we neared it, Ian suggested a rest. I was glad he did as I was really tired, but I certainly didn't want to be the one to suggest a rest, not when they have been climbing this trail for weeks now.

All around were piles and piles of things, much like in Skagway or Dyea, but here many crates were stacked on top of piles now covered with snow.

Sitting on the sledges was restful, and Leonard urged me to tie my satchel on, but I wouldn't give in. Beyond the Scales the mountains rose almost straight up. There were two notches in the mountains a little apart from each other. The one to the left, I was told, was the trail to the summit. The other was also a trail, but it was much more prone to smaller avalanches, so few actually went that way.

As I looked up, my eyes followed the line of men far enough away to look like ants marching up a very steep hill. It looked dreadful! To think I will only climb it once, but the men have each made over thirty trips up, many times going up twice in one day. I vowed not to complain nor stop and hold up the line. I can make the climb once!

We waited for a group returning from the top to pass before leaning down to pick up the ropes. We'd been walking about five minutes when a man stepped out of the line as he was going back toward Sheep Camp. It was our Indian friend! We had found him, and now it was almost time to say good-bye to this man who had been so much a part of our experiences on the trail. He spoke of our kindness to him and thanked me again for my hair cuttings. I had almost forgotten he had given me a haircut back in Dyea! I was now so used to short hair it would seem strange to have long hair again.

I reached into my satchel and gave him a small bundle tied up in one of my dish towels. He started to open it, but I put my hand on his, saying, "It's just a little something for your wife. Please thank her again for my warm fur lined boots. They have kept my feet so very warm. I think this might be something she will like." Then I gave into my impulses and hugged him. He hugged back though I do believe he was somewhat taken aback. He has always been such a quiet man. Even my men smiled at my actions, but I felt such joy at having met this special man I just did what I wanted to do.

He turned to leave, I thought, but instead spoke with the two other Indian packers with him. Then they immediately started to takes the ropes off of the sledges. Immediately they picked up some of our things and strapped them to their backs.

"We take. We paid toll today so we go free for day now. You part of my group and not pay. We help you up. Very cold near the top."

With that, the few remaining things were once again tied on the sledges, including my satchel. Now it was time to start up the last climb. It is about a half mile from the Scales to the top of the American border and maybe another quarter mile to the Canadian summit. But it is all up, and a very steep up, too.

So this is where I begin to take one step at a time. Thinking back to Skagway and Dyea, it has always been one step at a time. I've now learned to look at each day and to do what needs to be done then and not imagine what tomorrow might bring. I hope I will remember this always, for it is just as true here as it is in Seattle, Chicago, or back in Wisconsin on the farm.

We start off on the trail again, this time it is up to the summit and into Canada!

# 11

## OVER THE TOP - AT LAST!

April 15 - Early Afternoon to Sunset

As soon as we started climbing, the clouds came in, and the wind whipped up. No one wanted to stop since we were already in the line, so we just pulled our coats tighter around our necks and our wool hats farther down over our ears. We wanted to get over the top, and that was paramount in our minds. It was 1000 feet to the top, and then the terrible climb over the Pass would be over.

One of the Indians was first in line, but the pace was set by the man in front of him. Ian was next, Walt, then Tony pulling one of the sledges off to the side of the trail, the second Indian, Mark, me, Liam, Leonard with the other sledge, then our friend. The sledges, though much lighter since they were almost empty, were still too heavy to carry and had to be pulled by the side of the steps. Once again help had come to us, and I silently thanked God for our Indian friend. At the same time I felt rather sad because I knew this would be the last time we would see him.

As the trail made the final turn to go up the steps cut in the icy snow to the summit, the wind picked up much stronger blowing straight over the Pass and driving the snow right in our faces as it was kicked up by the boots of those in front of us. I just turned my head, looked down at the trail, and started up the steps.

There are supposed to be 1500 steps cut into the ice, but I didn't count them. I just had to take the next step. I found there was a rhythm to it. When Mark took a step on his right foot, I did the same. It was almost like a very slow march up the mountain - right, left, right, left. I learned later in the day this motion is now referred to as the Chilkoot Lock Step.

It wasn't long until the moans and groans of those in front became really pronounced. I tried not to add to it, but I did quite a bit of huffing and puffing. Soon I realized I had unknowingly grabbed onto the icy rope running beside the steps. A good number of those going up had stout sticks for support and to steady them with the loads they were carrying. One man further up the trail was carrying lumber on his back. I had watched him pass us before we started up, and marveled at his strength.

I thought we were climbing pretty well until I quickly looked back to see we had hardly moved at all, at least that's how it appeared. I couldn't see the summit as the line blocked any view of it. All I could see was men bent over at the waist, almost double. I could hear those in front and behind gasping for air, the groans of many, even some swearing at each step.

The wind was intensely cold, driving through any place where coats, hats, and gloves did not cover completely. The only way to keep warm was to go on, never stop. We passed a ledge by the side of the trail where three men were standing leaning on their support sticks, sucking in cold air. This was one of several resting points, and from the previous reports of the men, once a man stepped out of line it might be several hours before he could get back into the ever moving line. No one stopped to let others in. It was on to the top for everyone.

Time and steps passed, and I had no idea how long we had been on the stairs, how far we had come, or how much farther it was. I was actually afraid to glance ahead as I might find the top was still too far away.

Behind me, Liam offered help, "Don't even try ta look back down. The steps are very icy, and turnin' might throw ya off balance. Put ya head down and jest take the next step. You're doin' good, Freddie. It up 'n' up, jest one step at a time." Here he was telling me what I had been trying to tell myself. It's only the next step I have to take, then the next, and the next. Besides, looking up all I could see was the seat of Mark's trousers. Under other circumstances, this would have made me laugh, but now I didn't have the energy even to laugh. In camp tonight I must tell him there is a split in the seam of his pants, and then I must mend them. And I must do this quietly, not wanting to embarrass him.

I lost track of thinking about the steps, and followed Mark's feet. That's all I looked at. My energy was going quickly, and I didn't want to be the one who called for a rest stop. It was a grueling climb, and my lungs ached from breathing the very cold, frigid air coming through the wool scarf covering my nose. I thought of all the trips the men had already taken, and I prayed for the strength to go on.

The wind became stronger; the pace slowed. I slid my hand along the icy rope to steady myself. I slipped on the steps several times, catching myself with the rope. Had I been using a stick, I most likely would have fallen, and I wasn't carrying anything! How had these men done this day after day, trip after trip?

Up ahead someone stepped out of line, and in those brief few seconds as the line of men opened, I thought I could see the top. My heart raced with excitement. Could it be? Leonard must have seen me look up as he said, "Don't get too excited, Freddie. This is only the American summit. The Pass narrows to one hundred feet wide, with high cliffs on both sides. The wind is really bad there, and the Canadian summit is still further on. You're doing good. Keep it up."

I dared not tell him how tired I was, but I was so glad to hear that at least we were near the American summit. It wasn't too much longer when I heard shouts and cheers. The line scattered. I was up! Ahead we could see the North West Mounted Police Post and the officers with guns. I'd heard they were armed to keep Soapy Smith and his gang from crossing into Canada. Above them, the Union Jack, tattered and frayed, whipped in the wind. Mark took the pack off his back, and gave me a hug. We threaded our way through the stacks of goods looking for our things. Then I saw them, one with S-J 23 on it, and I knew once again we had all our things together in one spot.

As quickly as they had come, The Indians said good-bye for the last time. Everyone shook hands, and they were off. Stepping to the side of the trail, they sat down on their feet and quickly slid down in the groves made by so many others going down the fast way. I watched them leave, feeling very sad, but so thankful for the help they had given us along the trail and that help was given in friendship, without pay.

The men put down their loads and stretched to get the knots out of their backs. Leonard, Liam, and Tony then left to find one of the patrol officers who could check us across the border. I wondered what would entail, but we didn't have to wait long.

Bundled up almost from head to toe in a great buffalo coat, fur hat, and big fur lined gloves, a Canadian officer greeted us all. With the wind whipping the pages of his book, he asked our names, where we were from, and confirmed this was our last trip up. Then he looked at the Scotsmen's bond papers and their things, checking to be sure the bond seals had not been tampered with, and finally signed off on their bond papers.

It took quite a while for Tony and Mark to separate their things from ours so we could show proof we had the required amount of gear. While the men were busy doing this, I stepped behind a rather large pile so I could unbutton my coat, and get my money pouch from beneath my shirt. I needed to pay the Canadian duty. In the past I had given Leonard or Walt the toll money needed each day to climb the Pass, and last night I thought I should put the money in my satchel but simply forgot this morning. Was it really just this morning we started up? It seemed so much longer ago than that.

As the Canadian official was going through our things, I asked him how steep the trail really was. It looked to me to be almost vertical, yet I knew that was not the case.

"Well, the men say it feels like they're climbing a wall, but it's actually about a 35 degree angle up. I know you won't believe me, but if it were not so cold, it would be easier to climb in Winter than in Summer over the massive boulder strewn trail. In Summer the rains and damp fog makes everything very slippery. Then again, in Winter the wind wants to blow you back down the trail. It's hard both ways. But remember the steps are only a half a mile up. Anyone can do it one step at a time." There was that phrase again. I guess it is something to keep in mind for any situation we meet.

As the men finished up clearing the border customs, I just sat down on our pile. Once I got down, I realized how tired I was and hoped I could get up. If not, the men could either pull me up or leave me right here. I was too tired to think of moving on to the next relay point, Deep Lake, another six miles down the trail. Ian came over, sat next to me, and put his coat partially around me. I can't tell you how that made me feel. It was so bitterly cold up top, I just knew I would probably freeze, but here was this gentle man who, with his friend, had become so much a part of our experience along the trail sitting beside me trying to keep me warm. "Ya done good, Freddie. Ya done good." In those softly spoken words I knew I was truly blessed to have met these men, and as I reached to take his gloved hand in mine, I realized the feeling was mutual. We worked well together and for that we were very fortunate indeed.

Shortly, Leonard came over to where Ian and I were sitting, handed me the money pouch saying we'd eat a bite here as it had been seven hours since we left Sheep Camp, and we needed energy now. Liam came by with the extra hotcakes they had cooked this morning. He had packed the food wrapped in a towel inside his heavy coat to keep it from freezing! Soon the rest joined us, and we ate quickly as it was starting to snow, and we needed to be on our way down the trail.

Our meager, but refreshing, meal finished, the men immediately began putting all the things the Indians had carried on the sledges, even adding more boxes from the pile at the summit. Tied down and secure, it was time to leave.

Ian and Liam pulled one sledge, and Leonard and Mark pulled the second. The pack frames were strapped on top. From here it was downhill all the way! We threaded our way through the piles until we could see the trail stretching out before us. And downhill it was! The trail was crowded with men, but this time most of them were sliding down, dragging goods behind them or riding on make-shift sleds.

Now it was our time to start down. The first part of the trail was so steep, Leonard wouldn't let me ride. We started down with two men in front guiding the sledges to keep them from running away, another man was in the back of the sledge pulling back on a rope with all his might, and even then, the sledges seemed to have a mind of their own. The men were concerned about the heavily loaded sledges getting out of control and running into others struggling down the steep slope.

About half way down, the slope tapered off, and they felt it was now safe enough to ride the rest of the way down. Ian and Liam shoved off on one sledge, while Leonard, Tony and I climbed on top of the second, and off we went. Mark and Walt followed on the seat of their pants. I thought of poor Mark's trousers and hoped they would hold together until tonight when I could find some way to mend them.

What a ride that was! Snow flew out from the runners of the sledges as we raced along so fast it was almost a blur. Ian and Liam reached the bottom first, quickly looked around to make sure we were not going to crash into them, then got off the sledge, and I think danced a jig. We raced by them another few yards, stopping in the middle of Crater Lake, a small frozen lake at the foot of the first big hill. By the time I got off and looked around, Mark and Walt were getting to their feet very near Ian and Liam.

"That was great! I wonder if we'll have much more like this?" Walt was like a kid after a sled ride down a hill. I think we all felt the same way. We didn't tarry long because we still had quite a long way to go. Walt re-tied the ropes from the back to the front, and now three would pull each sledge making the work easier for all. All of them insisted I ride, and I didn't argue with them. I felt like a kid myself and wanted the feeling to last a while longer. I also knew this might be the one time I would ride.

Leonard and Mark moved things on the sledge and finally had a space for me to sit between some of the boxes, offering a little protection from the wind. Now the wind seemed to have changed directions coming at our backs, rather than our faces.

Seeing others put up sails, Walt quickly dug out the big piece of canvas, cut it in half, and after a bit of work, found a way to put up sails. We jumped on and went sailing down a frozen lake! What a ride! For the first time, everyone rode on the sledges under sail power with the wind filling the sails and carrying us along.

Too soon, however, the sails had to come down, and the men grabbed the ropes to pull us along. The wind had not stopped, but the canyon had gotten narrower, and there were many other sledges, make-shift sleds, and so many men walking with boxes on their backs, the men didn't want to run into someone and possibly hurt them.

I crouched as low as I could, tucked my head deep down inside my coat, pulled my hat down as far as it would go, and settled in. Without meaning to I must have dozed off. I seemed to be aware of the men talking as they pulled the sledges, but it was all rather fuzzy. I awoke and sat up as Tony shouted,

"Look over there! Happy Camp!" All eyes looked at the tents amidst the stunted fir trees, realizing we were almost back into the big trees and shelter from the winds.

We didn't stop as we still had about three miles to go. I snuggled down again, trying to remember what foods I had left out at Sheep Camp this morning, thinking what I had to cook tonight. Even when we reached Deep Lake we had to set up the tents, get a fire started, and make camp before we could rest from the long day.

The miles went rather quickly, and then the Deep Lake camp came into view. Nestled in the trees, the wind didn't bother us, and we quickly built a fire. Pots of snow were melted and coffee made. I couldn't find the sugar, but no one cared. Cold hands wrapped around hot coffee cups felt good.

Tents were set up in short order, and I started supper, hot oatmeal with the fried biscuits we'd forgotten to eat at the summit. It wasn't an exciting meal, but it was filling. I even added raisins to the oatmeal. As the men cut green boughs to put under the bedrolls, I put some dried fruit in water to simmer. It would taste so good later.

Talk centered mainly about moving things from the summit. The men would pull the empty sledges back up, load them, and return, but they all agreed this was preferable to climbing the Pass again. In the first place it was a shorter climb, and also the wind didn't seem to be nearly as bad on this side.

The ordeal of the Pass was behind us now. Ahead lay the lakes where we needed to find the other Scotsmen, plan and build our boats, and wait for the ice to break. The fear of the Pass was over. It had been a good day, and I whispered a silent prayer of thanks for our safe climb up and over the Pass.

# 12

## DEEP LAKE - THE FINAL RELAY POINT

### April 16 - A Warm Sunny Day

When I heard Leonard and Walt stirring, I started to get up, but Leonard whispered, "Stay where you are, Freddie. Ian and Liam have been up for a while and have breakfast already made. Yesterday was hard, so go back to sleep for a while." But I got up anyway to help get the men started back up to the Pass.

"G' morning, young lady. Sleep well?" Liam moved a crate closer to the fire so I could sit down and handed me a cup of tea. Ian dished up hot oatmeal, added sugar, and evaporated milk. "We're going to stay here today. We begged off saying we was too tired and needed a rest." Ian leaned close and sheepishly said, "Well, we sorta told a fib, and I hope you will forgive us, but we been planning this big surprise and thought tonight would be a perfect time. Hope the men don't mind us taking time off."

"Ya notice something?" Liam nodded his head toward their tent.

"The flag! You remembered! Oh, you wonderful men." Seeing the red plaid scarf tied to the top of the tent, I said, "I wonder where they are now?"

"Oh, they wasn't near ready to cross when we left so I guess we'll probably be at Lake Bennett afore she gets ta us."

I knew Ian was right, but I hoped she would come soon. Thinking of her made me think of Sister Margaret Mary and her traveling companions. I hope we see them after Malinda is with us, so the Sister will know she is fine.

Ian, Liam, and I enjoyed the warm fire and the sunshine for some time. Then later while I washed dishes, they looked through their food boxes surprised at some of the things they had. It was a long time ago that their things were sealed in bond at Skagway, and they had forgotten what some of the crates actually contained.

I looked up toward the Pass but saw only storm clouds. I thought of the men having to deal with the wind up there and possibly a snow storm while the three of us were here enjoying a rest and certainly better weather conditions.

"What did the men take to eat or do they hope to make a quick day of it?"

"They just took the rest of the dried salmon, some dried fruit, and headed out. Don't ya worry though, they're anxious to get the job finished." Ian stood to take off his heavy coat. "Oh, it feels good to take the coat off for a while. I've lived in it so long, I wondered if I'd ever go without it again."

"Say, Ian, we better get started on the surprise supper. Freddie, now you'll know 'cause you'll see us fixing it, but we want them to be surprised." I wondered what they could be planning, but decided whatever it was it meant a lot to them to prepare a surprise supper so I promised not to give even a hint to the men.

As Ian and Liam began fussing around, acting rather like school boys planning something devilish, I decided to take the short walk back to the end of the lake to see what the trail looked like beyond here. The valley was rather narrow, and the lake was quite long and emptied into a river just a little below us. I wished it wasn't frozen as I like the sound of a river as it rushes over rocks.

Sometime later I returned to camp and melted some snow in a big pot, and then I told the men I was going to take a bath and even wash my hair.

"Maybe we should do the same, Liam. The weather's good, and we can't let Freddie be the only clean one." Ian smirked as he went to his tent to get some clean clothes. Seeing him bring out clean trousers made me remember I had neglected to mend Mark's trousers last night. I must do it tonight.

I watched other men going along the trail. Everyone seemed to step a bit more lively, even those heading back up to retrieve more things. I guess just knowing the worst was over made everyone walk a little quicker.

Soon I heard Ian and Liam talking happily. Busy by the fire, they were cooking something, and I couldn't resist a sneak peek. I was really surprised! These two grizzled men were mixing up cake batter, using their gold pans for mixing bowls!

"What cha baking? A Prospector's Cake?" An appropriate name, I thought.

"Hey, pretty good, Freddie. That's what we'll call it - Prospector's Cake. Hope you like chocolate. I do, and since I'm the baker, I gets ta make what I want. Ian's just the one who thought of using the gold pans. Pretty clever 'eh?"

I could see they were having a wonderful time cooking. "I'd like to think the men don't like chocolate cake, because it would mean more for us, but I know Leonard does and the others would eat it anyway. Can I help?"

"Sure, Freddie. We'll let ya lick the pan. My little ones used to love that part the best." Ian had made a frosting of cocoa, sugar, and a little condensed milk, and now, he was scraping the pan with his spoon.

Soon I could smell the cake baking, and oh it smelled good. It reminded me of Mom in the kitchen at home. She was always baking something. I must write them letting them know the worst of the trail is behind us, and we are all well.

I sat by the fire looking at the beautiful cake, carefully turned out onto a towel as Ian spread on the frosting. When finished, he gently picked it up and took it inside the tent so it really would be a big surprise. And I got to lick the frosting pan!

But my mouth dropped open when I saw what Liam was fixing next. "Where did you get eggs?" I couldn't believe my eyes, but there they were, eggs shells burning in the fire and over a dozen more eggs ready to be broken in a pan.

"We packed over twelve dozen eggs inside flour sacks. Stitched 'em in and hoped they wouldn't break, and they didn't."

Ian was busy chopping cheese in small bits. Bacon was cooking in the second Dutch oven. Eggs, cheese, and bacon! Omelet! I wished the men were here right now. I could hardly wait to see the expressions on the men's faces when they came back tonight. Soon I took down my heavy coat from where it was airing on the tent and put it on. While the day was nice, sunset returned a chill to the air.

Hearing a whistle from up the trail, the same whistle Leonard used when he called the horses on the farm, I knew the men were back. I could see them pulling sledges piled high with boxes. Soon they dropped the ropes and collapsed onto the crates to rest.

I gave them hot coffee as Ian and Liam began to untie the sledge ropes, stacking the boxes and crates around camp.

"What a day! Going up was easy. Empty sledges are certainly easier to pull uphill than loaded ones. It didn't take us nearly as long to get up as I thought it would." Tony actually shivered as he drank his coffee.

Leonard cleared his throat and spoke. "But it had snowed up top, so we had to shovel our things out again before we could load up."

"Ya, but that downhill! Wow! And I didn't run us into any rocks like I did the first night coming back into Dyea." Tony was rather proud of his improved steering ability. Everyone laughed remembering that event. Funny, we laughed about it at the time not knowing what all we would have to go through before we would laugh about it again.

"If we can keep bringing loads like this, and if it doesn't snow any more at the top, we can have most everything down in three days. The big unknown is the weather at the top." Walt was now relaxed, having stretched his legs out in front of him.

"Say, you men hungry? If not, then us and Freddie will eat everything."

The men jumped up to get their utensils which we had stacked near the fire. They were ready, but supper still had to be cooked.

"Now, you jest sit down. We still have to cook it, but at least now you'll know what it tis." Liam shook his spoon at them, and they sat back down.

Ian took the lid off the Dutch oven sizzling with hot grease, and Liam took the towel off the pot with the scrambled eggs, and poured them carefully into the Dutch oven. Then he just sat there on his knees by the Dutch oven to look at the expressions on the men's faces. They were as surprised as I was, and those eggs with cheese and bacon smelled so good. It was indeed a surprise none of us could have imagined!

Tony jumped up, searched for one of his boxes, broke it open and pulled out a jar. "Serve up those eggs, men, and top them with this. It's salsa, a Mexican sauce used for so many things. Goes great on eggs! It's got tomatoes, onions, peppers, roasted green chilies, lots of spices. Mom makes it with apple cider vinegar. But watch out, it's also spicy hot! Try just a little first."

Between bites all we heard was "Ah," "Delicious," and "I can hardly believe this!" Leonard spoke for everyone, "Boy, am I glad you fellows are with us and not someone else. This is wonderful!" Two

129

men came over to see what all the excitement was about, saying should have come earlier as it sure "sounded" good.

Just then Ian came out of his tent with the chocolate cake. "Better ask our guests to get a plate and fork and join us. That is if you like chocolate cake."

I don't think I've ever seen grown men scramble so fast to get a plate and fork as those men did. Again, no one spoke except to say how good it was, and we ate every crumb! The two visitors wanted to know if we ate this way every night, because if we did, they wanted to join up with us right away. Ian and Liam just smiled, knowing they had really come up with a great treat for all of us.

After dishes were washed, the men just sat around the fire drinking the hot cocoa we had found and talking about what they'd bring down tomorrow. Leonard finally asked, "Freddie, what did you give our Indian friend for his wife? While going up today, we tried to think what it might have been, as we knew you hadn't cut your hair again."

"Oh, I gave her my small looking glass and a pretty comb I sometimes used to pin up my hair. I thought those little items might be something she didn't have and might like. Besides, with short hair, I didn't need the comb, and I don't want to see myself in a mirror until I get thoroughly cleaned up."

"Ay, you're a pretty lass, me Freddie. And I'm so grateful ta have met ya and the men folk." Liam gave me a hug, and Ian was next in line.

Time for sleep. Tomorrow will come soon enough, and the men will go back to the top, but I also know there will be a spring in their step. The Pass is behind and the river and Dawson City are ahead.

As I curled against Leonard's warm back, I thanked God for our group. We've been through some mighty hard days – days so very cold and miserable – only to wake one day to sunshine again. I prayed for strength in the days to come with God to guide us. Then with prayers for our family, I slept soundly all night.

April 19 - Last trip to the top!

The weather has been lovely these past days. The sun's been out, and while it is still cold at night, it feels so good to take off the heavy coats for most of the day. The men left early each day vowing to bring as much down as possible. Indeed each time they came in the sledges were piled high, and the pack frames were even used as small sleds with more boxes tied on them.

One evening as I washed supper dishes, I started to cry. I don't know why as I wasn't unhappy, but I did feel as though I wasn't doing my share. Here I was each day enjoying the warmer weather while the men worked so hard going back up to the summit.

Ian saw me and came over and put his arm around me. Leaning his head against mine, he said, "Now dry those tears, give me a smile. We're all exhausted and feel like crying, but the worst is past. My guess is in a few weeks, you'll be good as new." He took the towel he always seemed to use when he cooked and dried my tears. Ian and Liam have been like adopted fathers to me, so I just gave Ian a big hug.

I thought about that towel. It's been used at every meal we've cooked since Skagway. In fact, I'm sure if we were to look carefully we could probably tell what we have eaten each day just from the spots on the towel. I doubt if it will ever come clean, but then maybe it should stay the way it is. It has a story to tell all by itself.

This morning, knowing it was the last time to the top, the men actually walked with even a greater spring in their step as they picked up the ropes and started to leave, hoping they wouldn't have to dig out gear again. Ian gave me a big hug and so did Leonard. "Enjoy the day, Freddie. Should be another sunny one. How about some of that good soup for supper? That would really taste good, and some of those fried biscuits, too. Maybe you could even find the butter in one of the boxes."

I stood by the trail and watched them go until they were just specks in the distance. In the back of my mind I knew Walt, Leonard, and I came on this trip together, and we'll finish it together in the company of the other wonderful men.

Mark left me his trousers with the split seam, and I mended them while enjoying the sunny day. When I finished, I made the soup Leonard had suggested using the last of the fresh potatoes, dried vegetables and peppers, and a tin of beef. Biscuits were made and staying warm on top of a Dutch oven. Soon I heard the familiar whistle. The men were back. The soup and biscuits disappeared quickly, and Mark surprised us with some candy he found in one of his boxes.

Relaxing after our meal, the men talked about the last day up. Ian said it was actually sunny for a short time at the summit but still very windy. He asked one of the Canadian Mounties if a group of ladies had come over. They hadn't seen a large group, though they did say a few ladies were bringing things up the Pass. Mark said over 10,000 people had crossed the summit, and the Mounties guessed there are probably that many if not more still to cross.

Leonard interrupted with, "I saw some of them. The ladies were just getting to the top as we were leaving. I got a chance to speak with Malinda and told her we were at the far end of Deep Lake. She said they were stopping at Happy Camp. I told her the flag was flying and to come look for us. Deep Lake was only a few miles from Happy Camp, and it was an easy trail."

Walt also spoke about some unsettling news - bears are coming out of hibernation. Two men actually saw a big bear though it was across the valley from Happy Camp. So now we must be careful and watch out for the hungry bears. Others thought the noise in the camps would keep the bears away, but mothers with cubs might be another story.

Once in the tent, Leonard said Malinda had been told she was not cooperating with the group, and she would have to change or they would send her down the trail. She pretended to be sick a time or two but knew it wouldn't work for long. Malinda even said if she hadn't seen him today, she might have gone back down the trail to Dyea. She just couldn't imagine when or if she would ever meet up with us.

I slept fitfully, woke up, slept again but never very well. I couldn't imagine the torment Malinda was going through, and I really felt sorry for her and the way the trip had been described before she signed on.

Finally, I just got up and went outside. Seeing Liam by the fire, I sat next to him. We didn't speak for a while, then I softly said, "Couldn't sleep thinking about Malinda. So close to us but yet so far away."

"Ya, I was thinkin' the same. Poor child. Her parents would die if they knew the trouble she was in."

The moon was out, and the valley looked so peaceful. There were even men still on the trail at this late hour. Liam thought those on the trail were taking advantage of the bright moon. But when did they rest?

Finally, I went back to bed. Tomorrow would be here soon enough, and it would be time to start for Lake Bennett. How good it would feel to get the trail behind us, even though we really didn't know what kind of boat to build.

# 13

## DEEP LAKE - A NIGHT VISITOR

### April 20 - Ready for First Trip to Lake Bennett

I woke early, or if truth be told, I didn't sleep much. Creeping from the tent, I saw Ian and Liam drinking tea by the fire. I thought at least today I could make breakfast. The men were speaking softly. "Why so quiet?" I asked.

"Shhh a bit, Freddie. Don't want to wake the fellows. Here sit down and have some tea." Liam indicated the nearest crate.

"Oh, don't worry. Leonard and Walt are awake, and Tony and Mark will follow soon. They want to get an early start."

"Tis not them I'm a think' of. It's a night visitor who's still asleep."

"Who is it, Ian? Surely it can't be Malinda. Leonard said she was at Happy Camp last night."

"Aye, tis true, but it tis Malinda, and I think we will start for Lake Bennett a bit later." By this time Leonard and Walt were up and by the fire.

I couldn't believe what they were saying. How could Malinda be here already? Shortly Tony and Mark were up, and Ian and Liam told us the story.

It seems the ladies struggled to get things through Canadian customs, and tried to figure out how they could get their things to Happy Camp. Some younger ladies solved the problem. Seeing six men nearby, they offered a trade. The men could help transport their things to the lakes, and the ladies would keep them company at night.

The leaders were delighted, so off they went, the six men, eleven young ladies and three older women. "That is if you want to call them ladies," Liam added. He said one of the young ladies had taken a look at the final summit climb, turned around and left for Dyea. She had not bargained for anything like climbing an icy wall.

With sleds piled high, they were off to Happy Camp. As several young ladies prepared supper, the men put up the tents and were soon joined by three other men who wanted to share in the work to get the rewards the ladies had to offer.

Before supper was over, the ladies had picked their partners for the night. Malinda and one other young lady were busy washing dishes and were fortunate enough not to be selected that night, but she knew she would not be so lucky the next night. After everyone had gone to bed, she told her friend she needed to take a walk. Finally, after some time, very quietly, she went back to the tent, reached inside to get her small bag of personal things, and slipped away. Realizing she had forgotten her wool hat and gloves, she took the towel used to dry the dishes and wrapped it around her head. Of course it was wet and partially frozen, but at least it kept out some of the wind.

Then she started for our camp. She remembered Leonard saying we were camped only a few miles further down the trail. By the bright moon she found the trail and started running. Others on the trail asked if something was wrong since she was alone with no hat to speak of, and no gloves. The further along she went, the more frightened she became. How would she find us even if we had the flag up? She ran part of the way, and when she could run no longer, she walked, but she never stopped.

Seeing all the tents at Deep Lake, she searched for the flag, but it was really dark in amongst the trees. She stood for a while looking around when the moon peeked through the trees lighting up several tents, one of which was flying a big red plaid scarf!

Quietly, she crawled into the tent with the flag, not realizing it was Ian and Liam's. Those wonderful Scotsmen awoke with a start, realized who it was and told her she was safe. Liam gave her his warm wool cap right off his head, and Ian gave her wool socks to put on her very cold hands. She was exhausted, and shivering as much from fright as the cold. The men made a bed for her between them using two of their blankets. And now she was still sleeping.

Ian started hotcakes when everyone agreed to delay the start of the first trip to Lake Bennett. We'd just begun eating when Malinda crawled out of the tent. Everyone hugged her, saying how fortunate she was to find us, but at the same time, Ian, acting like a concerned father, said she took a terrible chance with the bears coming out of hibernation. But when he gave her a hug, she knew he was just concerned and not scolding her.

"Here, young lassie. Sit down to some good flapjacks." Liam had fixed her a plate.

"Not hotcakes! I've lived on undone hotcakes and under-cooked beans for over a month now. I can't eat another one." She started to push the plate away.

Walt quickly stopped her. "You've not eaten flapjacks like these. They're light and fluffy, perfectly done. Ian makes the best ever. Better than Mom's, but Freddie and Leonard, don't tell my Mom I said that."

With such a great recommendation, she took a tentative bite. Well, that was all it took. She ate at least six or eight hotcakes with syrup, and she had two cups of coffee before she finally put down her cup and plate, took a deep breath and said, "Thank you. Those were great. And I'm sorry I ate so many, but I've been so hungry for days."

I put on a pot of snow to melt so Malinda could freshen up, then got out her bag of clothes from our tent suggesting she could clean up and change clothes if she wanted. Even sitting by the fire, she shivered. I think she was still very scared of what might have been her fate had she stayed where she was for even one more night.

It didn't take long to make new plans. Malinda got cleaned up and decided not to change clothes just yet, while the men took down the tents and put them on the sledges.

As the men worked loading the sledges, the two men who shared the cake our first night here came by. Since their tent was very near ours, they had heard the commotion and come to see what all the excitement was about.

"We couldn't help but overhear all the excitement and some of what you've said. Maybe we can help, too. We've got all our things here from the summit and were planning to leave for Lake Bennett today. Maybe we can help each other."

This time I asked his name, and he introduced himself as Mandy and his friend as Elliott. Both were from Indiana and married. Mandy had daughter, and Elliott, a son.

"We'll take just our tent and bedrolls. We'll tent near you at Lake Bennett and maybe, with such a large group, the young lady won't be noticed if anyone comes looking for her."

"Fine with us. Join us in about an hour." Leonard said while he shook their hands.

"Say, we'll leave plenty of room for some of your things. Our sleds are not as big as yours, but at least we'll take what we can."

Once again, others have come forward to help. With jobs to do, everyone got busy. Pretty soon, Elliott returned with an empty sled, a pair of overalls, and wool shirt.

"Here, the young lady can wear these. They're sorta clean. I kinda washed them once. If that group comes looking for you, maybe they won't recognize you. Mandy has a daughter and from what he thinks that group was, you must have been traveling with the wrong kind of ladies. Mandy said he'd have killed the people if his daughter had gotten mixed up with their kind. 'Course, his daughter is only four right now, but a daughter is a daughter."

So with that, we got busy. Soon Malinda stepped out of our tent, looking for the world like one of the men. She had twisted her long hair up under Liam's wool hat. Walt picked up some old wood from the fire and started to rub a little ash on the lower part of her face. "You'll look like one of the men when we finish with you." Everyone, even Malinda laughed. Walt gave her a hug, and said, "Don't worry. We know you're a lady, and besides it washes right off. Maybe we should call you something besides Malinda."

Leonard popped up with "Freddie's short for Winifred, so what can we call you?"

"I really appreciate what you trying to do and especially for taking me in, but I have nothing to be ashamed of. I've done nothing wrong. Their advertisement was wrong or at least implied something other than what it actually was, and if they find me, I'll just tell them so. I'm named after my Grandma Linda. Everyone called her "Ma" so that's why my name is spelled the way it is. I really do thank you for everything you're doing to help me, but I just want to be called Malinda."

I agreed with her and said so. She has a right to use her own name, and we have no right to make her change it for any reason. It took courage for her to come to us so late at night, and I admired her for doing it.

Malinda continued, "That group has all the food and other supplies and some of those things rightfully should be mine. My money paid for them. But since I'm the one who left, I am not going to ask for them back. They should be satisfied with that." I think we all knew she was absolutely right.

Leonard and Walt made sure I was settled among the things on one of the sledges and Malinda safely settled on another. Then we were off to Lake Bennett. We hoped to find the other Scotsmen and camp near them if there was room for such a large group.

Shortly we came to a gorge with the river plunging over in a frozen waterfall. With the sun shining for the last several days, it had a thin layer of water running over it. Spring was really coming, and I was glad. Once past the waterfall the trail ran along the edge of the gorge. A log house restaurant sat near the trail, doing a good business this morning.

The snow was deep and piled above our heads on both sides of the trail as it turned into the woods. Here the trail was so narrow only one person or one sled could pass at a time. Like on the icy steps up the Pass, there were a couple places to get off to the side. This narrow trail meant people could not pass going both ways at once.

It was three or four miles to Lindeman City, and soon after the narrow part, we started downhill. Suddenly there was Lindeman City! Hundreds of tents lined the shore of the lake and even well back onto the very large flat area.

The place was a hectic scene of men sawing logs and building boats. We stopped to ask the way to Lake Bennett. Mandy had heard there were two trails, and we wanted the best way and hoped it was also the shortest.

While they talked with some men camped by the lake, Malinda and I stretched our legs and walked around. No one seemed to take notice of us perhaps because of the way we were dressed. I felt colder at

Lindeman City than at Deep Lake and pulled my coat tighter around my neck. The area was more open, and the wind blew quite hard. In contrast, the tents at Deep Lake were tucked under the trees and seemed warmer. In all this activity, a line of men moved steadily down to Lake Bennett.

Soon, the men were back; we climbed into our places again, and off we went. The trail led down along the lake to the river connecting the lower end of Lake Lindeman to the upper part of Lake Bennett. Though frozen, we could tell there would be some difficult rapids when the river was flowing. This would be a bad stretch of river. I was glad we were going to Lake Bennett.

Then we saw Lake Bennett. As far as the eye could see, canvas tents lined both sides, an unbelievable scene. The steep mountains came down very close to the lake and the streets of Lake Bennett City were lined with thousands of tents. The trail divided to go along both sides of the lake but we took the right hand trail. I wondered how we could ever hope to find the other four Scotsmen.

We wound through the tents until we reached a street actually named Main Street. Ian called a halt, climbed up a hill nearby to look over the area. On this hill men were building a church! Here among thousands of men, all anxious for the ice to break so they can get on the river Dawson City and the gold, they're taking time to build a church. It looked like this city planned to stay with permanent buildings and all.

Ian returned, pointed down Main Street, and off we went. Along Main Street we saw tent after tent of businesses. There were doctors, lawyers, the ever present saloons, hotels, a large mercantile, even a bakery. Main Street was long, maybe more than a mile, until it just stopped, and the tents took over.

At this point, Ian took the lead. I had no idea where we were going, but Ian must have had a plan. Then suddenly the air erupted with shouts and cheers, all in English, but even after weeks of listening to Ian and Liam, the Scottish version of English, when spoken fast and as joyously as this was, was difficult to understand. Ian had led us directly to their friends! Then I noticed a bright red plaid scarf flying high above the tent. The same type of flag as we flew for Malinda, now was flying for us. We knew right away we were home. Ian explained how Malinda happened to join our group. Then while the Scotsmen caught up on the news, we unloaded the sledges.

Malinda and I started to get pots and pans and the food unloaded. The other Scotsmen invited us to use their big fire, so we started coffee and heating water for tea. The other Scotsmen had cooked beans with bacon, and we made soup, and sat around the fire, telling tales of dead horses on the terrible White Pass trail, the avalanche we encountered, and ending with stories of triumph at crossing the mountains.

Tomorrow would come soon enough. Right now it was time for fellowship, good food, and relaxation. Friends were reunited. The day had been beautiful. Malinda was safely with us. What else could we possible need or want?

Malinda and I took a walk – time for some talk just between us. And oh, how I needed her to talk to.

We realized we both had lost weight and had other changes which the men wouldn't understand. But we were so glad to have each other to share our thoughts and concerns.

Later when all were asleep, I could not help but cry, knowing of the trials Malinda had been through while I felt so safe and secure with all "my men folks."

I prayed for all those we'd met who had helped us. God surely has been with us, and for that I was thankful.

# 14

## LAKE BENNETT - A BOAT TO BUILD

### April 23 - Final Trip to the Lake

It's very nice to sit around a fire and not worry about having to get wood as there are large piles of bits and pieces all over. These are the ends of boards cut when men are building their boats. The other Scotsmen arrived four days ago and were concerned about Ian and Liam when they heard about the avalanche. Now we're a group of fourteen - all camped with tents almost touching - it's quite a sight! We are a "jolly bunch," Ian says.

Andrew, one of the other Scotsmen, went to talk with some others he had met and was able to borrow a couple sleds for the men to use. Now, they will have two larger sledges, four sleds, and two pack frames to use. Since it is eight miles or more back to Deep Lake, it will still take several days to gather all our crates and boxes here. While the men were gone, Malinda and I sorted the boxes into a pile for us and a pile for Mandy and Elliott.

The other Scotsmen have already cut and dragged logs to the area and will soon cut them into boards. Each day they left to cut more trees, carrying an ax over his shoulder and others carrying guns for protection against bears.

There are tents of every size and shape from small two-man tents to large ones, almost like circus tents. Thousands of people are here, and thousands more will arrive before the ice breaks. Tents circle both sides of the lake, and from a distance almost looking like snow. The warm weather is melting the snow quickly, though it freezes again each night. With mid-forties temperatures each day the ground is a muddy mess.

Our meals are different now. Each day one of the Scotsman manages to bring in rabbits, ducks, or a chicken-like bird called a "tarmigan" though I don't think it is spelled that way. Once Bruce, another Scotsman, traded a few boards for a moose roast which we cut into steaks. We even had enough to make moose stew the next day.

As the days went on, Malinda grew exceptionally quiet. When I asked her if something was wrong, she said she felt like she had nothing to give to the group. I assured her she was giving more than she knew - just being here and giving me the chance to talk with another lady. Another time I dropped a small box and just sat down and cried. We decided it was all the pressure of the trail finally getting the best of both of us. Later we sat in the sun simply enjoying a good cup of tea.

The Scotsmen returned in mid-afternoon saying it was their turn to cook, and we didn't argue. Andrew and Bruce showed us what was for supper. They had helped some men drag some logs to their camp in exchange for some bear meat. They heard bear stew was really good, and they were also going to make sourdough biscuits. Seeing the puzzled look on our faces, Bruce only smiled and replied, "Now jest ya wait. I got the "starter" from some others here. It was used for all kinds of baking, from biscuits and bread to hotcakes. The starter always had to be kept warm so it could 'keep growing' for if it got cold, it would die." I wasn't sure what he meant by that, but then he unbuttoned his two wool shirts and pulled out a jar of some whitish-looking stuff.

"This here's the starter. I keep it next to me under me shirt every day, and it jest keeps on a-growing. If ya like it, then when we all leave on the boats, we'll give ya some. Just have to keep it warm though." It was good to get to know these friends for we had only met them once before, long ago in Skagway.

As I sat in the sun waiting for the men to return from the final trip back to Deep Lake, Malinda sat nearby writing a letter to her folks, explaining how she had been duped on her trip, of meeting us, and of the terrible night she had left and literally run for over two miles to get to us. She hadn't wanted her parents to worry and so hadn't written earlier.

Supper smelled so good; I was getting really hungry. The men wouldn't let us do anything, but we both watched as the biscuits were being made so we would know how much of the sourdough starter to use. "Necessity is the mother of invention," Andrew said as he picked up an empty tin which had contained evaporated milk at one time, and cut out perfect biscuits. "Haven't figured out what ta use for a rollin' pin yet." Then he put them on small metal pans and into the two

Yukon stove ovens. On the top of the stoves they were cooking some rice. The stew simmered near the fire.

The men came in early with sledges loaded. They had gotten a break at the narrow part of the trail and had been able to go right through each way. Everything was finally here at Lake Bennett! The dreadful ordeal of the trail was behind us! Now, we would need to build our boats to be ready to leave when the ice broke. Then it would be 550 miles downriver to Dawson City and the gold!

That would be number of tomorrows later. Now it was time for a good supper with friends. I was thankful we were all safe and through the hardest part of the journey.

Around the fire, the main topic of discussion was what type of boat to build. The four Scotsmen wanted to build a large raft for the six of them. We were still undecided. Walt suggested they walk along the shore to look at the boats others were building. With Tony and Mark going with us to Dawson City, we would need to build one very large boat, or two smaller ones. The longer they talked, the more they felt two boats would be more work but would be a better idea. In case of an accident, at least one would still be usable. More discussion followed, but I only heard the word "accident." I thought the worst part was over. What was ahead that I didn't know about? Malinda reached out and held my hand. "Don't worry, Freddie. Everything will be fine. The men are just thinking of safety first," she whispered.

Later as I closed my eyes to sleep, I could think of nothing but boats, big ones and little ones, but I realized so much was finished. No more terrors of avalanches. No more climbing 1500 icy steps. No more Soapy Smith or his gang. We were in Canada and soon would start to build our boats for the final journey to Dawson City. I wonder what Dawson City would be like? I decide to leave that thought for another night.

April 24 - Work to Do

While eating sourdough hotcakes, Leonard mentioned something he'd forgotten. It seemed as they were going through Lindeman City yesterday, they ran into the group of ladies and the men who now accompanied them. The ladies decided to stay there while the men build a barge big enough to tow a raft behind it, carrying all their gear. Leonard and Walt didn't think much of the idea but didn't tell them so. No one even mention Malinda.

The idea of two boats seemed the best way to build. Tony expressed reservations about the raft the Scotsmen planned to build. It might be fine after the rapids we would have to run when leaving here, but if the rapids were really much larger than the ones between Lake Lindeman and Lake Bennett appeared, a raft could easily break apart.

The beach area was a jumble of rocks, big and small, and between them the mud was ankle deep. But it was the noise that really got our attention. From the saw pits, where the men whip-sawed trees into boards, came a constant sound of profanity. To cut the boards, logs about eight feet long were set on end in the ground, and then a frame was built on top between the upended poles. This platform was about four feet wide and twelve to fifteen feet long. There was an opening along the center part of the platform in which the log to be sawed was placed. The man in the pit below would push up on the saw while the man above pulled up. As I looked at the saw pits, I couldn't understand why they were called "pits." The man below did not stand in a pit. He stood on the ground looking up at the man above.

After a line had been drawn the length of the log, the sawing began, and so did the swearing. Someone explained that the man on the top pulled up on the long saw and guided the blade along the line. Then the man below pulled down on the saw, getting a face full of sawdust with each down stroke. Each man felt the other was not doing his job. The one below shouted at the man above for not pulling the saw up as he should, while the man above shouted his complaints. The wood was cut only on the down stroke, and the shouting by both parties often erupted into arguments, even fights. We saw one man jump up and pull his partner from the platform, and a fight ensued. Others rushed to break up the fight, but this was just one of many we witnessed our first days here.

Boats of all kinds and in many stages of construction lined the shore. Some were actually being built by carpenters who had come to Lake Bennett just to build boats for others. Those who could afford them would have good boats with nice keels and sturdy oars. Most could not afford the carpenters. We certainly couldn't.

There were small two-man boats, built somewhat like a bathtub, vertical on the sides and back and with the front only slightly sloping. A group of about twelve were building a barge, big enough to live on. We talked with them, and they planned to put up several tents for sleeping and have a raised platform for the Yukon stoves so they could even cook on board. This group planned to travel day and night, sleeping in shifts, getting to Dawson City as quickly as possible.

Bigger boats could carry more gear, but the men couldn't use oars. A man in the back would use something called a sweep oar, like an oversized regular oar but used by sweeping it back and forth acting as a rudder and also giving some power down river. Most boats, however, were like our fishing boat back home, with sides curved down to a keel, the back was square, and the front was formed by the sides coming together in the front. We saw many, many of these.

But the ones the men liked best were the scows. They were flat bottomed, with vertical sides, and the front and back were the same, extending beyond the bottom in a long slope up. Men building these said they were very safe since they didn't tip over, though they were slower in the water. Most men with the scows planned to have both oars and a sweep oar in the back. Almost everyone also planned to have a mast and put up a sail to catch the wind. I could tell the men liked this idea best. After looking at a number of scows and talking with the builders, they had a good idea of how big they wanted to build our boats.

Returning to the tents, Walt got out some paper and a pencil. Using a couple of crates as a table, they talked, discussed, and changed their minds a dozen times while drawing up their plans. During this drawing session, Mandy and Elliott, who had gone looking for friends, returned. They had not found their friends but did meet three other men who were looking for some partners, and they decided to go with them. We told them how much we appreciated their help and asked if we could help any way.

"Could we use the sledges to move our things?" Elliott asked.

Walt snapped back, "Certainly not! Wouldn't think of letting you borrow them. Really, just kidding. We'll move you down there ourselves."

Malinda suddenly remembered she was wearing Elliott's overalls and wool shirt. "I'll help you move but I need to change clothes so I can return your overalls and shirt."

"Oh, Malinda, keep 'em. You look better in them than I do. I got other clothes anyway," he dismissed the whole idea of getting the clothes back.

Malinda and I got up to help. The men loaded sledges and sleds while we folded the blankets from the tent. It would take several trips even with everyone helping, but we really wanted to let them know we certainly appreciated their help earlier.

We met their three new friends and invited them to come for coffee after supper. They said they would if they could bring some cookies they had just baked.

The rest of the afternoon was spent drawing plans. Walt and Leonard leaned over the crate table, talking, gesturing with the hands, scratching their heads, and tugging on their scraggly beards. One scow would be about sixteen feet long and seven feet wide; the other about twelve feet long by maybe five feet wide. The idea of a sail appealed to everyone.

Supper tonight was roast duck cooked over the coals. Ian and Liam had been down to the lake and saw eight ducks swimming in a small inlet of the lake which was already free of ice. They managed to shoot six of them. While the ducks roasted, they cooked potatoes and canned green beans and carrots. They were somewhat apologetic about not having anything sweet for dessert until we told them that Mandy and Elliott and their new friends were coming over later with something to share. They had made "cookies" – sort of. They had mixed raisins and oatmeal into bread-like dough and baked them. We were certainly enjoying good meals now. Just a few weeks ago on the other side of the Chilkoot Pass, a pot of beans would have been a feast. Now it's moose steaks, rabbit stew, roast duck, and who knows what next.

During supper, boats seemed to be the main topic of conversation. Mark and Walt tried to talk the Scotsmen out of a raft for safety reasons, but they had their minds set on the quickest boat to build. Leonard argued that two smaller boats instead of one large one would take a bit longer to build, but would certainly be able to carry all the supplies and would leave more room for the men. He reminded them that the trip down the Yukon would take many days, but I really don't think any minds were changed.

Realizing the sun is up over sixteen hours a day now, I finally said good night and headed for the tent. Tony looked at his watch exclaiming, "Good time for bed. I didn't realize it's already eleven and I'm tired and

153

it is time to go to bed. Good night all. Tomorrow, it's woodsmen we'll be."

April 26 - Logs, Logs, and More Logs

For two days the men have dragged logs down to the beach. Our tents were a good bit away from the lake, but Tony had found two men just about finished cutting the last of their boards and asked if they could use the saw pit. With a shrug of his shoulders, one said it was fine by him. Others had asked also, so they could share.

Malinda and I walked up Main Street yesterday hoping to buy some fresh vegetables. We found a store, but they only had canned goods. We saw a barber shop and a post office, which reminded Malinda to mail her letter home. The man in the post office told us to tell our folks to send mail to the Ft. Selkirk or the Dawson City North West Trading Post. She quickly added that note to the back of her letter. How good it would be to get mail from home.

Instead of going back the way we came, we walked up into the hills to look over the lake. The scene was quite spectacular. Lake Bennett was very long, in fact we couldn't see the end. Malinda heard it was twenty miles long. Across the lake the mountains were quite high. The tops were still white with snow while the middle was dirty brown, melting snow with rocks protruding everywhere. Nearer the bottom, the remaining trees were green, probably spruce trees, like on this side. With the masses waiting for the ice to break, I wondered who would be around to attend services in the little church being built on the hill. It was a good thing the Scotsmen still have their flag up because we would surely have gotten lost in the mass of tents.

This morning as the men were leaving to cut trees, we told them we'd do laundry if they'd put out their dirty clothes. Soon the pile of dirty clothes was enormous. I didn't say anything since we had said we'd do laundry, but we really didn't expect we'd be washing *everything* they had. Leonard kissed me as he left, then whispered, "Next time say you'll wash a few things, not everything." Then he just smiled and winked, shouldered his ax, squared his shoulders as if he could take on the world, and off he went.

With laundry to do, we heated all the water we could, then spent hours washing, scrubbing, and rinsing clothes. With the tie-down ropes, we strung up a line between the tents. It was hard work, but we resolved never to tell, since we had a wonderful benefit from washing all the clothes. Our hands and even our fingernails were clean for the first time in so many weeks, and it felt oh-so-good to have really clean hands again.

Andrew was the first to return with Jason, Robert, and Edward, the other Scotsmen. Seeing the neat piles of folded clothes, they couldn't thank us enough. It seemed this was the first time they have had clean clothes since leaving Skagway months ago!

Robert and Jason said they would cook tonight but added they didn't cook anything but beans. We then confessed we had already cooked a big pot of beans with the rest of the left over moose meat. They looked a bit disappointed about not cooking, but at the same time they admitted our beans would surely taste better.

While drinking tea and resting on the ground, with a crate for a back support, Liam talked about the trees being cut. "They're not really big around, but they're at least fifteen to twenty feet long. Several boards can be cut from each if we are careful. The hardest part is dragging 'em back to the saw pits. We have ta go a long way up them mountains ta find the bigger trees, and dragging 'em in mud over bushes, rocks and tree stumps is surely hard work. Sure be glad when we finally cut all we need."

Enough is enough. I am tired, and I am going to bed. The others can stay up and talk if they want. Tomorrow I must write to Mom and Pops, but for now I am comfortable, curled up nice and warm and clean, and very thankful for how well things have turned out.

# 15

## LAKE BENNETT - SAWDUST AND BOATS

May 1 - The Mounted Patrol Arrives

Our days seem to run together. The men cut trees and haul logs from the hills behind us, and the pile grows higher each day. With the daylight getting longer, they work much too long and return for supper very tired and dirty.

This afternoon, I heard shouting coming from the water's edge. Looking up, I saw some men pulling their sleds over the ice. On the beach, men were screaming for them to get off the ice. Those on the ice didn't hear them and went right on. Suddenly, they turned toward the shore and ran as if being chased, frantically pulling their sleds and looking behind them. On shore men yelled for them to hurry.

Malinda and I hurried to the beach. We got there about the same time the men reached the shore. Then, we finally understood the problem. The ice is getting soft on top, and with the glare of the sun, they couldn't see the thinning patches. On those sections the weight of sleds and men might be too much, and the ice would break. The men were going down the lake when they suddenly heard the ice cracking beneath them. That's when they ran for the shore. They said it continued to crack even as they ran. The ice is not yet ready to break completely and move down river though. Some say it could be two weeks yet; others say a month. Until then, no one should go down the lake over the ice.

As Ian and Tony were washing supper dishes, a North West Mounted Policeman stopped by. We had seen him going to others and wondered if there might be a problem or if something terrible had happened. Soon he came to our area and introduced himself as Superintendent Sam Steele. He was talking with everyone, warning them about the thinning ice on the lake and telling everyone not to try to go further down on the lake as it was much too dangerous. Last year the ice went out on May 18, but he doubted it would be that soon this year since the weather has been much colder.

He asked what kinds of boats we were building, warning us, "Don't build boats to be your coffins." This really scared me.

"I don't mean to scare you ladies, but the boats must be built very strong. You have 550 miles to go, and in the first 100 miles, you have to run the Miles Canyon and White Horse Rapids. It's my job to see that boats are safe." Superintendent Steele went on. "What type and how many boats are you building?" Mr. Steele looked at our large group. "Several boats, I hope."

Leonard spoke first. "We're going to build two scows for six of us. One will be maybe sixteen feet long, the other about twelve feet long. Each will be about five to seven feet wide. I've heard the scow's a safe boat, not easily tipped over. Is that true?"

"Good choice. Yes, they're sturdy, and though slower, they'll ride well through the rapids." Turning to me, he added, "Don't worry. Women and children aren't allowed to ride through the rapids, and just before them, Mounties will check each boat. You ladies must walk. They even encourage men to hire professionals to take their boats through. Some men are building a tram on the cliffs above so gear can be portaged around the rapids."

The Scotsmen said they planned to build a large raft for the six of them. Superintendent Steele shook his head, admonishingly, "No! Please don't do that. They're not safe. I can't stop you, but I strongly urge you to re-think your plans. If you hit a rock, the raft could split apart, dumping you and everything you have into the icy river. I won't want to give you a boat number, but the law says you can build whatever type of boat you want. Please re-think your plans." He was almost angry at such an idea.

"My suggestion is that you do the same as your friends. Two scows will not be that hard to build, and will certainly be much safer." Noticing the pile of logs stacked nearby, he added, "There's probably enough logs right there to build four scows. Build strong, seal the seams well, and you should be just fine."

I asked, "When you came, I thought you were going to tell us that some of Soapy's men had crossed the border, but I can tell, this boat business is much more important."

"We watch the border pretty closely. We don't want his gang in Canada. One of Soapy's men actually got by us, but he tried the shell game with group of men, one of whom was a Mountie, though not in uniform. Well, he was caught and promptly marched all the way back to Dyea, put on a boat headed south, and told never to return. I guess the Mountie who marched him there wouldn't let him stop for anything until he was turned over to the ship's authorities. The Mountie returned two days later all smiles. It did us all good to see that scoundrel caught."

He shook hands with the men, tipped his hat to Malinda and me, and walked off to another group. Then he turned back and asked who owned the two sledges. Tony and Mark replied, "We do. Why?"

"Well, there are some men just down from the Pass who want to buy some. They're part of a large group with all their gear at Happy Camp. It's actually three families with children and some young people. The men came in here last night hoping to find someone who might want sell some sleds. I don't think they have much money, but they could really use the sledges. If you want to sell them, you might go see them."

"Great! We've wondered what to do with them. Where they are?" Superintendent Steele gave them directions to find them, and Tony and Mark left immediately.

As Superintendent Steele went to talk with another group, I noticed now straight he stood, his broad shoulders and back ramrod straight. He was here to help with any problems and thereby save lives, too. His stature showed he meant business. He had work to do, and I hoped people would listen to him, especially our Scotsmen friends.

Tony and Mark returned with the other men and gave them the sledges. The men were most grateful, saying they would be a big help. After the men left, Mark said, "We just gave them the sledges. Their families are here from Alabama hoping to get enough gold to buy a farm. They were share croppers and tired of working for someone else and living in miserable conditions. One man brought his wife and two young children, five and seven years old, and another came with three teenage sons. A third man stayed at Happy Camp with his wife and two boys. They were thankful for the sledges." Mark and Tony just said they couldn't take money from them. Mark even suggested they build scows.

The Scotsmen decided to take Superintendent Steele's advice and build scows. Ian stood up, stretched as if to take the kinks out of his back and said, "There's still an hour or so of light, and we have logs to drag to the saw pit. Let's put our backs to the task and get some of them moved. Tomorrow we've got to start whip-sawing logs. The ice went out in mid-May last year, and it might go out later this year, but boats have to be built."

Malinda picked up the empty coffee pot, rinsed it out and started more coffee. I put on water for tea or hot cocoa. "I wish we'd made some cookies today. Let's try baking a cake tomorrow. It will be a treat for the men after a hard day of work." Malinda searched through the food boxes for even a small treat, but found only dried fruit.

The men worked until well after sunset. Finally, more tired than I've seen them in a long time, they sat down by the fire, arched their shoulders up to take away some of the aches and pains. They just sat there for a few minutes not saying anything. Soon breezes had come up, the temperature had dropped, and coats were put back on quickly.

## Sunday, May 8 - Logs Become Boards

Last Monday, with logs at the pit, the men started peeling the logs. This was the first job to be done. Then the logs could be marked for sawing. Only then could they begin cutting the logs into boards. They worked out a job plan. Several jobs had to be done in a specific order. After four men peeled logs, another four would strike the cutting lines, and the last two men would whip-saw the boards. Since this was the worst job, they planned to change jobs throughout the day. This way each would take a turn "in the pit".

So far it seems to be working. Of course, the man below doesn't like it and gets pretty angry, especially at the man on top. But each knows that sooner or later he will be the man above and another man will be below.

The first night after whip-sawing boards, they came back very dusty, dirty, and full of sawdust. Leonard was very discouraged. Shaking his head, he said, "The way things are going, and as slow and hard as the cutting is, we won't be ready to leave for a month or two and will be lucky to get to Dawson City before the river freezes again!"

All day the area is a beehive of sounds. Aside from the swearing and arguments at the pits, we can even hear the timber crashing in the hills. The saws in the sawmill in town screeches and whines as logs are rammed through the cutters. Add to that the hammering of the boat builders, the rasp of hand drawn saws cutting boards the correct length, and men shouting to others to do his share of work, and it is noisy!

We also have dogs barking continually. The barking was not new, but now it is almost constant. Some said it's because wolves are around. I haven't heard any, but it could be true. Some dogs have puppies, about a month old now. The puppies are sure cute, just little balls of dirty fur. It's the dog owners I don't like. They shout at the pups, kick at them, and treat them awful.

We've had some wonderful days! One day Malinda and I actually rolled up our shirt sleeves, took some dried fruit, we climbed up the hill behind us. The pussy willows are in full bud. Berry bushes bloom with delicate flowers. One of the first to bear fruit is the kinikinnic - I don't know how it's spelled. The bright red berries add a lovely touch of color to the hills. The berries are supposed to be good to eat, but Malinda and I didn't find them tasty. The leaves are called "Indian tobacco," is used as a tobacco substitute.

The men are getting suntanned on their arms and faces. Walt has freckles across his nose though I don't mention it to him. Malinda likes them, but won't tell him so.

They work very hard all day. Malinda and I often make soup to take down to them about mid-day. We tried baking bread the other day, but dough didn't rise too well. We baked it anyway, but it didn't bake evenly. At least we tried.

Last year on my birthday, Leonard had asked me to marry him. I don't think he even remembers this year. When I look at Malinda and her situation, I realize just how fortunate I am to have a husband who loves me.

We don't hear much news from Outside. Papers cost a dollar, too costly for us, and the news is old by the time it gets here. I overheard someone say America was at war with Spain. I can't imagine men killing men for whatever purpose when I am here in this beautiful place, even with shouting men and barking dogs.

Yesterday as I went through the food boxes to see what we had and to re-pack in fewer boxes, I found our rubber boots! We can certainly use them here and along the river. Leonard and Walt were delighted, and the rubber boots were certainly easier to put on and take off than leather boots.

When we took soup to the men today, we heard men shouting loudly, pushing each other around. The fight was bad, with name calling and fists flying. The men finally decided to split everything right down the middle and go their separate ways. After throwing the cut boards into two piles, they stormed to their tent, and cut it right down the middle, making each half useless. Then they proceeded to cut flour bags in half, not just dividing them equally. Now each has half of fifteen to twenty bags of flour and sugar little of which can be used. Cans of food were divided and angry words echoed through the area. When others managed to put an end to the destruction, the fighting men stomped away in disgust. We found out later, these men were brothers-in-law. What a tragic way for friendships to end, and what terrible damage it caused the families.

The snow is melting fast now. Chipmunks and squirrels scamper throughout the area, foraging for any scraps of food. Birds are everywhere - sparrows, robins, and ducks of all kinds. Geese are heading north to nesting areas. The tap tapping of the woodpeckers is better than pounding hammers of the boat builders. Mosquitoes will soon arrive in hordes, and they are supposed to be huge! Then we will wish we were on the river!

The stack of cut lumber grows daily. Tony and Mark bargained with a couple of men and traded extra soup and biscuits for some cut boards. Walt thinks we can cook on the boats, but Leonard is against the idea thinking that some embers could fall from the Yukon stove and start a fire.

Speaking of the Yukon stoves, I thumbed back through my journal and realized I've never described them, and they are really quite ingenious. Made of sheet metal, they measure about eighteen to twenty inches from front to back and about thirty inches long. They have two holes on top for cook pots and a small oven. It's difficult to get the right temperature in the oven, but with practice Malinda and I were able to bake a lopsided cake, and even tried to bake bread, though the bread is baked too well on one side while it was almost undone on other side. We use the stoves for cooking, but usually the Dutch ovens are better over the open fire. When it was time to move from camp to camp, the stove sides telescope together, making a smaller package to carry. We've even used them in the tents to help keep us warm on very cold nights.

Another Sunday is over, and I thought of church friends back home. I must write the folks again before we leave. I know the news Mom reads in the Clinton paper is probably not always accurate and certainly doesn't tell what we are doing. I will ask them to share the news with Walt's family and with our friends at church.

# <u>16</u>

## LAKE BENNETT - A BIG SURPRISE AND TEMPERS FLARE

May 15 - What a Week!

On Monday when the men finished for the day, they returned dusty and dirty though pleased with the work accomplished. The stack of cut boards grows daily, and today they started building the first scow. Many logs have to be cut, and now they need more oakum to seal the seams. After supper, Leonard asked for some money. I'm trying to keep some tucked away for emergencies, but the balance dwindles away. As they left with the others, Ian whispered that he'd bring Malinda and me a surprise.

They returned empty handed - no nails and no oakum. When I asked, Walt quickly stammered that they had taken the supplies to the work area. Leonard gave me the change, and I was happy to see they hadn't spent much.

Wednesday, the wonderful smell of coffee, hotcakes, and bacon woke me. Bacon was the delicious surprise! Mark said they'd be late tonight, thinking they might actually start work on the second scow. Tony grabbed the extra hotcakes and some dried fruit, and left telling us to enjoy the day. When Liam and Mark volunteered to cook tonight, Malinda and I decided to climb the hills again. So off we went as soon as we'd cleaned up the breakfast dishes.

It was May 11, my birthday and the day Leonard had proposed, and he didn't seem to remember either event. I was silent, not even talking to Malinda. Finally, she asked what was wrong, and I started crying, which I seem to do easily these days. When Malinda put her arm around me, I told her about this special day.

"Look, the men are really busy. You know the day because you write in your journal and keep track of the dates. They have no way of knowing. For them the days all run together. Don't blame them." Knowing she was right, I dried my tears on my sleeve and tried to smile.

The weather has been beautiful the past few days. Wild grasses and lovely flowers bunched in clumps on the hills, some of which I recognized, and some I didn't. The blue forget-me-nots, shooting stars in deep shades of red, the red bleeding hearts, these I knew. Two others I didn't know. One was a little white bell shaped flower, and another smelled like a geranium. I picked some to take back for all to enjoy.

We sat on a rock above the lake and surveyed the area. The ice now has water on top which rippled in the warm Spring breezes. As the snow line slowly creeps toward the top of the hills, waterfalls and rivulets run down the mountains. It was a lovely day, and we thoroughly enjoyed ourselves.

With seventeen to eighteen hours of daylight now, the men work longer and longer. They return each night so tired that I wonder how long they will be able to keep up the hectic pace. But they won't stop until the work is finished, and I know they keep an eye on the lake ice and realize the time's getting shorter with each passing day. They want to be ready to leave immediately when the ice finally breaks.

As we returned, Mark was scrubbing potatoes to boil, and Liam was making a salad! I must have looked very surprised for Liam said in his quiet manner, "I just went up on the hills and picked some greens like we pick in Scotland. Hope ya like 'em. Maybe ya ladies can get more 'cause fresh greens is good for us. Oh, I see ya picked some flowers. Lovely! I do like flowers."

I asked if he knew the names of the two white ones. He looked at them carefully before replying. "One is a wild geranium and the other is like our heather. Both grow in the colder climates of the north." Liam is such a wealth of knowledge.

Noticing moose steaks were on the grill, I asked "Where'd you get the moose meat?"

"Oh, we traded a few boards for them. Seems two fellas shot a moose, and knowing it wouldn't keep now that it's not freezing, they went around trading meat for cut boards. We figured a couple of boards were worth the moose steaks." Mark turned the steaks over and moved the pot of potatoes closer to the fire.

Pretty soon, the rest came back, shaking sawdust from their hair. When they noticed the fresh greens, Liam repeated his story. I could hardly wait for supper, everything looked so good. We ate until we could eat no more and enjoyed every bite.

With dishes washed, Walt and Malinda took a walk. I think they are getting sweet on each other. I know Walt had a girl back home, but she got angry when he decided to go north to look for gold and left him for someone who she said "had brains enough not to go running after a fool's dreams." He is such a good man, and a good friend.

The Scotsmen, Andrew, Bruce, Jason, and Robert, went back to the work area wanting to sort boards. The rest of us enjoyed the fire as the sun dipped below the mountains on the other side of the lake. Leonard added wood on the fire, and Liam put on a big pot of water for tea. We enjoy having tea before bed, so warm and soothing. I snuggled closer to Leonard as he put his arm around me. I really did have a very nice birthday with good friends, and wonderful food even if they didn't know it was my birthday. It was one of the best evenings we've had in a long time.

When a nearby group started an argument, I looked at Leonard hoping he would say something to stop it, but he didn't move. Then the group broke into song and shouts of "Happy Birthday, Freddie!" I blushed and buried my face in Leonard's shirt. He had remembered and told others! Soon neighbors were giving me hugs, and wishing me happy birthday. Three men produced a birthday cake they had baked – really it was bread they had baked in a Dutch oven with a candle on top. Among them were the smiling Scotsmen, Walt, and Malinda.

Walt and Malinda told me to shut my eyes. "Hold out your hand, Freddie. Here's something from all of us to you." Walt said, putting a ball of fur in my arms. "Well, first of all, it's a girl, and we got her from some men who were abusing their dogs and new puppies. We've had her for three days down at the work site, and our neighbors have taken care of her at night. That's why we haven't wanted you to come down to the boats. You would have found her for sure."

As I cuddled the soft bundle of wiggling puppy, Leonard said, "She's part Yukon sled dog and part who knows what. And look at her eyes."

"Why one's brown and the other's blue. How strange! I think I'll name her Sky so I'll always remember the blue skies we've had here." Leonard had remembered after all!

Everyone enjoyed the birthday bread and tea, and I thanked each for making the day so special. I really didn't want the day to end, but soon the men drifted back to their tents. The last one to leave said, "She likes to sleep inside the tent, and we're a bunch of softies. We let her. At night she curls up right at my feet making a pretty good foot warmer. Happy Birthday, little lady. You and your friend brighten up our lives. Thank you for being the family we wish we had with us."

As I pulled the blankets close around me, Leonard whispered, "It was a year ago today you agreed to be my wife. Little did we know then we'd be celebrating the day in this frozen land. I couldn't imagine life without you here beside me right now." He pulled me tighter to him, and kissed me. I was blessed beyond measure to have such a good husband and wonderful friends. As I closed my eyes, I realized Sky had curled up on my feet, and indeed she was a good little foot warmer!

I woke in the morning with many puppy kisses all over my face. We laughed as Sky ran from me to Walt, then Leonard, and finally Malinda. She wiggles at both ends - head and tail - as each of us tried to pet her. At breakfast, Sky went from person to person begging food. I'm so glad she was rescued from the cruel men who kicked her. When the men left, Sky started to follow, but I called her, and she came immediately. Malinda and I did the dishes, shook the blankets leaving them to air outside, and started soup. Sky followed our every move even trying to play tug of war with the blankets.

Finally, exhausted, she curled up in a tight little ball near the fire and went to sleep. Malinda leaned up against a crate reading a book, and I sat resting against another crate writing a letter home. I didn't write about the terrible incident on the lake a few days ago when another man tried to go down over the lake. The ice broke beneath him in one of those soft spots, and he and his sled disappeared into the icy water beneath. It was a tragic sight. News of this type is most assuredly reported in the papers back home. As they say, bad news travels fast. I must tell the folks not to believe ninety percent of what they read in the papers. Good news is not nearly as exciting as bad news.

I wrote that the first scow is built and told them about Sky and the wonderful surprise birthday party. Remembering the Christmas gifts from Arwin, Leonard's brother, and his wife, Marian, to their two little daughters, I asked how the bike riding lessons were going. At Christmas the snow was two feet deep outside, and the girls couldn't ride their bikes. Now, the snow must be gone, and Mary Jane, at six, will learn to ride quickly, and Martha Anne, two years younger but more active, will be riding right along with her big sister. I do miss them. I told Mom I was sure the girls would love playing with Sky until all of them were so tired they would drop from exhaustion.

The work appeared to be going well until yesterday, Saturday. Leonard stormed back early silent, even angry looking, but said nothing. Walt followed, also angry. Leonard stood shaking sawdust from his hair and clothes. He didn't even stop to scratch Sky as he usually does. In fact he started to kick her away, stopping short of actually doing it.

"What's wrong, honey?" I asked.

"It's Walt! He's not pulling that blasted saw up like he should, and frankly, I'm very tired of having to pull it down and push it back up, too. He's not even keeping a straight line! We ruined several boards today, and the work is too hard not to do it right the first time." He stomped around, and pushed at Walt.

Then Walt shoved Leonard away and snapped back. "What do you mean I don't pull that saw. You know good and well I do, it's you who can't pull it down right. Admit it, you're just sorry it was your turn in the pit today." Thinking a fight would escalate any minute, Malinda and I stepped between them.

"Come on, Leonard and Walt, both of you. Stop it! Don't do this!" I was so angry with both of them I actually cried as I physically held Leonard away from Walt. "You two have been friends for so long, if something like this comes between you now, you'll regret it the rest of your lives. Remember how we have watched others fight and split everything, and how you vowed never to do that? Now stop it!" The argument had to stop immediately or the consequences would be dreadful.

Malinda pleaded with them to think about what was happening. "I've only met you, but I love you both dearly. Stop and think about what you're doing. Think of why you came north. Don't let this day or even several days like it end such a long friendship."

By this time the other men had run back. Tony grabbed Walt by the arms. "Hey, fellows. We're all tired, but we can work this out and not fight about it."

"Tony and I joined you because you are good men. Don't let one bad day destroy everything we've all worked so hard to accomplish." Mark pushed his way between them, pleading his case also.

Liam and Ian separated them further saying, "Listen ta yar friends. We're here ta help each other. Come on now, both of ya. This is yar friend. Remember that, and stop this fighting. You're the ones who insisted on sawing again today even though you've been a doing it for three straight days now. Tomorrow neither of you will be in the pit. We'll do it, and you can lay out the boards for the next boat. Remember we have to build four of them and so far only one is complete."

Ian finally spoke the words that calmed them. "Ya know, fighting will only tear us all apart. Ya think just because us Scotsmen are older, we can't handle the hard work? Well, ya're wrong, me lads. We can do it just as well as ya young fellows. So stop this right now! We won't stand by and watch anything like this happen to you, or to any of us."

By this time, Leonard and Walt were looking pretty sheepish. Leonard extended his hand, and Walt quickly grasped it and shook it hard. "I'm really sorry, Leonard. Maybe I wasn't pulling up like I should have, but I really did try to follow that line. The trees just have so many knots in them. And they're right, we can't let this tear us apart."

"I know, Walt. It's just I'm so tired, so hungry, and feel like I've been dirty for so long I don't think I'll ever be clean again. I know I wasn't giving it my best work, but I'm tired of all this sawdust in my clothes, my hair, under my fingernails and even inside my mouth. Forgive me, Walt."

I ducked into the tent, untied the money pouch and took out a ten dollar bill, precious dollars that needed to be put to good use right now. "Leonard, Walt. You're both pretty dirty." Looking at all the men, I added, "In fact you're all really dirty. So before you even think about eating, take this money and go to town. Take one of those hot baths. I don't know what it will cost, but you can put in a little extra. Now go and get cleaned up. You'll feel much better, and supper can wait."

Malinda added, "and you'll smell better, too!" With that, everyone laughed. Sky started jumping up and down wanting attention. Leonard and Walt both leaned down to pet her, bumping heads as they did it. I guess they thought it was funny, as they both sat down on the ground and laughed, and Sky went from one to the other licking their faces.

Supper was late, but the men looked and smelled so good when they returned. The Scotsmen had even

175

paid for haircuts and beard trimming. Malinda and I hardly knew them when they returned, but it was so nice to see everyone smiling and happy again.

That night, the argument replayed in my mind. I was so afraid for Leonard and Walt and for our group as well. Up to now, there had never been anything so serious. Sure there had been differences of opinion, but nothing like this. I was really concerned, and even Malinda admitted just how much this argument had hurt her. She does care for Walt. Sleep came later when I realized the crisis could have torn us apart but had been averted, and I prayed we would always stop and think before we acted in haste.

May 22 - Sunday Again - The Boats Take Shape

I do wish the church on the hill was finished. With all we have been through and what thousands of others have been through, it would be nice to share our praise in the lovely church overlooking the lake.

Sky is growing so fast. She's gained a lot of weight and is quite roly-poly now. I, too, am feeling much better and have gained back some of the weight I've lost. I finally had to let my belt buckle out a notch.

With the wonderful Spring weather, I would have thought the scurvy and dysentery, so prevalent among many here in camps, would be gone, but I guess it will take more than just warm weather. We have been very fortunate to have stayed so well except for a cold or two, and we would probably have had colds in Wisconsin anyway. I haven't always felt good, but at least I haven't been as sick as so many others have been.

Two of the scows are now completed. They even gave them several coats of the seam sealers, both oakum and pitch. Mark actually demanded it, saying the water would be so cold, the pitch and oakum might shrink causing the boat seams to leak. That dire warning was enough to make them do a second and even more thorough job.

Work on the other boats is going well. By Thursday, they thought they had whip-sawed enough wood, so all hands turned to boat building. But, yesterday, realizing they needed more boards, they again began the dreadful job of whip-sawing. They even cut enough boards to build raised seats for the men who will be rowing. Each boat will have one or two men on the oars and a man in the back using a sweep oar for extra power.

We've had a few days of rain though not enough to stop the work. It just makes the men chill easier in wet clothes. But what wonders it does for the hillsides! The hills are turning a brilliant green, and berry bushes are full of flowers, but we will be long gone before the berries ripen. We've seen some bears up high on the hills, but none come down among this hoard of people. The noise should be enough to scare them away. Some said the bears were the bigger, more dangerous grizzly bears. I can't tell the difference between them and the black bears since they all look brown.

After a rain the hills look like they are sprinkled with diamonds. Rain drops glisten in the sunshine and sparkle on the leaves of plants. It is actually warm out now. I remember it was just six or seven weeks ago that the avalanche occurred, and we were so terribly cold on the other side of the Pass.

Everyone works very long hours trying to finish the boats before ice goes out. Some say it won't be much longer. Already at the shoreline, the lake ice is melting, and we can even see patches in the lake which appear to be ice free. Most think it will be at least two weeks or more before the ice finally breaks, but the men are not slowing down their work.

Last night after supper, the conversation centered around packing the scows. They were glad they had built the scows which can carry more weight and still leave enough room for people to ride comfortably. The main concern was what would happen if one got wrecked. Equipment, food, and other supplies will be divided, making each boat self-sufficient. Then if something happened to one boat, the other one would have enough food and supplies to get us through to Dawson City. Even though we might be crowded on one boat, we felt sure that we could continue.

Today a new plan was set up. One man would help Malinda and me sort, repack, and re-label everything while the others continued work on the boats. It was actually rather fun opening the boxes as I'd forgotten about some of the foods and the kitchen supplies we had. I'm actually looking forward to getting to Dawson City, setting up our tent, and making it into our home. I may even finally make a good loaf of bread. Malinda is really good at it, but each time I try, it doesn't taste like the bread Mom bakes.

It's amazing to see the different types of boats, barges, scows, and canoes being built. When I think that most of the men here probably have never built a boat before, it is truly a wonder to see the designs. Of course, there are the boats built by the carpenters which are beautiful and surely seaworthy, but I am also sure they cost a lot of money. Even today, more men arrive to begin building boats. Tony and Mark actually traded the few extra boards we didn't need for some tins of beef and chicken.

Those who have finished their boats and packed them, now await break-up. Many sit on their boats playing cards, reading, writing letters, and smoking their pipes, anything to be ready when the ice moves out. Some boats are already at the edge of the shore ice ready to shove off.

Superintendent Sam Steele and his contingent of the North West Mounted Police walked among the boats inspecting each one for its sea worthiness and then assigning it a number. This number had to be painted on the boat, and no boat would be allowed to leave until a number has been assigned and painted on it. In addition, each man is required to give his name, address, and next of kin. This information is noted in the book the officers have, along with the number of his boat.

Superintendent Steel is called the "Lion of the Yukon" for his insistence on safety. Boat owners are required to check in at several police outposts along the way. This way, according to Steele, if a boat doesn't show up in a certain length of time, a search party will be sent out to look for it.

Our two boats have the numbers 12495 and 12496. The Scotsmen have the two numbers before us. We will be independent groups on the river, but we hope to stay together, at least until we get past the rapids. I really don't like to think about those rapids, but Superintendent Steele reassured me that Malinda and I would be required to walk around them. I'll still worry about the men though. It's just my nature.

Tonight after supper, the Scotsmen, and Tony and Mark quietly took out pencil and paper, writing letters home. This is the first time I have actually seen them writing though they could have done it before in their tents. Not knowing where the next post office will be, they, like me, probably want to assure family and friends they are fine, and the boats are almost finished. Soon the lake will relinquish its ice, and thousands of boats will be racing for the city of gold, Dawson City. And we will be a part of that number. I wonder how long it will take us to reach the city?

May 25 - Wednesday

The boats are finished! The Scotsmen built larger scows, one probably about eighteen feet long and seven feet wide. The other one is smaller about fourteen feet long and maybe six feet wide. The numbers are painted on them, and each has been thoroughly inspected. They are declared safe!

The men started packing the scows today, and I was very surprised to see how much room remains in each them. Even the smaller ones had enough room for the three who will ride in them. The larger scow will carry most of the cooking utensils though the smaller one will have a pot or two. Each scow will have a tent. If something does happen and a boat is wrecked, we'll still have enough to get us to Dawson City. We may not use the tents at night unless it looks like it might rain. In fact, we might not even stop at night. We may run by moonlight since the nights are so short anyway.

We've been so busy with last minute details, packing the boats and planning who would ride where that I forgot about how Sky would like being in a boat all day. But then I saw Sky sleeping in the boat on top of a crate and realized she'll do just fine.

Walking back to our tents, my thoughts turned to Ian and Liam. They have been with us since Skagway, months ago and have been like fathers to me. They've boosted my spirits, cooked breakfast when I didn't feel like eating much less cooking, and helped us in so many ways. I have their names and addresses in Scotland and have promised to write, but there will be a big empty place in my heart when they leave with the other Scotsmen.

Ahead, Ian and Liam slowed down to walk with me, and Liam put his arm around me. As I told them my thoughts, Liam said, "Don't worry, little one. Ya're going to have yar hands full soon what with getting to Dawson City and helping yar husband and all."

Ian broke in, "And besides, ya're gonna have ta get them baby things made. That'll keep ya busy."

"What are you talking about? Baby things?"

"Why, my little lady, surely ya know, ya're going to have a baby?" Ian held me at arms' length and smiled as he talked.

"Oh, I can't be having a baby. How would you know anyway?"

With a fatherly hug, Liam smiled and said, "Lassie, I've been with me wife through three pregnancies, though we lost the third little one, and I know the signs. Ya don't have ta be a doctor to tell. Ya're as bright as sunshine and blossoming something beautiful. Ya're a very lucky little lady."

I was almost ready to say something when Ian whispered softly, "We've been awatchin' ya, and I'm sure everything will be just fine. Ya just take it easy lifting the heavy things, but go on with ya're regular work. Women been having babies for a long time, and besides when ya get to Dawson City, if you're concerned, go see a doctor. Now, we won't say nothing to Leonard. That's up to ya to tell him the news."

I hugged them both. I never thought I could be in a motherly way. If it is so, how I wish I were home now. Home with Mom and Pops. Home where there is help if I should need it. Instead, here I am north of nowhere in a land just now shedding its frozen mantle of snow for a Spring coat of green. And I must tell Leonard, but when? Tonight? Or wait until we are on the river or even in Dawson City?

I never thought that this might happen when I am so far from home. And I wonder if I am really pregnant. So many questions are going through my mind right now, and I don't have answers to any of them.

Finally in the tent, curled up trying to sleep, I decided to wait until we are past the rapids. Until then, it will be my secret, only shared with two of the most wonderful Scotsmen in the world, and I love them even more, if that is possible.

Now, we wait for the ice to leave the lake. If only it would break, and we could leave. If only... If only... When... When will it break? When can we leave? For once, we are ready, and the lake is reluctant to give up the lock of ice that bars us from the river below. How long will it be? How soon before we hear the shouts of men and the cheers as boat after boat leaves for Dawson City and the gold just waiting for us there?

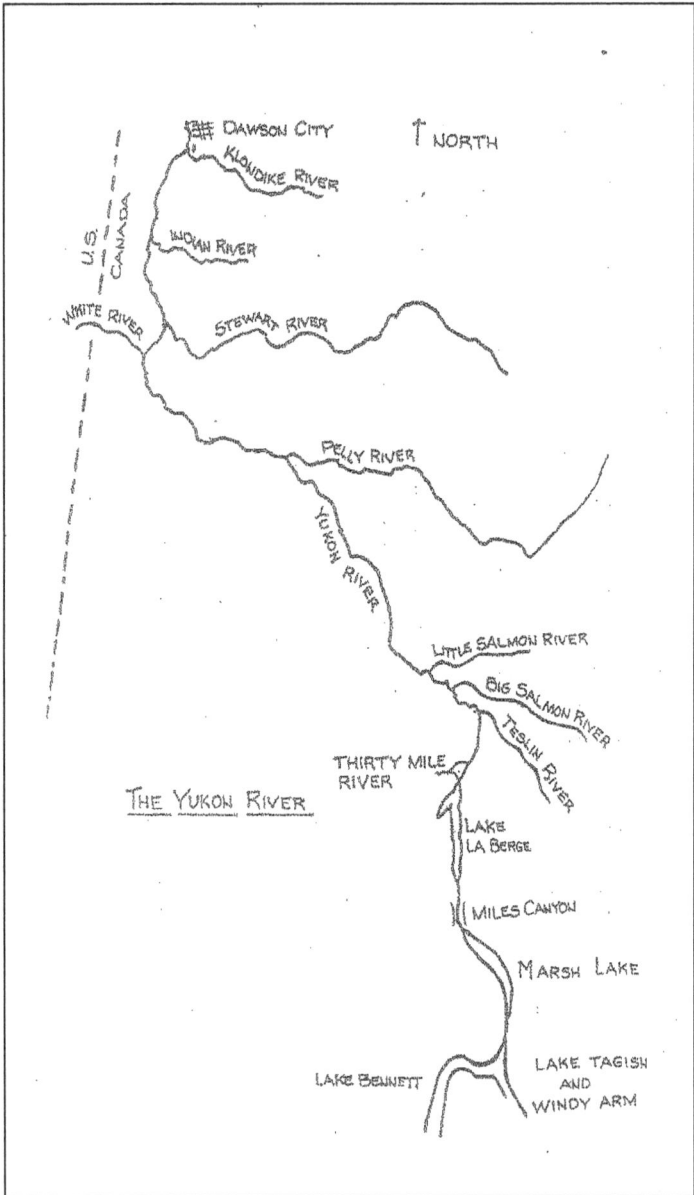

# <u>17</u>

## THE WAITING IS OVER – ON THE RIVER!

May 31 – On the River to Lake Tagish

On the Yukon River at last! I thought it would never happen. But let me fill in about the last several days before the ice finally broke.

May 28 - Waiting for the Ice to Leave Lake Bennett

These last three days of waiting didn't mean we had nothing to do. Wednesday the boats were finished, inspected by Superintendent Steele, and our numbers were painted on the bow of each scow. Then we started loading them with everything except stoves, tents, food, cooking utensils, and a few tools. While the men packed the boats, Malinda and I baked bread. Ian did the same. We knew during the river trip we would not really have time to bake bread. It takes time for the dough to rise, which it could do while we were on the river, but later it would take more time to bake it. By late this afternoon, Malinda and I had baked seventeen loaves of bread, wrapping them in the petticoat and dress I am not wearing. With only two dish towels, we couldn't spare them to cover the bread. I also made fried biscuits which Leonard likes.

We picked greens, putting them in cook pots with a bit of water to keep them fresh. At least we'll have bread and greens to eat.

It's supposed to take about two to three weeks to reach Dawson City. I guess much depends on the winds which can come up suddenly. But two or three weeks is a short time compared to the weeks or even months we spent on the trail and here building the boats.

This afternoon we were down by the boats looking at the lake. Superintendent Steele stopped to remind us to pack carefully and watch out for the winds. He's like a worried father, concerned when his children leave home to be on their own. He cares about all the boaters and said he has assigned numbers to many rafts, some built only of a few logs lashed together. He told of two men who used their sledge and strapped a couple of logs to each side. We didn't see how they could survive with the river water constantly splashing them. Everything would be soaked if it even stayed together.

As Liam and Ian cooked supper, Leonard, Walt, Malinda and I walked up into the hills to see Lake Bennett for last time. The men haven't taken the time to look at the view or see all the wild flowers. Now I insisted they come even for a short time. Our feet sank into the thick moss covering the hills, and we could actually hear water rippling under the moss. With the snow almost completely gone, streams were everywhere, some even ran through Lake Bennett City. We sure were glad to have our rubber boots!

Sunday morning, May 29th, dawned bright and warm. The whole valley was bathed in sunlight. Beautiful green water showed beneath the edge ice some of which was still quite thick, too thick to melt. Along the shore, men were doing laundry, hanging it on their boats. Everywhere men waited and watched and listened.

Steele had told us the river ran almost 2000 miles before it reached the open ocean. During that time it mixed with the white glacier-melt water and also the brown mud from the undermined river banks. It wouldn't be this color all the way to Dawson City.

Suddenly, with creaks, groans, and a deep rumble, the ice began to move! It was mesmerizing to watch. The surface of the lake was alive and moving! We could see cracks and splits, but it was like a giant picture puzzle of ice moving across the surface of the lake. The ice was headed out, and the river now rushed on its journey north!

Shouts and cheers rang out all along the shore. Boat after boat was dragged, pushed, and shoved into the river. It was time to leave! We wouldn't be able to leave as some boats boxed us in. What a sight it was, watching hundreds of men shove off on the final part of their journey to Dawson City.

We rushed back to the camp, took down tents, packed up the rest of our things and took them down to the scows. Everything was tied down securely. As Walt left with an arm full of things, two men asked if he wanted their tent. They planned to run day and night, not stopping for anything. Once in Dawson City, they planned to stay in a hotel like kings spending their gold. So Walt got a small tent, about eight by nine feet. Another man gave us a metal grill for cooking meat.

At the lake men yelled at those in front of them to "Get out of the way!" Some bigger boats were too heavy to push or shove into the water, and every man available lent his shoulder to the task of shoving them into the water. This went on for hours, it seemed. Indeed it really did take hours for hundreds of boats to be launched. It was already mid-afternoon before we pushed our scows into the water. We had helped others, and now different men helped us. Tony looked at his watch as we settled in the scows. It was almost four o'clock! We hadn't eaten since breakfast and were past the point of caring.

Out on the lake, the boats looked like an armada of children's boats floating on a park pond. Some were large, some small. There were skiffs and scows, canoes, kayaks, and square coffin-like boxes as Superintendent Steele would have called them. We even saw one very large raft carrying not only people but also a couple of horses and the hay to feed them. Some had already put up sails, others used only oar power. All were headed north, down the river with one goal in mind - Dawson City. Many ran prow to rudder with the boat in front. Some looked over their shoulders gauging the distance to those behind, not wanting others to pass them. Men pulled with Herculean strength, straining at the oars, always wanting to be the first in whatever group of boats he might be in.

It's different rowing on the river. We don't row the boats as we do on the fishing lake in Wisconsin. There, Leonard pulled the oars toward him causing the boat go backwards. In other words, the man rowing had his back to the direction the boat was moving. Here it is absolutely necessary to row so you can see where you are going, thus facing down river. So the men faced the bow of the boat and pushed the oars, moving the boat forward down the river in the direction of the flowing water.

We've spent months getting here, and now the gold fields are so close, if you can call 550 miles "close." Many days would pass before we reached that fabled city, and I wondered if they could keep up this pace all the way to Dawson City.

The first day Tony, Walt and Malinda were in one scow, and Mark, Leonard and I were in the other. We were close together, and the Scotsmen's two scows were near us. I got out the fried biscuits and gave some to Leonard and Mark. Tony pulled close enough for me to pass food to that boat. I thought it was rather clever the way I did it. I tied the biscuits up in a bandanna handkerchief, put the bundle on the broad end of an oar, and extended it for them to reach. Leonard agreed he wouldn't have thought of it, but he added he didn't think it would work too well with a cup of coffee. I told him the biscuits would probably have landed in the lake if I'd thrown them.

With the late start, Mark felt there was really no reason to stop for the night. But when I grabbed a blanket and looked for a place to lie down, I suddenly realized we didn't have Sky. Where was she? In our haste to leave, we had not thought about her at all. She had been running between all four of the scows, and I didn't notice where she was when we shoved off. I panicked. We couldn't leave her!

"Stop!" I shouted. "Where's Sky? I've got to go back and find her." Tears streamed down my face as I yelled to make them understand I wouldn't leave her. Never!

I shouted to the Scotsmen, who only shook their heads. They didn't have her. Leonard started to pull for shore when two men in a boat right behind us shouted, "Wait! Stop! Are you looking for a little dog?"

"Yes," I shouted. "I've got to find her." I screamed.

Holding up a dog, he yelled back, "Is this her?"

I nodded my head and fell down in the boat sobbing with happiness. Leonard pulled back on the oars to slow the scow. Sky was passed to me, and I hugged her tightly. Finally, I composed myself enough to give my heart-felt thanks to the men. They waved as they rowed on saying they had seen Sky and heard her barking as we left. They figured we'd forgotten her, and they had rowed hard to catch us. One added if they hadn't caught us, they would have kept her she was such a beautiful little dog.

Sky licked first one and then the other and ran all over the boat. Her welcome could not have been more eagerly expressed. As she snuggled down beside me, I covered her with a corner of a blanket and vowed never to leave her again.

May 31 - On Lake Tagish

Yesterday and last night we sailed the length of Lake Bennett, past the community of Caribou Crossing, and onto Tagish Lake. We stopped beyond Caribou

190

Crossing, to cook breakfast and make coffee. The fire felt very good after such a cold night. It was good to be on the river at last, but we were tired from lack of sleep. The men spread out the two canvas sails and went to sleep. Ian and Liam pulled out the regular sail they had packed over the trail using it to sleep on. Malinda and I put together a loaf of bread, a tin of beef, and dried fruit for each boat, and started soaking beans for supper. With a Yukon salad, as we call it, and the rest of the cookies, supper would be very filling. But after this trip, I'll never want to eat beans again. We've had them so often. They're filling and good for us, I know, but they're still beans!

A few hours later, we were back on the river. This time I made sure Sky was with us. I didn't need to worry though since she never left my side! The men hoisted the sails before we left, hoping to catch the breezes. As I settled into a place on the scow, I noticed the Scotsmen had hoisted their flag, the red plaid scarf. It was an appropriate display on the top of their mast.

The lovely bluish-green water of Tagish Lake rippled in the wind. The breeze filled the sails, and we fairly raced along. It was very relaxing to let the wind do the work. For the first time, the men enjoyed looking around at the snowcapped mountains in a land few knew anything about until last Summer when news of the gold strike captured the world's attention. Now, we were part of the rush to the Klondike. What an adventure it has been already, and we are not even at the gold fields yet!

We stopped to have supper as clouds began to gather, and thinking it might rain, we set up the tents. Walt didn't bother to set up his tent, but said it would come in very handy once we reach Dawson City. We were so tired, we didn't linger by the fire. I couldn't imagine why we were this tired when we've been riding all day. It must be we have worked so hard to get this far, and now everything was finally catching up with us. And so to bed where we slept very well, not even noticing the rain during the night.

This morning Ian and Liam again had coffee made and then fixed their wonderful light and fluffy hotcakes. I'm glad we are staying together. We sailed down Tagish Lake for several hours, soon realizing the wind was getting quite strong. Seeing a number of boats pulled off up ahead, we followed suit. By now, the wind was blowing quite hard, making it difficult to control the scows even with the sails down. The water whipped up waves which splashed over the sides getting us wet!

We spent the rest of the day on shore. The waves on the lake got higher and higher, making the boats rock quite a bit, even though they were tied securely to trees. This place was known as Windy Arm. Rightfully so! It was windy! Other boats continued to come in during the day, and no one left. Caution was the word for everyone.

Cooking in the wind wasn't much fun, but Liam and Tony made beans again adding syrup, sun dried tomatoes, and the tin of beef. That and a couple loaves of bread and salad, and we were well satisfied. With only enough salad for one more meal, Walt and Malinda went off to gather more greens.

Not knowing what future campsites might be like, we thought this was a good idea. I started to get up to join them, but Leonard gently pulled me back down saying he thought maybe Walt and Malinda might want to be by themselves.

June 2 - Thursday

Yesterday it was still too windy to try and cross Windy Arm. A few tried to leave, but we could see them return to shore a short ways down the lake. The men are getting anxious to leave. They feel like they're wasting time sitting around, but they also know it would be foolish to be on the river under these circumstances.

So the day passed with no activity and plenty of rest for everyone, even Sky, who curled up at the feet of anyone napping. She's a good dog, seldom barks, and doesn't chase into the nearby woods after animals. Maybe she is afraid we'll leave her again.

Today, the wind finally subsided, and again the race was on. By the time we finished breakfast, only a few boats remained. With a good breeze, the sails were hoisted, and we crossed Windy Arm without a problem. The river emptied into Marsh Lake about 5 miles further. This lake is about the same size as Lake Bennett, and it took us all day, even with a good wind, to reach the lower end and see the canyon beyond.

Here we pulled off. We had now reached the treacherous rapids. It was already late in the afternoon, and the men questioned whether to run the rapids now or wait until morning. We were not alone. Many other boats had stopped and were tied up. Ahead we could see the narrow gap of Miles Canyon with a red flag hanging on the left canyon wall. We wondered what the flag meant. We knew this would be the first of the rapids, the easier of the two rapids. In just three and a half miles the rapids will test the mettle of each man.

We agreed it would not be wise to attempt the rapids this late in the day. Besides, we needed to look them over and find out what was the best way to run them. I wanted to find the trail Malinda and I would take and where we would meet them below.

Most boaters camped in a swamp-like area, with scattered discards of those trying to lighten their boats once they saw the rapids. We found a small place a bit higher and much dryer though further away. We put up three tents, as there simply was not enough room for the fourth tent. The uninvited guests for the evening were the mosquitoes, hordes of them, everywhere, and we were miserable. After supper, the men went to see what lay ahead. Maybe I'm being foolish, but I didn't want to see what the rapids looked like. I just wanted this part of the river behind us.

None of us would sleep well with all he mosquitoes and thoughts of what tomorrow would bring. Again, I remembered I only had to take one step at a time, only this time it would be the men who had to face one obstacle at a time, that of back to back rapids with no way to stop between them to repair any damage which might occur.

I cuddled Sky close for warmth, but more for comfort. If I am indeed pregnant, I want to take good care of both the baby and me. I should tell Leonard about my condition, but I'll wait until we have gone through the rapids. I thanked God for bringing us safely this far and asked for safety tomorrow as the men run the rapids.

# **18**

## TO RUN THE RAPIDS AND BEYOND

June 3 - The Rapids!

Last evening, the men walked down the high trail above the river, looking over the rapids. Malinda and I didn't go. We could hear the first rapid in Miles Canyon very clearly, and I was not looking forward to this section of the river. We have passed so many dangers, and this is just another one. The last one, we are told.

Leonard thought the first set of rapids was not really a big problem. He said the red flag on the left bank indicated that side of the canyon was the dangerous side, almost certain to wreck any boat going that way. The right side was better, though a gigantic rock in the middle of the rapid presented problems.

They watched a number of boats going through. Those going on the right side made it fine, but Walt saw two going left. One hit the wall and broke apart, with the men barely able to cling to floating timber, and the second boat hit the center rock and spun off.

Each gave his impression of the dreadful White Horse Rapids. These were the worst rapids with water pounding furiously through the narrow confines of the canyon. "There are whirlpools in the center of the rivers, rocks everywhere, some barely submerged, others exposed." Tony said hundreds were on the cliffs looking over the rapids.

I asked about the trail Malinda and I would take. Mark thought it was a good trail though mosquitoes were everywhere. "You won't have any problems, but it will take time. It's not far from the canyon so you can watch boats go through, too"

"I really don't want to watch the boats. I just want this part to be over." Malinda sounded really scared, and so was I, not so much for us as for the men and the boats.

Liam kicked some wood into the fire with the toe of his boot. "Well, we can't leave until Corporal Dixson checks out our boats and feels we can handle the rapids."

"Ya, and we heard it would cost $100 dollars a boat to have someone pilot it through. That's a lot 'o money. Why just to haul our gear over the tram costs maybe five cents a pound. Me, I'd rather run the rapids myself." Ian was shocked at the costs, and so were the rest of us, but we would have to see what the Corporal had to say.

Corporal Dixson came by some time later, and after talking with the men, looking over the scows and how everything was tied down, he asked the men how they felt about the rapids.

"You ladies will have to walk. No women or children can ride through the rapids and walk the puppy, too. Men, I can't urge you strongly enough to tie everything down as tightly as you can. With that promise, you can pilot your own boats." I don't know if I was happy or sad, but I was definitely scared for them.

Corporal Dixson then gave the men some advice. "When you leave, stay to the right through the first rapids. Don't get too close to the right wall and stay well away from that big rock in the center." He knelt down on one knee and drew a picture in the dirt. "Stay right here. It's about two miles to the White Horse Rapids. Again, stay to the right. Pull with all your might to run the waves head on. You've got good high side boards, but you'll get wet. Once through, pull off to the right. Inspect for any damage and dry out everything. The ladies have a five mile walk. You men will be there much sooner."

Everyone was very quiet for some time after he left. Then Liam put down his cup and said, "Think I'll check them tie ropes again." With that remark, the men left for the scows. Malinda and I remained by the fire. I was thinking about tomorrow and wishing it were over. With all we've been through, and this being the last of the dangers, we just had to make it safely through tomorrow morning.

The men felt confident they could handle the scows. They suggested we eat just a bite before running the rapids and have a good breakfast at the end while things dried out. Liam even said he'd have it all ready when Malinda and I arrived.

I'm not sure any of us slept well, and when I got up I saw Ian had hotcakes and coffee made. He'd been down to the boats and saw the sun was not in the canyon, and no one wanted to make that run in shadows.

Everywhere men were making ready to leave. Walt told us we'd better start on the trail. I really didn't want to leave. As I tied a rope around Sky, Ian and Liam came over to us. "Freddie, Ian and I want you to carry this satchel for us. It's all our money and a couple of watches. If anything happens, at least we'll have money to replace our things." Then with hugs, they said they'd see us below in a little while.

As we left, I wanted to look back, but knew I really shouldn't, and I also realized I wasn't crying. Somehow, I knew the men would be fine. Sky tugged at the rope. When we got to the last point where we thought we could see the men, we did turn to wave, but no one was there. The men had already left for the boats.

From the canyon we could hear shouts of men and the roar of the water crashing over the big rocks. We had walked a couple miles when Malinda found a place where we could see the White Horse Rapids. I almost died when I saw them. They were terrible, and yet they were awesomely beautiful. I'm not sure how they got their name, but the spray looked like the white tails of wild horses. If there hadn't been boats floundering in the maelstrom, it would have been beautiful. As it was, it was awful. Boats were tossed around like toys. We could see some go through rather well, but most took on lots of water. Some slammed into rocks though they continued down river.

Suddenly Malinda shouted, "There they are! See the flag!"

I saw two scows running together, one with that red plaid scarf flying in the wind. I couldn't tell who was in the second scow, and I frantically looked for the other boats. "There are the other two!" Malinda pointed as a huge whirlpool suddenly grabbed a boat and spun it around. It wasn't one of our boats, but I gasped, holding my breath until it shot out below. Our boats were right behind. Leonard pulled hard on the sweep oar and another man strained at the oars, but I couldn't tell who it was. Both boats missed the whirlpool, though not by much. The rapids sounded horrendously loud up on the trail, and I could only imagine what it must have been like below. Water pounded against boats, rocks, and the canyon walls.

"Oh God! It's Leonard's boat! What happened?" I gasped, dropping Sky's rope and putting my hands in front of my face.

"He's fine, Freddie. He's fine. They must have hit something, and it looks like the sweep oar broke, but he's holding on." I saw Leonard holding on as the boat headed for a rock, bounced off, and spun around. The boat went down backwards, and Leonard was trying to climb back in the boat. Sliding around another rock, they spun around heading down river right. Then they were out of sight below the canyon rim.

I started to run down the trail with Malinda right behind me and Sky running in front. I stooped to pick up the rope, realizing my heart was pounding and my mouth was dry. Malinda must have felt the same, as she said, "I could sure use a drink of water right now. I wish we'd brought some with us, but I didn't expect to be this thirsty."

"Me neither, but let's hurry. I want to hear their story of the rapids."

Boats were along the shore everywhere. Malinda spotted the red scarf flag, and we ran to the men. The four scows had landed in different areas, and the men were busy bailing water and checking for leaks. Leonard gave me a hug saying "We did just fine, wet but OK. And it looks like the boats came through in good shape."

Things were already spread out to dry, and the men huddled together talking. Walt told of looking down Miles Canyon, seeing only the dark black walls of the canyon, over a hundred feet high and black as tar. He said it looked like the canyon had been sliced apart by a big knife. Walls towered overhead, and there was no place to land if they had gotten into trouble. And these were the smaller rapids above the White Horse Rapids.

Andrew, Bruce, and Jason were in one boat and somehow managed to run both sets of rapids without taking on much water. They were sure it was an accident, or just plain luck, since they didn't know what they were doing. Ian, Liam, and Robert, in their smaller boat, took on lots of water but missed the biggest rocks. Robert said they were headed right for the big rock when the water pushed them off to one side.

Tony sat quietly by himself, his head down, breathing heavily, deep in thought. I sat down beside him. "Everything's fine, Tony. Are you hurt? You're so quiet."

"I'm fine. I just needed to thank God for bringing us through." I then noticed the rosary in his hands. "I sure was scared when the sweep oar broke and Leonard was tossed out. I'm so glad you didn't see it,

Freddie. He was almost swept away from the boat, but managed to grab the side as he went over, but I couldn't help him."

I saw tears of fright in his eyes and knew he was really shaken up by the whole event. I put my arm around him, softly saying, "But Malinda and I did see it. We had stopped to look for the boats when Malinda shouted and pointed to Leonard. We even saw the sweep oar break. You did fine and everything turned out well. But thanks for sharing it with me. It's actually nice to know I wasn't the only one scared."

Walt and Liam joined us after checking the boats for damage. Liam said they'd had a pretty good run, and Walt agreed he and Mark got some help when the water pushed them away from some rocks. They even said it was great fun, and they might like to do it again. After a rather long pause, each also admitted that once was really enough.

Leonard didn't say too much, only that when he looked down Miles Canyon and saw how really narrow it was and then saw the White Horse Rapids, he just shook his head. He never imagined the rapids would look so terrible close up. He said the boat creaked and groaned, pitched around like a toy bouncing from one wave to the next. Now, the boat needed immediate attention for a few small leaks.

The entire area was spread with wet belongings. Some men, broken in spirit, sat beside wrecked boats. Those like us, who had made it through in fairly good condition, didn't rejoice. There was patching to do and healing of spirits before we could go on.

I was thankful the sun was so bright and beautiful. Walt had thought to put some bread and fruit where he could find it quickly, and Robert shared some dried beef he had in his bag. This helped put our minds back to the work needing to be done.

Clothes, gear, and boats soon dried, and leaks were patched. It was time to leave. Sky was curled up in Leonard's boat. Tony sat beside her scratching her ears. I don't know who liked it more - Sky who loved the attention or Tony who needed to give it.

I gave the satchel, with the money and all, back to Ian, and the men shoved the boats into the water. The afternoon was quiet. I know we were glad to have the rapids behind us and thankful we had run them in good condition. Seeing some of the battered and broken boats along the shore made us think of the men who had lost so much.

We drifted for some time until Ian and Liam pulled alongside of us. He said the others wanted to stop at an Indian village near Lake LaBerge for supplies. "Ya folks go on. Remember the Mounties said we was to go down the left side of the lake. Don't worry. We'll catch up. We won't be long. Find a good place for all of us."

So we went on. The river was smooth, inviting us to take it easy. Dawson City was about four hundred and fifty miles away, and Lake LaBerge, or some say Lake LeBerge, was a few miles downriver. We'd find a good place and wait for the others.

We stopped to check in at the Police Post. We were again reminded to go down the left side of the lake. But as soon as we entered the lake, the wind came up quite fiercely. Leonard and Walt struggled to keep the boats to the left side. Leonard was having a terrible time trying to use the spare oar as a rudder. Even Walt, with a sweep oar, had problems. One minute it looked as though we would be able to stay left, then a gust a wind hit us broadside, driving water across the bows and onto everyone. Though they tried, the boats were driven to the right shore, and there was nothing they could do.

We pulled into a cove as quickly as we could, landing on a nice sandy beach. Tony and Walt walked back to where the river entered the lake to wait for the other boats, hoping to get their attention. We felt awful not being able to go down the left shoreline.

As Malinda and I started supper, Leonard and Mark set up the two tents. Dark clouds had drifted in over the lake, and rain was likely. Out on the lake the wind continued to churn up white caps. Tucked in the cove, we were spared most of the wind, but our spirits were not spared the fear that our friends might not find us.

Sometime later, Walt and Tony returned. It had started to rain, but they had waited, never seeing the other boats. They could see some boats going down the left side, but they never saw our Scotsmen or their flag.

The night dragged on. We saw other boats going down the right side, but none looked familiar. Leonard and Mark stayed up, keeping a big fire going, hoping the men would see it and stop. Finally, thoroughly wet, they went to bed. I hoped and prayed tomorrow would dawn bright and sunny, and our friends would find us or we would find them. I couldn't imagine not seeing them again. It just couldn't happen this way, without even being able to say good-bye.

# <u>19</u>

## LAKE LABERGE - WHERE ARE OUR FRIENDS?

June 5 - Down the Lake and Beyond

I need to keep up with my journal writing, but I don't feel like it. Yesterday was bright and beautiful, the rain gone, and the hills sparkled. Malinda and I fixed breakfast, but cooked entirely too much. Everyone missed the Scotsmen even Sky, I think, as she stretched out with her chin on her paws as if waiting for Liam to come scratch her ears.

Leonard and Mark walked back to the river, hoping to find them, but an hour later when a nice breeze came up, the men hoisted the sails, and off we went. Others shouted for us to stay close to the right shore as winds could come up quickly. Having already missed the left shore, we took their advice.

The tree covered mountains here were not especially high, and the shore was mostly rocks with some sand and lots of washed up timber. At first we followed the shoreline closely, going in and out of the larger coves and bays, but with no sign of storm clouds, we started cutting across them in a straight line.

Breezes filled the sails, and we skimmed along the lake, absorbed in thought, wondering if we'd soon meet up with our friends. This morning I forgot to put together food for the day. Sometime later we pulled to shore, fixed something to eat and warmed up by a driftwood fire. I was chilled, and the fire felt good, warming even the very empty place in my heart.

As Tony added bits of wood to the fire, he said, "You know the men may have stayed at that Indian village though it didn't look like much of a village to me."

Finally Walt said what we knew we had to do. "We need to take advantage of these breezes and go on."

"Wait a minute. I want to repair that broken sweep oar first," Leonard replied as he left to look for the right piece of driftwood. A long slender tree trunk cut to the correct length solved the problem as Leonard had grabbed the broad blade when the oar broke and soon had it nailed in place.

On the water, the sails billowed in the breeze, and we were off down the lake, focused on the beauty around us. Lake LaBerge was thirty miles long, before it emptied into the river. According to the river map the men bought at Lake Bennett City, Dawson City was now only four hundred miles downriver. Since the river flowed almost straight north, when we get to Dawson City, we should be about two thousand miles north of Seattle. The lake was a clear blue-green, most inviting for a swim, but putting my hand in the cold water quickly changed my mind.

We sailed at a good clip all afternoon when Tony looked at his father's watch and said we'd been sailing almost twelve hours. We pulled into a cove, got a fire built and supper started. We were tired, maybe because we knew the real dangers were behind us. The mosquitoes were terrible, so we went to bed for self-protection, closing the tent flaps tightly.

This morning it seems a new attitude prevailed. While Malinda cooked oatmeal, I remembered to put bread, fruit, and a tin of meat on each scow. With no breezes today, the men had to row. A long time later, Leonard pointed to a number of boats pulled in on the right near the Police Post. Leonard and Walt went to the office building while the rest of us looked around for the Scotsmen.

Returning, Walt reported the Scotsmen had not checked in so they must still be behind us. The men at the Post cautioned us to be very careful in the next part of the river known as the Thirty Mile River. It was a dangerous section with whirlpools and a huge rock in the middle of the river. The current split around the rock, but many boats were wrecked because those at the oars were not paying attention.

Once away, we picked up speed as the lake emptied into the river. High cliffs dominated the right side and bald eagles kept watch from tree tops. Their pure white heads and tails contrasted so with the black bodies. One tree had a dozen eagles sitting on branches. A bit further on we saw two mature eagles with two immature ones, their colors a mottled brown and black with just a bit of white in their feathers. Their golden eyes scanned the river so I surmised there must be fish here.

Last year at this time only Indians used this river. Now, hordes of men and boats raced to Dawson City. The river was really fast, making a right bend, a beautiful green canopy over our heads.

Suddenly we heard men shouting. Ahead we saw whirlpools swirling in large circles and just beyond was one gigantic rock. Some boats were pushed against the rock, others were partially submerged on shore, and all around gear was spread out to dry. Some men shook their heads, looking at the damaged boats, maybe having lost gear. Leonard and Mark pulled hard on the oars keeping us away from the danger while behind us, Walt and Tony made a good run further away from the rock. For a mile or so below the rock, damaged boats were pulled out on shore.

Once past the danger, the race down river began again. Those in front kept an eye on those behind them, and those behind strained at the oars to catch up. This was a race for the gold, but to win the race, the men had to pay attention to the obstacles in the river. A wrecked boat would not get them to the gold fields.

Islands began to appear. In some places it was actually difficult to tell where the main current flowed, and sometimes our two scows went around the islands on opposite sides. Some islands were quite small, but a couple of times we didn't see Walt and his boat until we reached the end of the island.

Once we saw both Walt and Tony leaning over the side of the scow. I couldn't figure out what they were doing until I saw the string in their hands, and it dawned on me they were fishing, using only the line! Quite soon, Tony pulled up his line with a fish about twelve inches long. He had no sooner pulled it in when Walt also caught one. We quickly pulled the boats together, and Tony pulled up a very colorful, high dorsal fin. No one knew what kind of fish they were, but we sure looked forward to fish for supper! I wondered what other kinds of fish we might catch, but I knew tonight we would have a great meal of fresh fish.

The sunshine was glorious, making me sleepy. Sky was asleep on top of the rolled up tent, so I curled up and soon was asleep, too. I'm not sure how long we'd been on the river, but I heard Walt say it was late and time to stop. Sometimes one boat would find a stopping place but too late for the others to row in. Finally, with boats pulled together, we drifted until Mark noticed a nice cove far enough ahead, and we rowed in easily.

Tying up to nearby trees, the men talked about the problem of finding a good campsite. Mark suggested we stay together in the afternoon so when a campsite was sighted, both could pull in easily. The fast current on the river would make it impossible to row back upriver if one boat missed a pull-out point.

A good fire was started, water put on for tea, and tents set up when another boat pulled in. The men had also been fishing, saying these fish were called grayling, and they were exceptionally good to eat. What a treat those fish were! The men shared our cook fire, and were soon putting their gear in the boat to run all night. They wanted to get on down the river and thought a night run would be fine.

I'm not sure how far we went today, since our map doesn't show many land details, but we felt it was a good day. For some reason the mosquitoes were not bad, so we stayed by the fire watching Sky scamper up and down the beach. She has brought us a lot of pleasure. Finally Mark spoke softly, "We all miss Ian and Liam, but I'm very glad we met you on that rickety old ship to Skagway, and Tony and I are richer for being part of this group." We were all very glad to have met each other, and I thought of that crowded old ship that had brought us together and of meeting Ian and Liam in Skagway those many, many weeks ago. Then we all learned of Malinda's plight and the memory of Malinda running down the canyon to join us at Deep Lake. Before going to bed, I gave everyone a hug. And I prayed that Ian and Liam and the other Scotsmen were alright and that we might all be together soon.

June 7 - The Days are Long

The past two days have been absolutely beautiful. The water through the Thirty Mile section was crystal clear. We could look down and see rocks on the bottom. I spent as much of the time looking down as up at the mountains. The water was fast, and as we drifted the men relaxed and enjoyed the day.

Small streams tumbled into the river sometimes adding crystal clear water and other times muddy water. By yesterday afternoon the water had begun to lose its clarity, still, we just dipped our cups in anytime we wanted a drink and enjoyed the very cold water. Even after Thirty Mile, Tony and Walt still caught grayling which we enjoyed at supper. Last night, some men passing us were surprised we were catching the fish. They had been trying all day with no luck. One asked Mark what he was using for bait, and the answer surprised everyone. He was using bread crusts! Walt was using bits of bird feathers, and that also worked.

We stopped for the night on a large sandy island, because we found fewer mosquitoes on the islands. The tents were set up, the scows securely tied to downed trees, and a nice stringer of grayling hung in the water tied behind a scow. These would be for breakfast. We even took off our rubber boots, enjoying the feel of sand between our toes.

When I got up the next day, the men were standing around the fire looking at large bear paw prints coming from behind our tent and right to the boats. Then the trail left, going between the two tents and back into the bushes.

Mark stood in the back of the scow, looking very disappointed, holding up an empty stringer. The bear had ever so quietly come into camp, walked by the tents to the scow, helped himself to our stringer of grayling, and then he thanked us so nicely by quietly leaving us to sleep in our tents. Even Sky didn't bark. Maybe she had some natural instinct telling her not to make a sound, or she might well be the bear's breakfast. Anyway, while it lasted we enjoyed the fish. Today the men caught nothing, but they haven't given up hope. The fishing continued, but the fish must have decided bread crusts and feathers weren't good.

The river is fast, and as we drifted, one man remained alert at all times. Downed trees hang from the river banks ready to snag or upset a boat. Sometimes the scows drifted together still moving at a good speed. This is some of the most beautiful country I've ever seen. Mountain after mountain spreads out before us. The hills are covered with wild grasses and flowers. Bushes, now in bloom, will later set into blueberries, cranberries, strawberries, and blackberries. We will be long gone before we can enjoy them, but fresh fruit would be so delicious.

The mountains grow lighter and lighter as they march off into the distance. Finally, they are just a pale blue-gray against the brilliant blue sky. Snow remains on top of the mountains and down in some cracks and crags. Some days the skies are gray with rain clouds, and the mountains blend with the sky somewhere miles away. We see rain clouds that seem to be just over the next hills, but we don't get rain. We've had our share of cold, wet weather on the trail and a few rainstorms on the river.

It won't be too long until Summer is officially here. We are so far north now it is light almost twenty-four hours a day. Oh, the sun does slip behind a mountain just before midnight, but a few hours later, it peaks from behind another adding sparkle to the water. I wish I could paint a picture of this beauty around us.

At times the sun is unmercifully hot, probably well into the nineties, and the men strip off their shirts to enjoy the warmth. Occasionally riffles appear over sandbars, and we must be careful, or we might end up stuck on top of one.

When we pull to shore for any reason, we are greeted quite forcefully by the local inhabitants, the hordes of mosquitoes! Walt calls them by another name - "moose-quitoes!" It's a constant battle trying to cook and wave my arms to keep away the nasty, biting swarms. Tents are set up facing the fire, and before we go to bed, the men build up a smudge fire to deter the mosquitoes. Sleep is next to impossible, however, and we can't seem to find our mosquito netting. I can't figure out why they are so prevalent in some areas and not in others. Around bushes they are terrible, but we've also had evenings when we could actually sit around the fire and not be driven insane.

We kept looking for Ian or Liam, but to no avail. They must have stopped at the Indian village. I don't think I will tell Leonard about the conversation with Ian and Liam until we get to Dawson City. I could be pregnant, but I don't want Leonard to be concerned. I may be getting bigger in my waist, but since the pants and shirt I'm wearing are much too large, I may be just imagining it.

Tonight we have a wonderful campsite. There is grass all around the tents, and not far away the hills rise gently, covered with a nice growth of trees. It's nice to see so many trees after seeing Lake Bennett and even Lake Lindeman so completely denuded of trees used for boat building. It will take a hundred years or more for those mountains to be covered with trees once again.

After supper, Leonard and I walked up the hills to the woods. It's nice to be by ourselves for a little while. The sun had dipped below the hills on the other side of the river, and the twilight patterned the forest floor in light and shadows. It was really quite peaceful. The silence was broken only by song birds or the scampering of tiny footed creatures scurrying beneath the thickly carpeted floor. Occasionally, louder sounds broke the quiet as tree branches snapped up when larger birds took flight, maybe dislodging a pine cone or two, dropping them on the leaves below.

Soon the wind picked up, and I told Leonard it sounded almost like the moans of lost souls –miners and even boaters - saying "Hurry! Tarry not here in this land of death!" Leonard said I have a vivid imagination, but in the depths of Winter when it is fifty degrees below zero, and men are caught in a storm, they would certainly freeze, and their ghosts could now be telling us to hurry along.

Back at the tents, we found the others looking over the river map. Though not drawn accurately, it does give us an idea of where we are. The river gets wider every day, and with all the islands, it is hard to tell which channel is the best one to take. We know some of the channels are dead ends, and those we definitely don't want to take.

After studying the maps to find our location, Walt thought we might be only a short distance above the Hootalinqua Village, another Police Post check-in point. From the maps it looks to be a tricky landing there. The Teslin River comes in from the east, just before the village, adding what looks to be a large volume of water to the Yukon. This means we'll have to stay close to the right side of the Yukon, ready to row across the incoming water to the Police Post.

We sat by the fire a while enjoying a nightly cup of tea, remembering it was Ian and Liam, who long ago in Skagway, got us drinking tea. We talked about where they might be, on Lake LaBerge or through the Thirty Mile section? They added so much to our lives with the softness of their voices which took the edge off any disagreements. Walt even mentioned he missed the smell of their pipes as we rested by the fire.

We thought of the wonderful omelet so lovingly prepared as a surprise at Deep Lake. I still can't imagine how those eggs managed not to freeze or break inside those flour sacks. Leonard said if he had known there were eggs inside, he might have handled them more gently. Tony remarked that if we'd known there were eggs in the sacks, we would probably have eaten them earlier and not enjoyed them as much as we did when they were prepared as a surprise. He was right, of course, which made us all laugh. What wonderful memories we will have about those eggs when we return home and make an omelet for breakfast. That one memory will be with us forever, always waking from deep inside, reminding us of very special friends.

## 20

### RIDING AN INCREDIBLE RIVER

June 9 - Two Very Long Days

Yesterday morning as we ate breakfast, many boats passed, all in a hurry to get down the river. Several waved, but no one stopped. With almost twenty-two hours of daylight, it's hard to sleep, but I was surprised when Tony said we actually slept six hours. I got food for the day ready, wrapped it in oilcloths, and we pushed the scows into the water before six-thirty. Our next stop would be the Police Post at Hootalinqua. I held out hope we would hear news of our friends.

Sky took her look-out post on the front of the scow, sitting on a crate looking down river. If we could only teach her to watch out for rocks and trees in the water, we could do other things like watch this magnificent scenery. Yesterday, Malinda sewed up a tear in a blanket, and Tony handed me a pair of trousers, asking if I could mend the seam in the back. We sewed on buttons and patched a few torn shirts, too.

Soon, Tony noticed a river coming in on the right. It had to be the Teslin. There was a large island in the middle of the Yukon, and about half way down the island, the Teslin entered the Yukon. We needed to be

215

on the right of the island in order to land at the Police Post. Had we been on the Teslin, it would have been easy to pull out. As it was, the men had to row very hard to cross the incoming river and find a place to land.

The main current pushed us to the right, though we landed beyond the Post. Walt and Tony didn't fare quite as well, landing further down from us. Tony and Leonard went to the Police Post to check in and inquire about the Scotsmen. I stood on the seat of the scow searching the area for the red plaid flag, which I was sure Ian and Liam would be flying. There was no sign of either their scows or the flag. Shortly, Leonard returned, shaking his head. He told the officers what had happened, and the officers said they would telegraph Lake LaBerge to see if the Scotsmen had checked. If he had news, he would telegraph to Big Salmon or Pelly River to let us know.

The scenery along the river was the most spectacular I have ever seen. Each bend in the river opened another vista. This was really a wilderness country. There were few cabins anywhere. This morning, we saw two beavers, placidly swimming across the strong current. I doubt we would have noticed them had Mark not heard the whacking sound they made by striking their broad flat tails on the water to warn other beavers of possible danger. Once he heard the sound, he quickly spotted the beavers. All I could see was the head and the familiar "V" in the water.

I thought Malinda was sleeping in the other scow as she was curled up on crates at the front end, but evidently she was watching the scenery. Suddenly she sat straight up, pointed to the opposite bank and whispered for us to be quiet. There in a small eddy was a mother moose and twin babies! Leonard and Mark quickly pulled back on the oars, slowing us down. Mama moose lifted her big head out of the water, where she was foraging for some delicious greens, to stare at us. Water dripped from her snout. Her eyes watched us, alert to any possible danger. The twin babies were standing in the water close to shore, just watching these two strange objects in the water. Obviously mama felt we were not a threat to her or her babies as she soon put her head back in the water, and quite quickly came up chewing on some sort of big green plant she had rooted from the bottom. What a special sight it was.

I thought back to the train trip across the country and the beautiful Rocky Mountains and the lush green valleys beyond the Cascades in Washington. They had been such an awesome sight to see, but now as I traveled down this river, I knew this was truly a wilderness. What would happen in the years to come with the influx of so many because of the gold rush? I wondered if any would stay to make it a home, or would they go back with their gold and forget this beautiful country?

Then I thought of the people who have entered our lives and have added so much to our experiences. People like Mr. Hale, who brought a message from the men that first day on the trail, and the next day helped move our things to Finnegan's Point. A special person like Sister Margaret Mary will always be remembered for her visit that eventually changed the lives of Malinda and everyone in our group. There was our Indian friend, who we simply called "Friend" since we couldn't understand his real name, and of course, Ian and Liam who will always have a place in my heart.

I told Leonard I wanted to talk to Malinda. The scows pulled together, and I grabbed the edge of the other boat, and Malinda grabbed ours so we could stay together.

"Malinda, do you remember Sister Margaret Mary and the time we met at Sheep Camp?"

"Of course, I do. How could I ever forget her? I wouldn't be here now if she hadn't listened to my plea and then done something to help. Why do you ask?"

"Well, I just remembered she said she and her three friends were going to go down the Yukon to the Pelly River. It didn't register this morning until Leonard mentioned the Big Salmon and the Pelly River Police Posts. Just now the words 'Pelly River' rang a bell, and I remembered."

Malinda looked down before replying. "You know, she left so quickly after we first talked, I never really had a chance to thank her for helping me. I wish I had some way to tell her I am now with you folks."

"So much has happened since then, but I, too, was wondering about her. Thanks to her, you were able to leave the ladies and join us. You'll note I use the term 'ladies' to be polite only."

I asked Leonard if they could tie the scows together, because Malinda and I wanted to do some laundry. Walt found a couple short lengths of rope, and quickly tied the scows together around the oarlocks at the center. He handed one end of the second rope to Leonard who found another place to tie up.

Soon, the River Laundry Service was in business as we floated along. With buckets half filled with water, we used the bar soap to scrub shirts, socks, and long underwear. Tony got busy rinsing the clothes in the river. He even slapped them on the top of the water which sounded much like the beavers slapping their tails on the water. Then he gave them to Mark who draped them all over everywhere. The trousers were harder to wash since they were heavier to handle, but soon even they were stretched out to dry.

When we finally finished, with clean hands and clean clothes draped all over the scows, Walt said we were going just as fast tied together and suggested we might consider a night float. We could stop for supper and tie the scows together more securely. The men could take turns sleeping, always having two men by the sweep oars for control.

Leonard liked the idea, especially since the nights were never very dark. He quickly pointed out that it might not be a good idea to do this every night since we probably wouldn't sleep well. Tony and Mark studied the river chart of what might be ahead tonight. Not seeing any difficult areas until we got to Five Finger Rapids about 120 miles downriver from Hootalinqua, they decided to run through the night.

Quickly, Tony pointed to the boats stopped along the right bank further down river. Grabbing the map, he thought we were close to the Big Salmon Police Post. We pulled in just beyond the mouth of the Big Salmon River, past a rather small river entering on the right, and Walt and Mark went to check in and see if there had been any word on our friends. Shaking their heads as they returned, I realized there was no news.

He had asked about this next portion of the river, and if a night run would be fairly safe. One Mountie said the next fifty to sixty miles were pretty obstacle free, but he cautioned us of dangers such as floating trees, called snags, and choices between several channels to take. He couldn't tell us where the best current might be as it shifted from channel to channel. And he warned us not to go through Five Finger Rapids at night.

Tony looked at the map and finding Five Finger Rapids said we couldn't get that far even if we wanted to. So now with a night run in mind, we continued down river until Mark spotted a small eddy with some sand and grassy area.

Walt got a fire going, while Malinda and I mixed up hotcake batter. This was the quickest meal to prepare. Leonard and Walt re-tied the rope around the center oar locks, and using a long, straight tree branch two inches in diameter, they secured it tightly behind the notch used by the sweep oar. Since the boats were really stable individually, they felt this would really make them very stable.

They finished about the time the hotcakes and coffee were ready. Mark suggested the men take three hour shifts at the stern. While it's twilight at night, he knew everyone was tired, and the men would have to keep a sharp lookout for obstacles.

With supper finished, the scows were shoved back into the river, and the night float began. Tony and Leonard took the first shift. With coats hugged tightly around us, Malinda and I curled up on crates in the larger scow and covered up with a blanket. It wasn't the most comfortable place to sleep, but we were warm and eventually we'd get some sleep. Walt curled up in front of the other scow, while Mark pulled up his knees sleeping on the seat. Sky curled up at Walt's feet.

All was quiet for a few minutes. Then for some reason, I started laughing. I thought I was quiet about it, but Malinda asked what was so funny. I said I actually didn't know, except here we were, trying to sleep on two boats, drifting down a river we knew nothing about, with a river map that was not accurate. For some reason it didn't sound funny, but I couldn't stop laughing. Soon she was laughing, too. Mark asked what we were laughing about, and try as we might, we couldn't tell him because our somewhat quiet laughter suddenly exploded into a burst of uncontrollable laughter.

Leonard just shook his head and asked if we wanted him to sing us to sleep. That did it. We laughed all the more. Finally, so tired from laughing, we tucked our heads under the blanket and were quiet.

So thus went our night float. I slept fairly well, waking only a few minutes while Leonard and Tony traded places with Walt and Mark. The next thing I knew, Leonard was pointing out a place to stop for breakfast. Over hot coffee, the tale of the night float was told. Things had gone smoothly, though a couple of times they had to row the double scows out of the way of snags. According to Tony, who liked to read the map, he thought we had gone about fifty miles during the night. He pointed to the map, showing where the Little Salmon River came in, saying we had passed that point a while ago. Now, we were stopped at the upper end of an island with another island right ahead of us, and he found such a place on the map matching what he saw.

Looking ahead on the map and finding Five Finger Rapids, he showed us how far it was to that point. As near as they could figure, we still had about forty miles to go before we reached the rapids. He doubted we could go that far today until he looked at his watch and saw it wasn't even six o'clock yet.

Malinda and I fixed breakfast, and the men studied the map. The river made big deep bends first one way and then another and the number of islands increased dramatically. This section of river would require careful watching of both the current and the map. Still, the men were determined to get as close to the rapids as possible today, then look them over so we could run through early tomorrow. Walt mentioned another set of rapids beyond Five Finger Rapids which the Mounties said would give us no problem except the possibility of getting hung up on a small rock field in the shallow water just before the rapids. We were told to take the right side of the river in both rapids. In Five Finger Rapids it was imperative we take the far right channel, even though it looked narrow, it was the only safe passage through.

Again on the river, after separating the scows, Tony gave the map to Malinda and showed her how to follow it as we went along. Then he and Walt took over the oars. Leonard and Mark decided to follow them down the river today.

The day was beautiful and sunny, and already I could feel the heat reflecting off the water. The current seemed to be even faster than it was yesterday. With many rivers and streams emptying into the Yukon, it was no longer a nice clear river. Each stream or side river dumped more dirty brown water into the Yukon. For a while the dirty water seemed to run as a separate river beside the Yukon, their waters not mixing. Then slowly and inevitably they mingled, and each time the Yukon was the loser, getting muddier and muddier as it went along.

I searched in my satchel for my soap and towel and finding them, I told Leonard I wanted to wash my hair. Oh the water was cold! It's one thing to put your hand in cold water; it's quite another thing to pour it over your head. I immediately got a headache, but I knew I had to finish. It didn't take long to rub the soap in my hair, but it certainly didn't lather up like I wanted. Leonard later told me the lather was dirty brown. Finally, the rinsing over, I shook my head much like Sky shakes when she gets wet. It felt good to have somewhat cleaner hair, and I knew it would dry in the sun in short order. Malinda must have looked back, seeing what I was doing, for when I saw her she was washing her hair, too. Then Leonard asked for the soap, and before you knew it, all six of us had washed our hair.

We came to a big bend in the river filled with islands and channels everywhere. Walt pointed between two large islands, and waving his arm indicated that was the way to go. We followed, and very soon the river took a sharp bend the other direction. We had made one giant "S" on the river.

Sharp cliffs rose first on one side of the river and then the other. Islands were everywhere. Some were so small we could see across them to the other side. Others were quite large. Some were rocky with only a few bushes or maybe a tree or two. These would be a hard place to camp, though they might offer protection from mosquitoes and now black flies, too.

Most islands had driftwood piled on the up river end. Some piles were quite large.

When we first encountered these driftwood piles, I had been concerned there might be snakes in them, but Mark relieved my fears by informing me there were no snakes in Alaska or the Yukon. It was much too cold for them. One evening after gathering wood, Tony came back to the fire with a little tiny creature in his hand. He said it was a vole, a mouse-like animal which lived up here. He told how he had done a lot of reading before coming so he might know what he'd see. He didn't remember for sure, but he thought these voles lived under the snow during the Winter.

After eating bread and beef, the men continued rowing all afternoon. Only a few times did they drift, but most of the time they searched for the right channels through or around islands. So far we have been very fortunate not to go down some blind channel and then have to row back out to the main current.

The sun began dipping lower in the sky when Tony said it was almost eight o'clock and definitely time to stop. We needed to eat and get a good night's sleep. Looking up from the map, Malinda thought we were getting close to another large bend in the river, and if this was true, we were only about six to eight miles from Five Finger Rapids.

It took us more than fifteen minutes to find a suitable stopping place. The best places, low and relatively flat, seemed to be on the left hand side of the river, but remembering the Mounties' warning to take the right hand channel through the rapids, the men didn't want to cross the river which has gotten considerably wider in the last few days.

In front, Walt's boat pulled quickly to shore. There was a trail up a slope about twenty feet high, which looked flat on the top, and there were trees large enough to anchor the scows, though the landing area was not too big. We followed and found the area was actually larger than it looked.

We climbed the trail and found, to our utter amazement, a very large flat area, covered with mosses and very tiny green plants. There was even a fire pit, so someone must have used this area not long ago. There were many very tall trees but very little undergrowth. The tree trunks were straight with branches starting quite high up. It almost looked like a cultivated garden of immense size. My foot sank down in the moss, almost to my ankle. What a soft bed we would have tonight!

We didn't sit around the fire too long after supper, though we did enjoy our usual cup of tea. What conversation there was centered around the upcoming rapids. Walt felt we should stay close together approaching them. Not knowing how big the rapids were compared to the ones in Miles Canyon above Lake LaBerge, they wanted the opportunity to stop and look them over, if possible, before we ran them. The Mounties told them women and children could ride through, but Walt wanted to be careful anyway.

Tomorrow will come soon enough, and right now I am very tired and looking forward to a nice comfortable night's rest. I think again of our friends, wondering where they are. Prayers tonight are for safety tomorrow and all our tomorrows for us and for our friends.

# 21

## FIVE FINGER RAPIDS AND BEYOND

June 10 - Rapids Ahead!

Malinda and Walt had coffee and hotcakes made when I got up. Each time we make them, I think of her comment at Deep Lake, saying she would never eat another hotcake. Now, we use our sourdough starter and make them quite often.

Breakfast finished, it was time to get back on the Yukon. Everything was taken to the scows and tied down tightly. It was less than five miles to Five Finger Rapids. This morning, Leonard and Tony rowed the bigger scow with me sitting up front and Sky standing on the crates, her tongue out and her tail wagging. She must think this is going to be fun. After all, she missed the "fun" of the rapids in Miles Canyon.

We had been told to be on the right side of the river and take only the right channel through the rapids. With the higher water from the snow melt, the other channels would be entirely too dangerous. Even the right channel would have some big waves.

Rounding a bend in the river, we saw the huge rocks which formed Five Finger Rapids. The right shore was absolutely vertical, the left side less so. In the middle of the river were four standing islands of solid rock, three about seventy-five to one hundred feet high and one slightly shorter. Each island was topped with its own little forest. I really saw how it got the name Five Finger Rapids. Spreading my hand out with the four fingers and the thumb representing the five river channels, it looked like a giant hand had raked the river.

The men pulled toward the right shore with Walt right behind us. Leonard stood up in back, and shouted for Tony to row both oars while he took the sweep oar. I turned to see Mark taking the sweep oar in the other scow. The current quickly increased, and Tony shouted for me to hold tight to the rope around Sky with one hand and onto the boat with the other. Closer and closer and faster and faster we went. My mouth was again dry, just like it was above the White Horse Rapids, as Malinda and I watched the men run those terrible rapids. I decided it was not thirst, but fear, that made it so. I saw the channel and tightened my grip on Sky's rope and on the scow.

Suddenly we were swept so close to the right wall I could almost touch it. Waves crashed over the front into my lap. Tony pushed the oars with all his might giving us extra speed through. I didn't look at Leonard, but I heard Tony shout, "Left! Left! Left!"

As quickly as we started, it was behind us. I looked at Leonard who raised his fist in the air to signal Mark and Walt we were through, and all was well. I turned quickly to watch Mark and Walt run through, only to find that they were already through and were drawing up beside us. Malinda was as wet as I was, probably from taking the same wave right across the bow. Sky was one happy, wet puppy. I think she probably would have done well in the other rapids, and she certainly seemed to like the ride. Then I remembered Leonard hitting the rock and falling out in the terrible White Horse Rapids, and I realized she probably would have been pitched into the maelstrom of water. I don't think she would have liked that one bit!

We continued on passing several nice sized islands. Tony and Leonard were both rowing again, but the speed of the river was almost enough to keep us going at a good pace. It seemed only a very short time when Leonard again stood up. Rink Rapids were ahead. I hadn't had time to dry from the last waves, and here we were about to encounter Rink Rapids. They didn't look like much, and I was glad to see it.

Again we were told to stay to the right and watch out for submerged rocks. Walt and Mark were right beside us and signaled us to go ahead, than they both pulled back on their oars to slow them down, giving us more room to maneuver.

The current caught us and pushed us away from the right side and into the main flow. The rapids looked quite tame to me, and Leonard didn't seem too concerned about the change in position until suddenly we heard scraping noises, and then we stopped. We were grounded on the rocks!

Mark shouted to us as they passed telling us to stay to the left side of the river once we were off the rocks and through the rapid. He said they would pull out as soon as possible and wait for us. If we got separated, we should stay to the left for about five miles, just past the very large group of islands shown on the map, as this might be a good place to stop. Then they were gone.

Tony and Leonard both leaned well over the sides trying to see what held us. They thought we were stuck on two rocks as if we had tried to run between them, not realizing the space was too narrow. Tony took one of the oars and pushed hard against one rock on his side while Leonard used the sweep oar to give us some leverage from the other side. We didn't move a bit.

All the while the other scow was getting further and further away until it ducked between the left shore and an island, and then was out of sight. I remembered how difficult it was to stay to the left side at Lake LaBerge, and how we ended up on the right side, staying up late watching for Ian and Liam. I knew Walt and Mark would wait for us, but how were we going to get off these rocks and join them?

I don't know how long the men worked different techniques to move us, but nothing seemed to help. It seemed a long time since we hit, and we were still sitting right where we were. With the strong current, Tony thought the best thing was for both of them to be on left side pushing on that one rock. By doing so, the current might swing the stern to the right side enough to push us off, causing us to pivot around the other rock. We'd run the rapid stern first, but since both ends were the same, it wouldn't make much difference except we would be going down river backwards. Seems to me, I remember them running stern first in the White Horse Rapids.

Anything was worth the try. Both pushed with all the strength they had left, and suddenly, just as Tony had said, the back of the scow began to swing out and down. Tony quickly moved to the front and pushed on the oar.

We were off! We were going down river stern first, but at least we were going down river again. Once through the rapid, which wasn't much really, the men turned us around so they could see where they were going. By the time the men had the scow headed down river and were settled at the oars again, we had gone to the right of the islands. I wondered if we would miss Mark and Walt, since we missed the left channel. The current kept pulling us to the right no matter how hard the men rowed. The number of islands increased to dozens, not just three or four. With so many islands, I was worried that the other scow would be out of sight behind one of them and we would miss them completely. There were many large downed trees in these channels, and any one of them could snag the other scow.

Along the right shore the cliffs were light brown, like gravel from a river bed mixed with sand. About three fourths of the way up from the river, there was a white layer. It was very distinctive. I pointed it out to Leonard who said the Mounties had mentioned that this was a layer of volcanic ash. Sometime hundreds of years ago this section of the Yukon River country was covered by the ash from a very large volcano. He said we would see it further down the river and should notice the color of the White River, which also contained large amounts of the ash in addition to glacial silt.

Soon we spotted Walt's boat coming around the upriver end of an island far to our left. He and Mark were trying to row against the current! Leonard signaled them as they pulled around the island and into the main current. We quickly joined them running past a number of islands. By this time we were thoroughly confused as to what might actually be the left river bank and not an island. Mark pointed to the left, saying we absolutely had to stop there. Both scows were able to pull into a grassy meadow-like area at the end of a deep bend in the river.

With a fire made, Malinda and I, still wet from Five Finger Rapids, moved in close to get warm and dry off. The men took off their rubber boots to dry their feet. They must have taken a good splashing from waves. However, it was not the splashing that caused the wet feet. It was boat damage!

As we stood by the fire, Mark told of taking a wrong channel and getting stuck at the end by a big pile of driftwood. Finding no way through or around it, they had to row against the current to find their way back to the main channel. But, while they were turning around, they hit a big rock right below the center of the boat. Malinda had noticed water coming in quickly from a broken floor board, and Mark had stuffed one of the sleeping blankets in the hole to stop the water. It held, but now major repairs were required before we could go further.

As if that weren't enough, Leonard described the water coming in our boat behind the rowing seat which he thought it was probably caused by a seam splitting open. Our boat, too, would need repairs. With still over two hundred and twenty five miles to Dawson, repairs were now absolutely necessary.

Tents were set up, and Malinda and I started cooking while the men unloaded the scows. They needed to do a thorough repair job, and by turning the boats over they could work on them more easily. There was not too much either Malinda or I could do, so we just made a big pot of stew. When the coffee was made, the men just filled their cups and kept on working. By the time the stew was cooked, the scows were empty and turned over. What we saw was not good news. Walt's scow had not only split a board but actually had broken out a section about two to three inches long. A replacement board was needed. Tony examined the larger scow finding several split seams, probably when we first hit the rock. But before they could be repaired, the scows needed to dry somewhat.

The men ate with bowls of stew in one hand while gesturing with the other hand how they would make repairs on Walt's scow. Seam sealing would not be much of a problem other than the time it took. Malinda and I stayed close to the fire, making more coffee and cooking some fruit for later. There was not much we could do on the repairs, but we could at least repair their spirits with hot food and drink.

We saw a number of boats continuing down river. A few men in one boat waved; most just hurried on, probably glad they were not repairing boats. Tony tried to point out a particularly small boat on the far side of the river, but by the time we saw it, it was just rounding the bend, going out of sight. Tony surmised it was so small the men had to sit on top of their gear to row. Mark wondered how they managed the big rapids, but thought they probably just bobbed right through like a cork.

The afternoon was spent re-sealing seams and trying to figure how to replace the broken board in

Walt's boat. Tony finally suggested we break apart one of our crates and use those boards to make a patch both inside and outside, leaving the broken board in place between the patches. The new seams could be sealed well on both sides, and it should hold quite well.

The question of which crate of food to unpack was solved when Malinda opened a crate of evaporated milk. If these cans got wet, no damage would be done - not like flour or sugar bags. We could put those cans in other crates we had already opened. This sounded like a reasonable solution, and soon cans of milk were piled on the ground. The men took the crate apart, careful to remove and save all the nails.

With the boats turned over to dry overnight, and the crate torn apart, the men finally sat down by the fire. This was really a beautiful place to stop. The river was very wide, with high cliffs on the other side and the soft grass under our tents. It was much later than we thought, as soon the red rays of the short sunsets painted the river in gold and shades of red. It was time for sleep.

Tony and Mark stayed up by the fire, discussing the needed repairs. I was simply glad to go to bed. We were now over half way to Dawson City. The dangers of rapids were behind us. Surely the rest of the river would be more relaxing.

I tried to sleep but just couldn't seem to relax. My stomach kept fluttering, and I wondered if drinking the river water, with all the silt and dirt, might have caused some problem. I usually tried to let the water settle in my cup before drinking, but when I have been really thirsty, I hadn't necessarily waited very long.

Suddenly, I heard Mark say, "Oh my! Look at that!" I crawled out of the tent and looked at the biggest moon I have ever seen rising just over the sagging roof of an old dilapidated and long abandoned barn where we had made camp. It was bright orange, reflecting the sun just now setting below the hills beyond us. Knowing this was truly a spectacular sight, I woke the others. There in the middle of a very short night, by a warm fire, we enjoyed a true marvel of nature. That moment will be etched in my memory forever. How thankful we all were to have experienced such a sight with friends, and how I did wish that Liam and Ian could have been with us. I do wonder where they are right now, and I pray we will meet up with them again along the way somewhere.

June 11 - Underway After Repairs

I woke to the song of birds twittering in the trees. No one else was awake, so softly I crept out of the tent and added wood to the still burning embers of last night's fire. I looked up, searching for the big orange moon, but saw only the setting white moon I was so used to seeing.

I shook out the still-wet blanket used for emergency boat repairs and turned it over to continue drying near the fire. The night had been warm, the blanket not needed, but it still needed to dry. I picked up a bucket and walked down to the river, filling it for coffee. As I put it on to boil, I realized I was actually the first one up this morning.

I was thoroughly enjoying listening to the birds when behind me I heard Mark remark very quietly,

"Come stand by me, but be quiet. Look toward the river, and you'll see a covey of ducks just up from where you filled the bucket."

Sure enough, there were several mother ducks with about twenty or so little fluffy ducklings floating peacefully on the current. They didn't seem to mind the cold water, and apparently they, too, were headed down river this lovely Summer morning. I wondered how many other mornings the early riser had seen such sights. I also wondered if others going down river took time to enjoy this incredible country through which we floated. I hoped we were not the only ones, for then others would have missed some of the most beautiful experiences one can have.

Soon others emerged from the tents, yawning and stretching out the kinks and knots from last night. The sun was already shining on the upturned boats and creeping fast toward the fire pit. While I cooked oatmeal, the men grabbed a cup of coffee, and walked down to examine the boats. There was lots of talk about what to do, but neither Malinda nor I paid much attention. We quickly folded up the blankets, stuffing them in one of the canvas bags we had found along the trail so long ago.

Then, with bowls of hot oatmeal and steaming cups of coffee, the men discussed how to make the repairs. Boards would be nailed across the broken section inside and also on the bottom of the boat. The board on the bottom would be nailed over the hole running parallel to the boards already there. This way, they hoped, there would be less friction on the patched section. Then the seams would be sealed both inside and outside.

Having lost half a day yesterday and a portion of today with repairs, Mark suggested this might be a good night for another night run. He pointed to the map, noting it was about fifty miles or so to Fort Selkirk. There we could rig for the night run, but we would have to really hustle to get there. Filling cups with the last of the coffee, the men went to work. Malinda and I cleaned up, prepared food for each boat during the day, and carried things down to the other piles on the shore.

Sky dragged a piece of wood down, I suppose thinking we needed it. She is growing so fast and is such fun. Each night by the fire she goes from one to another, accepting a scratch behind the ear or rolling over to enjoy a good tummy rub.

Walt came to help Malinda and me take down the tents and rolled them up. He and Malinda took them down to the scow, and I followed with pots and pans. Malinda and I then poured water on the fire while the men turned the larger scow over and shoved her into the river, being careful to tie it securely to a nearby tree.

As Leonard and Mark applied large amounts of pitch and oakum to the bottom side of the smaller scow, the others started packing boxes and crates into the larger one. Less than an hour later, the second scow was launched, and everyone watched carefully to see if the patch would hold. Seeing no water seeping in, crates were packed in, and both boats were pushed into the water. Another day on the river had begun.

Numerous islands divided the river. The men were getting good at telling where the faster currents were, and the morning passed. Tony and Mark and I were in one boat today, and the others with Sky were in the larger boat. We really liked the idea of changing places, even though the boats were never very far from one another.

Mark read the map today though I was actually holding it and trying to follow where we were. Our scow was first down the river. We thought, if the patch was not going to hold, at least the other scow would be behind us and able to come to our aid.

Early on we passed others who had stopped to cook breakfast, or maybe they were just late getting back on the river. Once while looking at the map, I heard lots of squawking and chattering from birds overhead. I looked up to see many small birds actually chasing an eagle upriver. They would dive at the eagle, sometimes actually hitting it, while the eagle flew a zigzag pattern trying to get away. Tony thought the eagle had probably gotten too close to the nests of the other birds, and now the smaller birds were giving the eagle a "blue ticket" out of the territory. The little birds were sure feisty. They were protecting their young, and no eagle was going to come near them; nature at work.

So the day passed. Islands were everywhere, some in groups of a dozen or more, and many just big islands by themselves. Earlier the boats might have taken opposite sides of the bigger islands or taken many channels through the many islands, but having rowed back up river once was enough. Playtime, as I secretly called it, was over. The work of going down river was paramount in the minds of all.

Sometime around mid-day or even later, the boats tied together so we could share a meal and just drift a while. We actually found drifting was almost as fast as rowing, and it was certainly a lot less work.

The Yukon River is an endless parade of eddies, whirlpools, and riffles. The water actually talks to us in hisses and gurgles as the silt from hundreds of small streams empties into the river to continue its journey for hundreds of miles to the sea.

We saw others drifting also, but we didn't see the funny little boat Tony had seen last night. I'd really like to have heard their description of bobbing like a cork through the White Horse Rapids or even Five Finger Rapids. What determination those men must have to want the gold so badly they would risk their lives in such a small boat!

The sun was quite hot now, and soon after eating I was very sleepy. Sky had jumped over to me when we tied together, and even she was curled up in the bottom of boat in some shade offered by several crates. I rearranged some of the blanket bags and the tent, and then stretched out, closing my eyes, but still hearing the men talking. Each day I have realized what good friends these four men have become.

I tuned out the voices and listened instead to the swishing, gritty sound of the sand and dirt in the water as it washed along the bottom and sides of the scow. The sound is not unlike that of sandpaper being rubbed over a board. Actually it probably had the same effect, though it would take a lot of this sanding action to make the boards smooth.

I sat up quickly when Leonard shouted "Look!" On the nearby shore a big bear swaggered along the river, followed by two of the cutest little cubs. Sky jumped up with her paws on the side of the boat, and Mark quickly reached forward to grab the rope collar we had put on her.

"We don't need her to go chasing Mama bear. She would lose that fight for sure." He held her tightly, but Sky neither barked nor tried to get away. Maybe she knew better, but I think it was really because Mark was really holding her tightly.

The mother bear was a beauty. Her dark brown fur rippled over her massive shoulders as she walked. Her head swung from side to side, always keeping an eye on her two cubs. The cubs were more interested in chasing each other or nipping the ears of the other to care what was going on out on the river fifty feet away.

Very shortly after we passed the bears, Mark mentioned we had better untie and be on our own. We were approaching a part of the river named Hell's Gate. "That's all the map says. It shows lots of islands to the right, but the channel seems to be to the left." He leaned over to show the other boat the map, pointing where we were. Quickly ropes were untied, and everyone's attention was on the many small islands on the right.

Walt stood up on the seat to get a better look and motioned for us to move even further to the left. Just as we were almost past the smaller islands, a portion of the right side of the river looped off, cutting long narrow islands all along the shore line. Now the place to be was definitely on the left. A few quick strokes of the oars, and we were in the main current, breezing along. No one could understand why it was named Hell's Gate as there really didn't seem to be much in the way of danger. If the miles marked on the map were accurate, Tony thought we had come forty miles already. The current was moving us along quite fast. He also said it was only about ten miles or so to Fort Selkirk and the confluence with the Pelly River. Before reaching the Pelly River though, the map showed lots of islands, some grouped in twos or threes, and others just big islands blocking what might be the main current. Those ten miles would require our complete attention, and Fort Selkirk was on the left shortly after the Pelly River came in on the right. Just beyond the Pelly River, the Yukon turned sharply to the left. Now all of us watched carefully where the current took us.

Those ten miles actually went quite quickly. Soon after the Pelly River entered the Yukon, Walt pointed to the Union Jack flying above cabins down river on the left, indicating we had reached the Fort Selkirk area. The Pelly was a big fast river with several large islands in its mouth, and lots of floating logs. Jammed on the islands were trees, roots and all, showing the force of the river tearing away river banks uprooting entire trees and sending them down river. The current was really fast, and the men had to strain to row across to the shore.

Reaching shore, they jumped out, grabbing the bow ropes and securing us tightly to large tree trunks resting on the shore nearby. Sky bounded off the boat and up the trail. At the top she stopped, and sat down as if to say, "Come on. There are people to meet and things to do. Hurry up!" This morning I had started beans

241

soaking in a big pot now wedged between two crates. I would add a tin of beef, one of tomatoes, some dried onions, and some syrup. Then with fried biscuits, supper would be good an also quite satisfying.

Mark and Leonard walked back up river to the Police Post to check in and look for mail, this being the first place where we could get some mail. The Yukon Field Force men headquartered here were checking boats instead of the NWMP.

Mark spoke with one of the officers who said Fort Selkirk was originally a Hudson Bay Company post established by Robert Campbell in the late 1840s. Its main purpose was to establish trade with the Indians of the area. However, things had not gone well, and the Indians had burned the post to the ground in the early 1850s. This post has been here for only about four years.

Getting the pot of soaking beans and the other things needed for supper, Malinda and I hurried up the trail to start supper. Walt and Tony rearranged the crates in the scows so we could sleep better, and also cleared the area by the sweep oars, giving those at the oars more room to stretch their legs.

Mark and Leonard soon reported back that there was neither word of the Scotsmen's boats, nor any mail for us. Mark also said the Field Force advised us not to stay here for the night as the area had no store or any supplies and was settled only by squatters and Indians, and neither group was particularly friendly to those going down river. But we didn't plan to stay here anyway. Other boats stopped to check in and fix supper, and all stayed right at the brow of the hill overlooking the river. No one ventured anywhere near the few tents and log cabins of the settlers.

As soon as supper was finished, Tony and Mark collected all the pots and such, saying they would wash them in the river. They really didn't like it here, but Mark did say it was pretty looking down the river.

Across the river, we could see very high black cliffs, probably 300 feet high, though Leonard thought they were even higher. The cliffs were almost vertical. The Pelly River had cut through them, and quite a large amount of water joined the Yukon. Looking down river I could see the cliffs continued for some distance.

Back on the river, with Mark and Leonard taking the first shift in back with the sweep oars, the rest of us settled down. It is still too early to sleep, but we each found our place for the night. If it had been dark out, I'm sure the stars would have filled the sky.

This has been a long day. The patches on both boats held well, and we have already gone over fifty miles, with a night float still ahead. We should be well on our way to Dawson City when we stop again for breakfast.

# 22

## ANOTHER NIGHT FLOAT WITH A BIG CHANGE

June 11 - Ready for Another Night Float

We didn't waste any time around Fort Selkirk and were thankful to get away from the unpleasant area. Once settled, Sky again took up her post at the front of the scow watching logs float down the river. We stayed to the left side of the river, passing a number of islands. Most of them had grass, small bushes and a few trees growing in the middle, but the shoreline was quite rocky.

Then just after passing some high cut banks on the left, Sky began barking fiercely and acted as if she would jump overboard. She had never acted like this, and we searched the river bank for something that might have disturbed her.

"Look! Over there!" Mark shouted, pointing toward the trees ahead of us. "There's a big fire back in that grove of trees. I wonder if someone needs help."

Quickly, we pulled for the river bank. I couldn't imagine why Sky had barked so. She didn't do this even when she saw moose or bears on shore. The men tied up to some logs, and that was when we noticed the funny little boat pulled up on shore. It was just part of a boat, probably cut in half when men divided everything. Somehow the men in this boat had managed to continue down river in this very unwieldy looking craft.

I looked around for Sky but couldn't find her, though I heard her barking as she ran down a trail. The barking changed to yipping, and then we saw two men, being lovingly kissed by a puppy. Sky had found Ian and Liam! What a reunion with big hugs for all! Sky thought she deserved hugs, too, as she bounced from one person to another.

Ian motioned for us to sit down so he and Liam could tell their story. It seemed the other four Scotsmen wanted to stop at the Indian village to resupply some much needed food items. At first Ian and Liam could not understand why the others had pulled out bottles of whiskey, but they quickly understood when the others started bargaining with a couple of Indian men for the comforts of women.

Liam wanted nothing to do with such a plan, and Ian was outraged at the thought. It seemed neither Ian nor Liam had known the other Scotsmen before they met on the train across Canada and decided to join up going North, like we had done with Tony and Mark.

Liam said that while building the boats, he and Ian realized the other Scotsmen drank too much but they always waited until we had gone to bed. When we were ready to leave, the drinking had slowed down so Ian thought the liquor was gone.

After telling the others what they thought of the proposed events, an argument broke out. The others tossed everything out of the scow and divided it, with over half going to the four of them. Some flour bags were cut in half before Ian could stop them. He sorted the tinned foods, giving the others two for each one he took for Liam and himself. Liam wanted one Yukon stove. The others said "Never!" and threw it in the river.

The others took both tents saying Ian and Liam could use "the stupid sail Ian had carried over the Pass which was never used much anyway."

Grabbing a saw, two other men started sawing the smaller scow in half right in back of the rowing seat. Ian argued that half a boat would be no good, but the others grabbed them, pinned them to the ground and cut it anyway. Then they shouted obscenities and started toward the Indian village. Liam said their final remark was, "We better never see ya on the river or we'll kill ya!"

Ian and Liam got up, wondering how they could go down river. They looked over the mess on the river bank, piling their things in one spot. Ian opened some crates to take more food, yet both wondered if they could find a way to go down river. In the crates labeled "food," he actually found bottles of whiskey concealed under a few food items. Packed this way they had gotten the whiskey through the Canadian customs.

While Ian sorted the crates, Liam looked over the two halves of the boat. Suddenly he said, "Hey, Ian, we're in luck! 'Member when we built them scows, we had boards left over and took time to nail them beneath the rowing seat? 'Member we sealed 'em tight thinking it might keep them scows from sinking if one end sprung a leak?"

Ian and Liam looked at the back section and sure enough, the cut was made in front of the seat. It looked watertight since they didn't see any signs of water in the back section. Since both ends were constructed in the same way, they just turned it around, piled in everything, filling every inch of space available. Grabbing two oars, they shoved off into the river. They wanted to get as far away as possible before the others returned. They had meant to take the other Yukon stove, but in their haste, they had forgotten it.

They stopped at the Police Post at Lake LaBerge, showed them the little boat, and told them the story. Since this type of incident wasn't unusual, the Mounties couldn't do anything to help, but they did assign them a new number since the original number was on the half left behind. So that's why, when we inquired about boat #12493, the smaller scow, we never got a report on it. It didn't exist. Their new number was #24147, meaning 2 - two men, 41 and 47 being their ages. They wouldn't tell us who was which age. The Mounties even painted the new number on the side of the little boat.

Their story didn't end there, however. They took the left side down Lake LaBerge, never finding us. We told them about the wind pushing us down the right side. Ian said the half-boat was very hard to row using the oars as paddles. They couldn't cut them shorter until they reached the Police Post and used a saw there. Also, the boat wasn't loaded very evenly because of the constricted space.

They were on the lake and the river many hours each day, making progress, but encountering lots of problems handling their half-boat. They had to sit on top of their gear and paddle, which was not easy at all. Each night they stopped extremely tired, having worn themselves out paddling from up top. It was only after they took a day to rearrange and pack more carefully that they were able to make better time on the river.

However, big problems arose at Five Finger Rapids. They were able to go through the far right channel but hit the wall just as they entered. Several of their crates were flung overboard, along with the few pots and pans they had taken. Ian grabbed one pot, but that was all. After Rink Rapids they pulled ashore to check their things. They had lost some crates and bundles because they had very little rope for tie-downs.

That night they looked everything over, finding they had lost a canvas bag of clothes, and three crates containing all of their tinned beef, chicken, and vegetables. They had three bags of flour, some oatmeal and rice, a bucket of lard, matches, and lots of cooking spices. They could keep clean because they had the laundry soap, and, having candles, they could see in the dark except it was never really dark at this time of the year! They found a small supply of cornmeal, evaporated onions, and a few other things. They had no sugar, no tea, no meat of any kind, no beans, and only a little dried fruit.

"Them men even tossed our guns in the river. We tried to snare a rabbit with a small rope but had no luck. With one pot for cooking, we've lived on very little." Liam spoke, shaking his head in disbelief. "It's pretty hard to enjoy fried cornmeal, rice, or plain oatmeal every day." I could tell both needed a good meal.

"After the big rapid, we stayed on the river a long time each day. We kept alookin' for ya, but never saw either of yar boats. Then, yesterday we noticed water coming in and knew we had a leak. We pulls to shore and unloads quickly to find a seam split and leaking bad." Ian got angry just thinking about it.

He went on, "We stuffed in a bag of flour since we only had one blanket and needed it at night. We thought the flour bag would settle in the split and seal it up. But the river only rotted away the bag with all the dirt in the water, and tonight we knew we was in trouble. So here we was, stuck with a leaking boat and no way to repair it." Liam said they heard a dog bark and saw two boats, hoping whoever it was would stop. Maybe one boat would have some oakum or pitch.

We were sad to hear their story but were quick to assure them there was room on our scows, and though we might be a bit crowded, we insisted they go with us. Malinda and I quickly got out the biscuits left from our supper and even the left over beans the men had saved for later on, in case someone got hungry during the night float. It certainly wasn't much for these two hungry men, but they were delighted to have something besides fried flour or corn meal cakes. We even made tea for them, and they were most grateful for everything, and we were more than glad to see our friends again.

While they ate, Tony examined how they used the sail as a shelter. He showed how they had actually made a triangle of it with two parts forming the sides and the third part a floor of sorts. They had only one blanket for the two of them, and it looked like they slept in the middle of the floor section, pulling the ends over them for added warmth.

Between bites, Liam confirmed that was exactly what they did. They had been caught in the rain on Lake

LaBerge and again on the river, and it was mighty cold. I remembered the rain at Lake LaBerge, but we must have missed the second storm.

As Ian and Liam ate, Leonard told them we planned to run all night, but if they were too tired, we'd stay here and leave tomorrow morning. They wanted to leave now. Already Tony and Mark had their things in our boats, even made an area for them to sleep and gave them another blanket to use.

When the men finished the meager meal, Ian and Liam folded up the sail-tent and gathered up the rest of their belongings. With Sky bouncing beside them, we prepared for the night run. Malinda and I would sleep in the front of the smaller scow, with either Leonard or Mark at the sweep while the other one slept on the rowing seat. Ian and Liam would be in the front of the larger scow with Walt and Tony on duty there. There was little room left for feet anywhere, but we really didn't care. We had our friends with us again, and tomorrow morning when we stopped for an extra big breakfast, we would take some time to re-arrange everything.

So the little half-boat Tony had seen yesterday had been them. Since they were on the far side of the river, we had not recognized them nor they us. It had taken Sky to get us together. I don't know how she knew they were in amongst the trees, but I don't question the miracles of God's help along our journey.

The night was coming quickly, if twilight can be considered night. Mark knocked apart the half-boat, packing the better boards for repairs if needed. He even saved the board with the #24147 painted on it to give to the Police Post at Stewart Island, and tell them the story of why the boat was no longer on the river.

Now, settled down under two warm blankets, I soon heard the so familiar snoring of both Ian and Liam. I vowed never to tell them they snored, because it was such a joy to be back together again. We were a good, compatible group, and I was so happy to see everyone helping to make room for our Scotsmen. I looked over at the two sleeping men to see Sky curled up right between them, almost as if to say, "I'll help keep you warm, my friends. Welcome home."

# 23

## GOOD TIMES AGAIN WITH FRIENDS

June 12 - Down River to Stewart Island

I woke early and just sat in the bow, watching the beautiful river and country through which we floated. Islands everywhere looked most inviting for a breakfast stop, but we drifted on, not wanting to disturb Ian and Liam. There has been no sign of any settlements for some time. No cabins, no campfire smoke, no trails. It was as though the land was unpeopled and unspoiled. This country would be a tough place to live, not very forgiving to those who didn't come prepared to cope with the loneliness, the dreadfully long and cold Winters, and the short three-month Summers, but it has captured my heart.

This is a vast land, hundreds and hundreds of square miles of unspoiled beauty. I wondered how long it would remain so. I think back to Lindeman City and Lake Bennett with hills stripped bare of trees, and I can't imagine how long it will take for trees once again to cover the scarred land.

Other rivers emptied into the Yukon, some very small, only a stream trickling over rocks. Each added more dirt and drifting bits of debris to the Yukon, dumping its refuse into the once crystal clear river we remembered in the Thirty Mile portion.

Soon Ian and Liam yawned and stretched. Sky got up to greet them with puppy kisses. Liam scratched her ears, and Sky, loving every minute of it, just wagged her tail in delight.

Leonard and Walt looked for a place to stop for breakfast. Mark was trying to pin-point our location, and with the map and Walt's help, they looked out over the land with cliffs and cut banks, and finally noticed a stream coming in on the left. The high shale-like cliffs on the right matched with those on the map, showing we had reached mile 435 or close to it. If correct, the night run got us about fifty miles closer to Dawson City.

We stopped near a stream, tied up, and started a fire. The day was sunny, though now fluffy white clouds floated across the blue sky. It was nice to have a good clean stream to fill the pots for tea and coffee. The stream was so cold, we just dipped our cups in and enjoyed a drink without having to let the silt settle first.

While Malinda and I made breakfast, the men rearranged the scows. Though Ian and Liam didn't have a lot of things, what they did have filled our open spaces. Two men would now sit on the bench seat to row while the third would remain at the sweep oar. Malinda and I would sit on crates in the bow. It didn't take long to eat and get back on the river. Stewart Island, about fifty miles downriver, was our goal for the day.

Some of the islands had an abundance of wildflowers. Pink briar roses twined over bushes. Lupine in shades of blue and lavender and yellow buttercups added color to the hills. We passed a valley, burned possibly by a lightning strike, just now starting to recover. Hundreds if not thousands of pink fireweed plants now blooming added a beautiful contrast to the burned tree stumps. New shrubs and small trees had begun to grow, giving the overall area a much softer look.

The lazy morning of drifting, and the warm sun, made me yawn. The night run had been good, but no one slept well, and the men needed rest. Tony suggested we stop to eat and maybe take a nap. No one objected. We pulled out on an island to avoid mosquitoes if possible. There was a pool of clear water left behind when the Spring runoff passed maybe a week ago, and it was delightfully warm.

Malinda and I told the men they could sleep if they wanted, but we wanted to take a bath in the pond water. We asked them to warn us if danger threatened, as we didn't want to be surprised by some big moose. Walt laughed, and asked how he would hear anything if he was asleep? But they good-heartedly told us to enjoy ourselves. And we did! What a nice warm bath! There were bushes nearby where we spread our clothes. We even washed our hair, and it felt so good to have clean hair. Malinda's dark brown hair gleamed in the sunlight. The warm sun dried us quickly, so we dressed quickly and wandered down the beach a ways. We picked a few flowers, wiggled our toes in the sand and enjoyed the peaceful surroundings.

Suddenly we stopped absolutely dead in our tracks. Coming from behind a large bush, we saw the paw prints of a very large bear. They must have been over a foot long, with the print of the claws extending another four inches beyond the pad print. This was one big bear!

Immediately and without a second glance at the paw prints, we ran screaming back to camp, and you can be sure the men heard us before they saw us. Breathlessly, we excitedly told them what we had seen, and Leonard, Liam, and Mark took off to see the prints for themselves. Tony shouted for them to stop and come back, not wanting them to meet up with some angry bear, but they were gone.

Walt and Ian hurriedly put cook pots and blankets in the scows, making ready to shove off if the bear came around "trying to be friendly" in a bear sort of a way. The men returned, calmly picked up the last few items and helped push the boats into the river. It was only after we were on the river that Liam commented the prints were probably from a very large grizzly, a big male by the size of them. And, he added, the prints were fresh, since no sand had fallen in the depressions made by the bear's feet.

We searched the island as we drifted by, hoping to see the bear but saw nothing. Walt taunted us, saying our screaming would have been enough to wake the dead or certainly scare a bear. I hoped he was right, but I would have liked to have seen him from a distance.

With that excitement over, the afternoon seemed calm and peaceful. We saw smoke coming from a cabin tucked in close beside a stream, but we didn't see anyone. Maybe it was the cabin of a prospector, trying his luck on the small stream, or maybe of an Indian family here for the Summer and the salmon run.

The Yukon Field Force at Fort Selkirk explained to Mark how the Indians used nets to catch the salmon, which they dried or smoked for use in Winter. Mark had asked about fishing, but the officer said there was no chance of catching any salmon. Since the salmon were returning up river from the Pacific Ocean over 1700 miles away to spawn in the streams where they had hatched five or six years ago, they would not eat again. When the salmon found their home streams, the females would lay their eggs and the males fertilized them. Then both died. Their last act would be to lay the eggs of the next generation.

It was quite a story. How they could swim upriver for such a long distance, find the exact stream where they had hatched, and only then spawn? What other tales of nature would we hear? What other wonders of nature would we see? I certainly didn't know, but I was awed by the magnitude of what this land had to offer.

The river now spread over three hundred feet from one bank to the other. Sometimes the current took us to one side; sometimes it showed up on the other side. Often two islands would be side by side with the current running between them. Sloughs appeared frequently, some with sand islands almost blocking the entrance. We could see sandpipers skittering in quick little running steps along the sand, stopping to eat an insect or two before running on. Ducks and their ducklings swam in the slower water, occasionally turning tail up to grab a bug in the water.

Liam, who had been looking at the river map, stood up on the seat. With the map in one hand, he described what he thought was the White River coming in on the left. Showing Tony, he pointed out the very large sandbars and lots of islands. He added that the unusual color of the water really made him think this was the White River. This was a major river joining the Yukon, and the map showed all the major rivers emptied into the Yukon before Dawson City on the right side except the White River. That and the gray/white color of the water made him certain this was the White River.

The incoming water was almost the color of milk. It was heavy with silt from the melting glaciers up river and from the volcanic ash we had seen so often along the river. It looked like thin mud and probably was.

The White River valley opened wide, allowing us to see miles and miles of wide meadows with the mountains fading softly off into the distance. It was quite a change from the country we have been going through. The two rivers ran side by side for several miles before their waters commingled. Now, the Yukon seemed sluggish, very heavy with mud, an undrinkable dun colored river.

With only a few more miles to Stewart Island, we stayed close to the right bank. Leonard wanted to be in a good position to stop. Soon Ian pointed to the Stewart River, its mouth a tangle of upended trees with roots in the air and branches ready to rake over any boat passing beneath them. A sandy island divided the Stewart River into two channels as it entered the Yukon. We saw tents up on a cliff about twenty feet high with the Union Jack snapping smartly in the wind. Leonard pulled us close to the right, but it was a dangerous place to be. We had to duck to keep from being hit by overhanging tree branches and even the roots of upended trees.

I held the rope around Sky tightly not wanting her to be swept overboard. The men were looking ahead, when I heard a twig or a branch snap on the bank directly above my head. I looked up and for one brief second I saw a very large bear right above me, just looking down at the scow. He was jet black with a beautiful white "V" running from one shoulder down between his front legs and back to the other shoulder. His eyes looked directly at me - or Sky, I'm not sure which - and his ears were turned forward to catch any sound.

The scow spun around a downed tree trunk and pulled to shore. I was so stunned at the sight of the bear, I couldn't say a word. Sky had not barked or made any sound, not even a growl. When I finally found I could breathe again, I stammered and stuttered, "Bear! A bear! A big black bear right above us on the cliff! He is huge!"

Everyone looked where I pointed, but there was nothing to be seen. The bear had vanished as quickly as I had seen him. By the time we landed, we were many yards down river. I looked back, but there was no sign he had ever been there. I knew I had seen him. It was not an illusion. He was real, and he was big. No one said a word, as if they were not believing me, yet giving me the benefit of the doubt.

A steep set of crudely built steps leaned at a slant against the bank and up to the Police Post above. Someone said there was a trail leading directly to the top about a quarter mile further down, but we opted for the shorter way up. Sky bounded up the steps with me holding the rope around her neck. We checked in at the

Police Post, and Ian and Liam told their story and gave Mounties the board with their new number #24147 painted on it. The Mounties were most appreciative of the information and happy to have the board with the number on it. They kept records of boats and boat numbers, even the numbers of wrecked boats.

One officer said this place seemed to be the final breaking point for many men. Just beyond was an island unofficially named Split-Up Island or Split-Up City where men, tired from the trip and wanting to rush on to Dawson City, argued violently, with friends and family members, eventually splitting everything. It was tragic for all since then no one had enough food or other essentials to see them safely through the northern Winters. The officers even expressed concerned about the food the Scotsmen had, as it was much less than the required amount, but we assured them no one would go hungry.

I told the Mounties about the bear I had seen, emphasizing I was the only one who saw it, since the others were busy handling the boats. The Mounties said a big male grizzly bear had been sighted several times though no one had seen him that close. He described the bear as a three year old, though he couldn't understand why he stayed around so many noisy men. The officers always carried rifles wherever they went, in case of any bear problems. I was sad to think the beautiful bear might have to be killed. Yet, I knew even with the Police Post and the cabins here, the bear was not as afraid of humans as I hoped he might be.

The officer told us of three islands down river about five miles. From this end they looked like one big island, but as we passed them, we would see narrow passageways dividing them. There was a nice place to stop at the end of the third island, but landing at the far end might be a little tricky. If we stayed close to the islands, we would be fine.

We thanked him and started back to the boats. At the steep steps Sky balked, so Leonard carried her down. Once at the bottom Sky barked in delight and scampered to our scows, jumping in before the rest of us were off the steps.

The next five miles went quickly. Mark spotted the islands, and we stayed close to the right side so we would not miss the landing, and we pulled in easily. It was indeed a nice place. The sandy beach had a good place for cooking, with logs nearby to sit on. We opted to set up the tents in a grassy area beyond the sand. Walt loaned Ian and Liam the little tent he had been given at Lake Bennett.

As Malinda and I looked through boxes for something for supper, Tony and Walt stood nearby, looking for all the world like a couple of schoolboys in trouble for doing something wrong. They had their heads down, their hands behind their backs, and almost sheepishly said, "We've got a little something for supper. Thought you might like a change from beans, oatmeal and hotcakes." We looked at them wondering what they had, when Tony took something from behind his back. Unwrapping it, he showed us a big cut of meat. Walt produced five nice big potatoes.

"Sorry, the trading post only had five potatoes, but five were better than nothing."

"I just couldn't resist this nice piece of moosemeat. Now get the fire going, and we'll roast the potatoes and have moose meat steaks. I'm hungry."

What a feast it was, but even beans would have been just fine now that our "family" was together again. As I curled up to sleep, I realized it was probably only sixty miles to Dawson City. I wondered if we could really get there tomorrow as we wanted. Most of all I wondered what we would find there when we did arrive.

I thanked God for everyone who made up this special group of friends, and prayed that whatever happened to the group in Dawson City, we would always stay in touch. Most of all, I prayed for our safety tomorrow, our last day on the river.

June 13 - Dawson City Is Just 60 Miles Away

We woke early, ready to get to Dawson City. Tony looked at his watch, shook his head, and commented, "It's only a little after 4:30!" But the call of Dawson City was in our blood, and nothing could stop us now.

After a quick breakfast, the tents were rolled up and put on the scows. We didn't even tie anything down. Sky scampered along the sand as if she knew something big was happening today. The scows were pushed into the water; we jumped on and headed for the City of Gold! With no rapids or rain in sight, we shouted "Ho for the Klondike! Dawson City! And the gold!" We finally let our emotions get the better of us, and those at the oars pulled with every ounce of strength they had.

261

The river grew even wider, filled with islands. There was a steady wind blowing upriver all morning and the men actually had to row. Before long, however, the wind kicked up pretty good-sized waves, and Walt had a hard time finding the current.

Tony told me to put the tents lower in the scows as the wind was picking up corners causing them to act as sails, pushing us back up river. If the men stopped rowing even for a few minutes, the scows either stood still or were actually blown back up river. Waves crashed over the sides, soaking everything and everyone. My teeth chattered, and I couldn't get warm. Sky curled up in a little ball, her wet fur shedding water as waves washed over the sides. She looked miserable and shivered as much as I did.

After an interminable length of time, Leonard signaled the other scow to follow us to shore. It was impossible to shout and be heard over the wind, but Leonard kept pointing to the left bank where there appeared to be shelter among some trees. Try though they did, we couldn't get over in time. The wind pushed us away from the shore as quickly as the men could take a stroke to move us closer. The wind slackened for a few minutes, and the men finally rowed to shore in a small cove, pulled the scows up as far as possible, and tied them to a tree. A second rope was wrapped around a big rock for added security.

Tony and Walt told us to get inside the protection of the trees and start a big fire. They needed to re-tie things so nothing would blow away. Malinda grabbed a big pot and the canister of tea. Mark took the pot from her, motioning for us to get to the trees, and said he would fill the pot in an eddy we had just passed.

In among the trees and thick bushes, the fire was quickly built, and though we were cold and wanted to stay by the fire, everyone looked for dry wood. I was thankful it wasn't raining for we'd never be able to get dry, and then we would have been in very serious trouble. Mark returned with water, and Tony brought the leftover biscuits from last night's supper. Leonard was shaking so much he couldn't hold still.

I was really surprised at how much protection the trees offered. Just a dozen or so yards away, the wind was whipping up a gale, yet amongst the trees, the air was almost still. The smoke from the fire went straight up through the tree tops.

When two other boats pulled in next to ours, Walt went to help them tie up and returned with our wet blankets he wanted to dry by the fire. The men from the other boats came with him, and shivering and shaking moved in close to the fire. The blankets were wrung out and draped over nearby bushes and rocks, and everyone huddled by the fire, letting the soothing hot tea warm us inside. The others also had water pouring in their boats so fast they were almost swamped. One man tried to bail but realized it was a losing game. Then they spotted our boats and managed to pull in just below us.

Walt had grabbed the river map after tying up the scow and was now looking at it, wanting to see how far we had come before the wind storm. One of the men from the other boats pulled out his map. Theirs was somewhat different, giving mileage more often, but not showing the river current or shoreline features as well.

With heads bent over, studying the maps and looking across the river for any landmarks, they finally shook their heads and said they had no idea where we were. Even though wet and cold, Walt tried to add humor to the miserable situation saying, "Maybe we're not on the Yukon anymore. Maybe the wind blew us to another river."

After his attempt to lighten spirits, Leonard retorted, "Well, if we're on some other river, there better be gold in it, or we're going to have a hard time explaining why we've come all this way to find nothing."

We needed something more than tea to warm us up. Finally, I asked for some help, and Malinda, Walt, and Liam came with me, with two from the other boats. We grabbed some pots, one containing the rest of the moose meat from last night, and Liam and Walt picked up a food crate. I looked quickly through another box and found some dried fruit. The men from the other boats quickly grabbed some of their food boxes.

As Ian cut up the moose meat for stew, I added dried onions and a tin of carrots and peas. The new men pulled out two loaves of bread they baked yesterday, now wrapped in oilcloths. They shared cocoa and coffee, and best of all, they opened a tin of cookies they had been nibbling on for several days. They must have baked dozens of cookies, for the tin was quite large and was still over half full. Either that or the cookies were not very good, so they hadn't eaten many.

While stew simmered, Leonard and Walt walked through the woods back toward a bend in the river. When they returned, Walt said the river was still kicking up good-sized waves, and all along the shoreline more boats had pulled in. He said we were on an island and the waves were crashing even more on the other side. Not a single boat could be seen out on the water. I wondered how long the wind would blow, keeping us here, so close to Dawson City and yet so far away. Sometime later, we shared our moose meat stew, enjoyed slabs of fresh bread, and munched on cookies.

Tony looked at his watch, and asked if any of us knew how long we had been here. Some thought an hour or two, and I guessed maybe four hours. Tony said it was now almost three o'clock! We had been awake almost eleven hours and had gone just a few miles. Studying maps again, Ian found where we had stopped last night, and thought we had come about twenty miles. If true, Walt thought we must be on Ogilvie Island.

One of the other men was anxious to get back on the river and wanted his three companions to leave. An argument broke out and tempers flared. Leonard stepped between them saying that if they were going to fight, they could all leave right now. And he wouldn't stand for the language they were using in front of his wife and Malinda. I was proud of him and our other men who stood firmly by him. I guess the other men believed them, for they apologized to us ladies and were silent for some time.

Finally, the one who had wanted to leave came over to Malinda and me. He hung his head and apologized, "I'm sorry. You're good ladies like my wife, Elizabeth, back home, and I'd never use that kind of language in front of her. I guess I've just let my guard down up here. Please forgive me." We knew how tempers could erupt especially when Dawson City was so close and yet no one could get there in this wind.

Liam spotted a fairly good sized log, and with Ian's help dragged it closer to the fire. Shortly others brought more logs or rolled rocks closer to the fire. It became apparent the day was wearing on with no relief from the wind, and we knew we would be here for the night. Dawson City would have to wait until tomorrow.

With slow and deliberate steps, the men walked down to the scows to bring back the tents. If the wet tents could be set up near the fire, they might dry enough so they wouldn't drip on us tonight. I think this was one time we were glad the tents didn't have a floor. The ground under the trees was dry, and with dry blankets we could sleep fairly comfortably, even if the tent was wet.

Since there was not enough room for all the tents around the fire, the other men started another fire a short distance away and set up their tents. I proposed that we eat together, and they agreed on one condition. They would cook but wouldn't tell us what they would fix, and we didn't argue since one of them had been a chef back in Kansas City.

Sky lay near the fire, her fur nice and dry now. She was content as long as she was with us. Leonard whispered that she had bared her teeth during the argument. Now she was asleep, dreaming about chasing rabbits for her feet moved as if she were running.

Soon dark clouds came over the hills on the other side of the river, and it looked like rain. What else could keep Dawson City? Rain we could manage, but not both rain and the strong wind. It would be a long night for us.

Sometime later we heard, "Bring your bowls and let's eat while it's hot!" We didn't have to be called twice. And what a treat! We had the best chili I have ever eaten, made with bear meat and spiced just right.

"You men eat this way all the time? Because if you do, I want to go with you! This is really good." Mark liked the chili, I could tell.

I broke his fantasy bubble of going with them by softly saying, "We're only one day away from Dawson City, and if you don't like the way we've cooked, then you can cook all day tomorrow." He almost choked at that thought and quickly tried to withdraw his remark. "No, no! I didn't mean that at all. We've had good meals. I was just making a remark. Really, I didn't mean it that way." Watching him almost choke on his food as he stammered, trying to take back his remark, made us break out laughing. I could just see Mark cooking. He might do a really great job of it, but he much preferred to row a boat and haul gear up a mountain. Somehow, I just couldn't picture him cooking, or for that matter, I couldn't picture me hauling gear up a mountain like he did. In the end I believe we both did our own jobs well.

With the chili, we had cornbread made in a Dutch oven. There was not a morsel nor a crumb left. At least I thought we were finished. Then Michael, the chef, took a towel off a pan and started dishing up chocolate custard! Well, I thought I was in heaven that is if the angels in heaven served chocolate custard! Right now, he was our earth angel. After everyone was served, he handed me the pan, saying we ladies could have any left in it. Malinda and I used our fingers to clean all around the edges. My mother and even Auntie Pete would have scolded me severely for doing such a thing in front of others, but they would just have to look down from heaven and forgive me. Secretly, I knew Auntie Pete would have licked the pan with me.

Soon it was time for sleep. It was raining, but not hard, and we hoped tomorrow would be bright and beautiful. Dawson City was so close, yet we didn't know what we would find there. The Mounties had told us to look for the scar of a slide on a mountain behind the town. He said it could be seen on the right as we made a bend in the river. I wondered who would be the first to see it. It would mean the end of the river trip and the beginning of a different part of our journey. This new part would not be by foot up a trail or on a boat down a river. Other than that, I had no idea what we would find in Dawson City, but by this time tomorrow we would know. Soon we would be home, for a while anyway, in a land far from Wisconsin and family. It was for them and for us we had made this journey, this wilderness experience, and now it would be up to us to make our dream of finding the gold become a reality.

# <u>24</u>

## THE SLIDE ON A HILL ABOVE A CITY OF GOLD

June 14 - The Final Run to Dawson City

It rained off and on all night. Sheltered in the trees as we were, we really couldn't tell if the wind was really still blowing. Mark, the first one up, shouted, "Everyone up! No wind! Dawson City here we come!" We stumbled from the tents into a glorious day! The sun was shining, the river calm, our spirits high! What more could we want! The men camped by the other fire were gone. Walt heard them leave just before he got up.

With only forty miles to go, we wanted to jump in the boats and row like mad, but Ian reminded us it would take the better part of the day to get there, and not knowing what we would find, it was probably a good idea to have breakfast first.

Walt and Liam scratched among dying embers, rekindling the fire, and added more wood which Liam had put under a canvas tarp. Mark got some water while Leonard and Ian took down the tents, rolled and tied them on the scows. I hoped there would be no wind, because I knew the men would row down the river anyway.

The coffee made, Malinda and Liam then started making hotcakes. Bedrolls were folded and wrapped up in the canvas sail. Soon the smell of hotcakes and coffee drew those packing the scows back for a nice breakfast. We ate standing up, not wanting to waste even a minute by sitting down. I was just as anxious as the others to get on the river and to Dawson City, but I just didn't feel good. My stomach was fluttering again. I just couldn't be getting sick on this our last day on the river. I sat down on a log and put my plate on the ground. I had something to say, and I was going to say it now, while we were all together around the fire.

"Now that we're almost to Dawson City, I need to say something."

Everyone looked at me, though they continued to eat. "First, I want to tell each of you just how proud I am of all of us. We've come a long way from Seattle to Skagway, to Dyea, over the Pass, and now we've almost finished the river portion of our journey. We've lived in miserable, terrible, freezing conditions. We've had good days, and we've had bad days. But through it all we have cared for each other, worried about each other, and learned to accept and love each other. And I just had to tell everyone how I feel after all these months we've been together. I know I will never forget what has happened, and I'll never ever forget any of you."

By this time, I was leaning over resting my elbows on my knees. I loved everyone, and yet I couldn't look at them. I started crying, and between sobs, continued. "I don't know where everyone will go once we get to Dawson City, and I just couldn't let you leave without saying how much each of you means to me." Sky sat right at my side, and I found myself scratching her ears.

Leonard kneeled beside me, gave me a hug, then holding me at arm's length, and said so sweetly, "Freddie, what's wrong? You're crying again, and you should be so happy. We've almost made it. Just one day left. Instead of crying, you should be happy."

I stood up quickly, kicking over my plate of half eaten hotcakes. "I'm scared! I'm so far from home, and I think I'm pregnant!" It just came out! I know I should have said something to Leonard before this time, but I never could find just the right moment. Besides, I really wasn't sure I was pregnant.

It seemed like an eternity before anyone said or did anything. Then sounding like a hundred people speaking at once, everyone shouted. "Wonderful!" "We love it! Our own little baby!" "Sit down and take it easy!" But it was Leonard I heard. "Oh, Freddie, I'm so happy! I've been wondering why you've been so quiet recently, and I should have asked, but I couldn't be happier."

Ian and Liam stood off by the side and just smiled. Finally Ian spoke. "We was wondering if ya had said something while we were separated from ya. Now we all know, and everything's gonna be just fine!"

"Leonard, I have to tell you Ian and Liam surmised about my condition when we were building boats back at Lake Bennett. I didn't believe them, but they said they had wives who've had babies and knew the signs. I wanted to say something after we were through the rapids, but then Ian and Liam got separated and I didn't say anything."

Malinda was now standing by my side all smiles. "I'm so happy for you and Leonard. What

271

wonderful news! And I'm so glad you told all of us together. By now we are all family, and this will make us more of a family."

"But I don't know for sure. And I don't know what to do. I don't know if there is a doctor in Dawson City. I wish I could talk to Mom and Pops." When I sat down again, Sky put her chin on my knee, and I rubbed her head.

"Well, one thing I know. You can't see a doctor until we get to Dawson City. And in a city as big as Dawson should be, with all of us thousands coming in now, there is sure to be someone you can talk to." Walt was always one to put things in perspective. He kissed me on the cheek before he continued. "You're like a sister to me, since I've always considered Leonard a brother and you're his wife! I can assure you, you'll be just fine." Walt was a dear man, and he was indeed like the brother I never had.

"Well, I hadn't meant to say anything just now, but I guess I'm just tired enough, and dirty enough, that my emotions got the better of me. But it's said, and now we need to get this breakfast over and get on the river. I can hear Dawson City and the creeks of gold calling." I was up and ready to go.

"Now just ya wait one minute. I've not had me say. Now Freddie, ever since Ian and me told ya what we thought way back at the lake, we've been a thinkin'. Well, we even went to the store back there, and the one thing we made sure we saved and brought after our split with them other men was a special treat for everyone. Now ya' just sit right here, all of yas." Liam was smiling from one ear to the other.

272

He and Ian quickly went through their bundles and returned shortly carrying something behind their backs. "I knows you folks don't drink, but we got this to celebrate the occasion. I was just sure ya would say something before the river trip was over, Freddie."

Liam brought out a bottle saying, "This here is apple juice. I never tasted it so I don't know what it's like, but everyone get your cups. We've got to celebrate this good news. Freddie, ya and Leonard's already got your gold, and we're so happy for ya." With that he opened the cork on the bottle, and as everyone poured out half empty cups of coffee, he poured the apple juice. When everyone had a little, he lifted his cup and gave a toast, "Here's to a new little life in this land gone clean mad for gold. May the good Lord watch over us all and especially you, and may there be much joy and happiness for all your family here, that's us I mean, right here beside you. 'Cause we's all your family."

But before anyone could move, in a voice almost commanding us, Ian said, "Now just ya waits one gol darn minute. We ain't finished. This here's for the little one." He handed me something wrapped in the towel that has been used at every meal since we started. Stained though it was, it looked like linen to me. Here were these kind men, thousands of miles from their own families acting for all the world like they were going to be grandpas! And, when I thought about it, they were! They were as close to being fathers to me as any men I have ever known other than Pops, of course.

"Go ahead, open it." Both Liam and Ian were almost dancing with excitement.

I carefully laid the towel on my lap and slowly unfolded the edges. There inside was the smallest pair of overalls I have ever seen. "Why, they're darling. Where did you ever find such a small pair?" I held them up by their white shoulder straps. Everyone was as taken aback by the tiny size as I was.

"We saw them in the mercantile store in town. They're just like the big men's overalls only they is littler. The store owner said the company gave 'em to him so he could display 'em, showing what the big ones was like. Well, we just had a better use for them. We told him why we wanted 'em, and ya know, he was so excited to think some young lassie had hiked over that dreadful Pass and was getting ready to go down the river, and she was going to have a baby! So he just ups and gives 'em to us." Both my grandpas-to-be were as proud as could be of their little surprise.

Everyone wanted to look them over and even wanted to take them from me, but I held on. This was a precious and wonderful gift. Finally Leonard said, "Just let us look at them, please."

Holding them up, he said, "Look. There's even a hammer holder and real pockets."

Tony pulled out his father's watch, and trying to put it in the bib pocket, said, "There's even a watch pocket, but the watch is too big. Anyone got a smaller one?"

True, the overalls were in every detail like the big ones. There were bib pockets, hip pockets, front pockets, and they even had silver buttons and a snap the same size as the adult overalls. They were just smaller. Quite a bit smaller. From the shoulder straps to the bottom of the legs couldn't have been more that fifteen to sixteen inches.

"Well, I have an announcement to make. If it's a boy, they'll be just fine, and if it's a girl, she'll be the first girl in Dawson City to wear bib overalls." I was happy and then realized I was no longer worried. I had been so worried about how Leonard would feel about becoming a father, but now I knew he seemed happy with the idea of being a dad. Ian and Liam were so right, back at Lake Bennett, when they said women have been having babies for a long, long time, and everything was going to be just fine.

"Do you have any idea when this baby will be born?" Mark asked after being so quiet until now.

"No, I don't have any idea, and I just know I have a good reason to get to Dawson City now. But if we stay here all day talking, we won't ever get there. So let's get things put together and move on down the river. I really do think I hear the call of the gold, or at least the call of Dawson City."

There was a new spring to our steps as we finished cleaning up, making ready to leave. I tucked the little overalls and the towel inside my bedroll, keeping them safely stowed away as a very real reminder of our adventure. Then I gave the bedroll to Leonard, who tied it tightly on the boat.

Soon we were drifting down a peaceful and smooth river. A spirit of togetherness permeated the very air we breathed. It was more like a feeling that we shared, something special that no one else knew. Indeed, we did! We knew where the gold was, and we also knew some gold couldn't be mined.

Tony and Mark proudly smiled as if they, too, were soon going to be fathers. Each had younger brothers or sisters, but neither was married. Yet, there was a new light in their eyes. Of course, Ian and Liam were and always will be my special "Father figures" and soon to be "Grandpas" to the baby. Walt and Malinda, sitting in the back of the scow, talked quietly, but I caught just a quick glimpse of Walt holding her hand.

Leonard just smiled. He used the sweep oar moving us away from a floating tree, but I'm sure his thoughts were somewhere else. Sky was in her position in front, watching the water and wagging her tail. I reached over, ruffling her fur. She has been such a good companion to me, and I also know that when the baby is born, she will add another little person to her list of those whom she will protect.

Larger islands and sandbars appeared at the mouth of small streams which emptied into the Yukon. In places there were steep cliffs beside the river, though in other places the land opened wide. The current was strong and carried us along at a good rate. We'd been on the river for quite some time, and no one mentioned being hungry until Malinda got out some dried fruit and two loaves of bread.

"I found this bread wrapped in a towel by our tent went I got up this morning. I guess no one noticed it when Mark got us up with the good news of no rain and no wind. The other men must have left it there for us."

Tony started to get out his knife to cut the bread, but quickly put it away. "Let's just break the bread and pass it around. Somehow bread always tastes better to me when I simply break some off, especially when Mom has just finished baking it."

How well I remember doing just that in the wonderful kitchen back home. Even after all these months, I can almost smell the bread baking on the day we left. How often that aroma and wonderful memories of that last morning have come back to me. I truly believe bread is the fundamental tie binding families together.

Soon the river narrowed through a stretch with steep banks, overgrown with brush and trees. Here and there were areas that had slipped away, leaving behind high sand and dirt banks. Swallows flitted around, doing acrobatics in the air, catching little bugs, I suppose. I scanned the cut banks, looking for their nests but couldn't see any. Their iridescent blue-violet color sparkled in the sunlight.

The scows were drifting very close together, and we were enjoying each other's company. Walt and Malinda were studying the river map, pointing first to the map and then to some feature beside the river. When he noticed several of us looking at him, Walt scratched his head and said, "I'm not sure where we are. We've been on the river for a long time, and I admit I haven't been watching the map too closely. But if my guess is right, we're less than ten miles from Dawson City."

Suddenly, everyone came alive! Less than ten miles? Leonard motioned for both scows to get to the right side of the river. Not knowing what the landing would be like, he didn't want to row back up this river should we miss it by not paying attention.

Scanning down the river, we could see no sign of the slide or scar on the mountain, just beyond the city, which was to be our landmark. All eyes were now on the hills on the right side. No one spoke, and I'm not sure if anyone really breathed.

Then, just before a large group of islands on the left and before the river made a big right hand turn, Walt stood up on the back of the scow. His eyes searched ahead. Suddenly he shouted, "There it is! There's the slide!"

We all looked, and sure enough there was the slide on the hill. Immediately, both boats rowed to the far right. As we rounded the bend, before us lay Dawson City. Boats lined the shore. We could see men everywhere. Buildings along the waterfront, and dirty white tents were crammed together, some even going up the nearby mountains.

The men pulled back hard on the oars, slowing us down and looking for a place to land. Seeing nothing but boats tied to boats, Liam quickly grabbed a boat and held on tight. Behind us, Tony and Mark did the same. The current was terribly strong, and it was all they could do to hold on to the other boats.

Quickly, Malinda and Ian grabbed a couple of ropes from their scow and threw them to a couple of men who had hopped across the other boats to help us. Mark and Leonard double tied the scows to the other boats, and Liam used ropes to tie bow and stern securely. We were in Dawson City at last. Those who had helped us didn't say a word, and just as quickly as they came to lend us a hand, they left as if it was something everyone did every day. We were simply another group landing.

No one jumped off. No one moved. For a few moments no one spoke. It took the words of our fine Ian to get our attention. "Well, we're home. This is where we've been heading for so many months and so many miles. Much has happened and much is left to happen. Thank God we are here. Thank God. This City of Gold! And tonight, I'm atreatin' everyone to supper out. No more cookin' - for today at least! Now, let's go see what this place has to show for itself! Dawson City, we're here to see ya and to get the gold!" He was right, of course. Thank God, we had arrived safely and were now ready to stake our claim for the gold!

# 25

## REALITY SETS IN

June 16 - Thursday - Saying Good-Bye to Friends

Since arriving, we have been busy but not the way we anticipated. From the river we could see buildings along the main street, called Front Street, and tents, tents, tents everywhere. At first they just looked dirty, but close up we saw most were ragged, torn, and generally not really fit to live in. Some may have been here since the discovery in late 1896 and through 1897.

After securing the scows, we finally stepped ashore in the City of Gold. We were elated to have reached our destination, but at the same time we were also overwhelmed by what we saw. Dawson City was not the city we had anticipated with nice hotels, large mercantile stores, or areas where we could set up our tents while we panned for gold.

We found hastily built, false front two story hotels, saloons doing a roaring business, dance halls, a few cabins on Front Street, and dried mud everywhere. The streets were ridges of dried mud, which in the rain would be a sticky mess. Squeezed in all this were a few log cabins and shacks. The best looking buildings were the government buildings - the NWMP headquarters and government houses. There were a couple of very ornate buildings, probably hotels or dance halls. One even had bay windows with fancy iron-work decorations. Hundreds of men wandered the town. They looked haggard, tired, dazed, worn out, and lonely, and yet there was something about them I found fascinating. These men, like us, had endured terrible conditions on ships north, bitter cold and freezing temperatures on the trail, built boats to float over 550 miles down an unknown river, only to arrive here and find what we found. The fact that we all made it this far is a testimony to our strength and endurance. I pray we'd have those same qualities in the days to come.

The first shock came when we learned the rivers and creeks were all staked. There is no place we can stake our own claim! In fact, the creeks were all staked before word of the discovery even reached the outside world. The gold rush was over before it began! Had we all come over 4000 miles for nothing? Had we left home with dreams of a fortune to be left now with only the dream? Had we come this far to have our dream fade before our eyes? Many of those men wandering along Front Street must think so.

Oh, there is plenty of gold in Dawson City. It passes from one person to another, in barber shops, cafes, in saloons, dance halls, the "red light district," but for most here, there was little chance to find your own gold. You could work for someone else, or you could find a service others needed, who would pay you. Many had come this far hoping to find enough gold to change their lives. Now, they walked up and down Front Street in search of something else, and they knew not what.

We've seen men trying to get mail at the Post Office, which was inundated with piles of mail, but since no one had an address, the mail just collected there. Some spent entire days going through the stacks, hoping to find a letter to them. They leave discouraged but no doubt will return another day looking for any word from home. We even tried to look for mail but gave up. There were just too many crowded in the Post Office.

Men looked for friends they had met on the trail who may have said, "Look me up when you get to Dawson." How could they find someone in this mass of people? The town is laid out in squares, but only the main streets are named. There are no addresses, no names or numbers on tents, no way to identify where a person lived. He might say he lives three tents from a certain corner, and that could be true one day, but then another tent might have been crowded in, and so their "address" would be wrong!

This is a dismal picture I have painted, but I want to write of another side to the situation here. Only a few who made the trek from Skagway or Dyea have even gone out to search for gold. Some men said they'd found something within they didn't know they had. These men and women have weathered all kinds of conditions on a horrendous trip, and found within themselves strength they never knew they had. Some wouldn't have changed a thing. Others would never make such a commitment of time and money again. Sure, they wanted the gold, but to some the trip itself turned out to be an opportunity to see what strengths they possessed. They have passed that test, and now they must decide what to do next.

Along Front Street many men were selling their outfits for pennies on the dollar, trying to get enough money for a ticket on the first steamship out of town. Others sat on the river bank and watched the muddy river continue its trip to the Pacific Ocean, not knowing what to do next.

Prices are high. Food is very expensive. Lots on Front Street lease for $12 to $15 a square foot! Ian and Liam insisted they would treat us to supper, and although we tried to discourage them, they would not hear of it. They had seen a small café off Front Street and were adamant that we would be their guests. And we did have a delicious supper - big, thick, juicy moose steaks, potatoes, fresh vegetables, thick slices of freshly baked bread with butter. We haven't eaten like that since we were at Mrs. Palmerston's, and there we had pot roast, not moose steaks. I have no idea what the cost was as Ian simply got up from the table and paid before we could offer to help.

Our most pressing problem was to find an area for the tents. With many crowded so close together, it was a daunting task. After supper we split up, going in different directions looking for any amount of sufficient space. Malinda and I went back to the scows and waited for the others to return. The sun would be up almost twenty-two hours a day, so it would be light for a long time while they looked around. We could sleep on the scows again, though we certainly didn't want to do it.

I think Malinda felt even more at a loss for what to do than the rest of us. She had no money, no food, no tent, no way to earn money - at least no way she wanted to earn it - and she didn't want to be a burden to us. I assured her each in his own way contributed to the well-being of the entire group. I tried to remind her of how badly we all felt when the Scotsmen weren't with us, and how great it was to have them back. Even though they had lost a lot of their outfits, none of that mattered. We managed with what we had then, and we will manage now. Somehow, we would find the gold we had come so far to get, though to myself I admitted I certainly didn't have the slightest idea how we would do it.

Tony and Mark returned first. They had found nothing, not even so much as space for one tent, much less three. Later, Ian and Liam came back with the same report, but they did find a notice in the Post Office to them from Scottish friends who had come here last year. It seems these men had written to Ian and Liam in Scotland telling them about the gold and suggesting they come. Neither Ian nor Liam had ever mentioned this. When I asked what they planned to do, they said they'd tell us later when Leonard and Walt came back. I wondered what sort of a tale it would be.

Soon Leonard and Walt returned, climbing over the boats tied to shore and to the scows. They, too, were very discouraged, even saying we would have to sleep on the scows again tonight, but maybe we could spread out using some empty boats nearby.

With everyone back and tales of disappointment were told, and when I could not stand the suspense any longer, I asked Ian and Liam to tell their story of why they came here and what the notice from their friends had said. I listened carefully, as did everyone, and must admit it sounded like something from a story book.

Ian and Liam come from a small village outside Glasgow, Scotland. They are indeed sheep ranchers, as I long ago suspected, but that is where my knowledge of them ended. I will write the tale as they told it, fascinating as it was, for I certainly could never make up such a story.

Three of their friends had come to Dawson City in 1897. They had been in San Francisco when the first ship, the *Excelsior*, docked, and hearing the tales of those returning with gold, they had written home, telling their families they were going north to the Yukon. It seemed these three had money. They got tickets to Skagway immediately. Once there, they hired enough packers to carry everything they had over the White Pass and down to Lake Bennett, and they only made two trips over the Pass! Once at Lake Bennett City, they hired other Indians to take them by boat as far down the lakes and river as possible before everything froze for the Winter.

They got all the way to Stewart Island when it became apparent it would be impossible to go any further by river. The ice was forming too quickly. The snows had come and the country was deep in a blanket of white. Even that did not stop them. They simply hired others to take them by dog sled to Dawson City.

The three men found that all the creeks and streams had been staked, but they had money and started buying claims men wanted to sell for a quick profit. Many wanted to get out before the Passes became completely snow bound. During the first Winter, there was little or no food to be bought anywhere in Dawson City, and men either had to leave or starve. These three men had come prepared to spend the Winter, bringing lots of food and really warm clothes. After acquiring several claims, they hired men to work for them, paying them a portion of the gold recovered. They could see even without washing much of the pay-dirt, there was plenty of gold to be had. It was then they decided to write home, telling others to come or send money for shares in the gold mines. Ian and Liam were just two of five who came, though they came separately. The other three arrived a few weeks ago, according to the notice. Many others wanted to come, but they simply couldn't leave family and home. So they sent money with Ian and Liam, money to be used to buy other claims or to buy shares of the claims the first three had already acquired. I almost fainted when Liam asked if I knew how much money I carried as I walked around the rapids. Of course, I had no idea. I hadn't even thought about the money, only about their watches and other possessions they had wanted to keep safe. Well, they had over $10,000 in bank drafts and notes.

In the last letter they received just before they left Scotland, they were told that when they arrived in Dawson City, they should go to the Post Office and look for a notice which would be tacked up inside. Finding it, they were to follow the instructions. I was thinking this was almost like a scavenger hunt we used to have as children, when we were given a list of things to find, and we had to follow instructions to find them.

They found the notice which instructed them to purchase whatever foods and other items they might feel necessary, then hire someone with a wagon to take them to Grand Forks, a mining town out on Bonanza Creek where it joined Eldorado Creek. There they would find their friends and would have plenty of work to do. It seemed this area was one of the richest in the district.

They were told not to worry about a tent or any other such thing as the men had already built a large log cabin hotel for themselves and their friends and were renting out the remaining rooms to other prospectors.

The first arriving friends had registered all the claims in a company name, which they did not mention, and all who came, or sent money if they couldn't come, would share equally in the gold. Ian and Liam planned to spend the Winter in Grand Forks, helping with the mining. Next Summer, when the Winter clean-up was finished, they would return home to Scotland.

Needless to say, no one spoke while they told their story. We were spellbound. We were so excited for our friends and so happy for their good fortune. Later as we talked, there was not the slightest hint of envy or jealousy among us. We had all come so far together, and we had learned to love them as the dear men they were. Now, we were just very excited and happy for them. How could we be otherwise.

Now I wanted to learn more about our friends. Their stories would be our link to them in the future. I wanted to maintain our friendships and to know about their homes and families. Why now and not earlier, I don't know, but right now it was important to me.

We talked for a long time telling our own reasons for coming. Tony and Mark wanted to get enough gold to help their families who worked outside of Los Angeles in the orange orchards of Southern California. Right now their families worked very long hours, being paid a small amount for each box of oranges they picked. Some of the time they might earn as much as $10 a week, and with that they had to pay rent and eat. It was hard, tiring work, and everyone in the family from small children to grandparents picked the oranges. Now, Tony and Mark hoped to bring home enough gold to buy some land for themselves and their families. Leonard told them our story, and we had all heard Malinda's story.

Each had a specific reason for coming, and each reason was really to help their families. The stories only reinforced our determination to follow our dreams and somehow find a way to take home the gold we came to get.

As the sun began to descend beyond the hills on the western side of the Yukon, we knew we needed to settle in for the night. Even though Leonard had mentioned we might sleep on other boats, we still fixed our own bedrolls in the places we had while on the night river run. We were still a family, not wanting to let go of anyone just yet.

With the sun almost behind the hills, the dirty brown river was soon painted in vivid, brilliant shades of red and orange, and along Front Street lights from the windows of the hotels, saloons, and dance halls sparkled like diamonds on this river tapestry as beautiful as any king might have. It was ours for free. We were rich indeed, even without the gold.

This morning, after we fixed coffee and oatmeal, Ian and Liam left to find someone with a wagon. I watched them as they walked away, finally knowing that today they would leave to follow their dream. At least they had a place to live.

Tony and Mark were going to the Police Post to ask if there was a list of jobs available. If they found no such list, they would start up the creeks from town asking if anyone needed help. Leonard felt confident he and Walt would find some kind of work. Foremost in Leonard's mind, however, was finding a place for us to live. He said a few nights on the scow might not be too bad, but no more than two nights. By then he wanted a place to put our tent and Walt's. Maybe we could find a house or log cabin to rent or a couple of rooms in a hotel for a modest amount of money.

Malinda went with Walt, but Leonard wanted me to stay with the scows. He felt that no one would take anything, but he wanted me here in case anyone returned, so we'd know where we might find them later. I sat on the scow, watching people aimlessly wander from one group to another. Everything in Dawson City seemed so disorganized. I knew there was a Police Post here because we'd seen the Mounties when we went for supper last night. Their job was to keep the peace and help those who might need assistance of one kind or another.

As the morning wore on, the sun became almost unbearably hot. It was ironic in a way. Less than three months ago we were freezing on the trail, and even then had heard temperatures in Dawson City could be as cold as 50 degrees below zero in Winter. Now I sat in sun so hot, it must be close to 100 degrees, and there was no shade. Sky actually stretched out flat on the bottom of the scow, probably the coolest place there was, with the cold Yukon River flowing just below the boat.

Leonard returned saying Walt and Malinda were looking for a place for themselves as they're now talking about getting married. Oh, how I had hoped they would not leave us. I knew Leonard and I would do fine, but I liked Malinda and Walt so much and didn't want them to leave us so soon.

Leonard and I had a bite to eat, but soon he left to meet a man who might have work for him. Before he left, he took one of our sails and using the oars managed to put up a small shade over the scow. It really did make a difference during the afternoon, but I felt completely useless just sitting there.

By late afternoon everyone had returned. Ian and Liam would leave early in the morning. They had managed to buy some tools from men wanting to sell their outfits. They even bought a good amount of tinned foods, flour, sugar, and such to add to their now dwindled supplies.

Mark returned saying Tony was cutting wood for the Mounties at the Police Post. Both will cut wood until they can find work at a claim. Mark had come back here to get their tent. One of the Mounties knew a lady with a small back yard who said they could set up their tent and stay there if they would cut her some wood for the coming Winter, too. He wanted to set up the tent before she changed her mind or before someone else changed it for her by offering to pay her for the tent space. He did say the two of them would stay on the scow tonight as he was just putting up the tent now.

Tomorrow they would move their things and then would show us where they would be.

Walt and Malinda returned, having found nothing - no work, no prospect of work, and no place to stay. Tonight would be our last night together as a group. It will be so different without our dear Scotsmen, even though we had been separated for many days on the river. I tried not to let my feelings show, but I would miss them.

Although wanting to go to bed, we talked for a long time. Mark and Tony had a place to set up their tent and a job cutting wood until something better came along. Malinda was the first to curl up under a blanket. I followed shortly with Sky at my feet. The men continued to talk, but when I awoke sometime later, I noticed everyone was asleep. I listened to Ian and Liam snoring, knowing this would be the last night. I began to think of the many nights that snoring meant good friends were nearby. It would now be quiet, but I would miss that sound even if at times it had wakened me from needed sleep.

I sat up and stroked Sky, more for my benefit than hers though she wagged her tail in appreciation. Looking toward the heavens and seeing a few stars even in the twilight of the night, I thanked God for bringing us safely to Dawson City, and for our friends who have been good companions throughout our journey. I prayed for God to watch over us now as we went our separate ways.

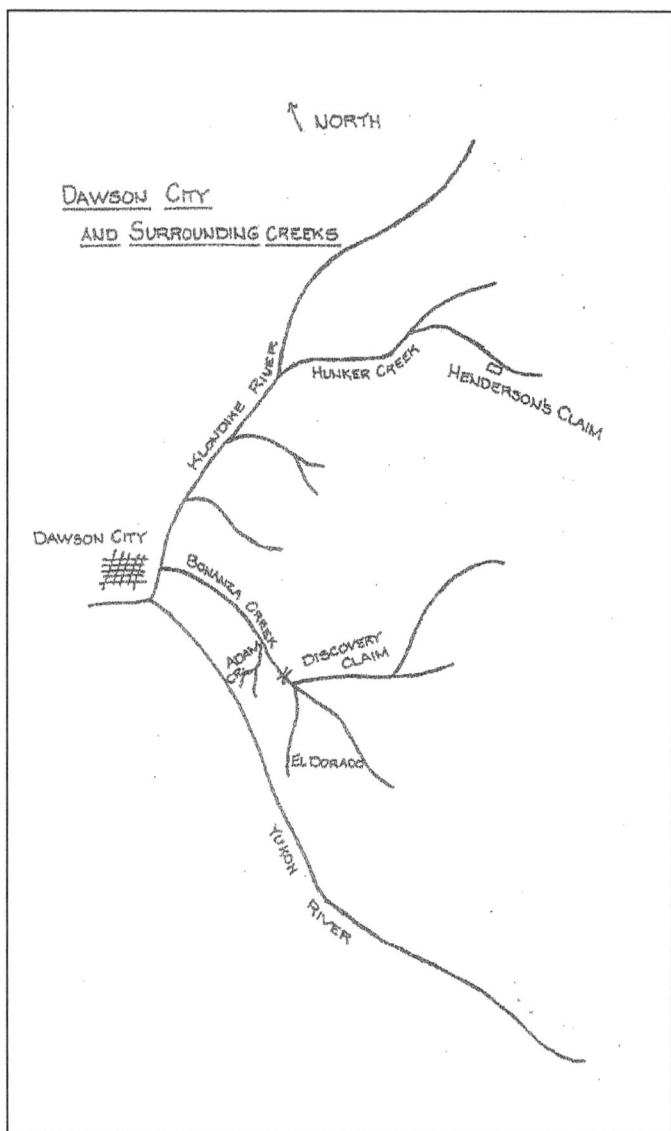

NORTH

DAWSON CITY
AND SURROUNDING CREEKS

KLONDIKE RIVER

HUNKER CREEK

HENDERSON'S CLAIM

DAWSON CITY

BONANZA CREEK

ADAM CR.

DISCOVERY CLAIM

EL DORADO

YUKON RIVER

# <u>26</u>

## A HOME OF OUR OWN

June 18 - Saturday and We Have a Home!

Friday morning was busy. The wagon arrived to take Ian and Liam to Grand Forks, and we helped load up their belongings. There were hugs and tears, too, and promises to come visit whenever they came in for supplies. I certainly hoped that promise would be kept. But how would they ever find us?

Tony and Mark left next, with us helping take their things to the small back yard. The lady who owned the cabin was very nice, telling us to come visit anytime. Her husband was working for someone else on a Hunker Creek claim and didn't get home often. They had arrived shortly after the discovery, but alas, too late to stake a claim.

Her little cabin was quite nice, though small. The yard was not big but plenty big enough for Tony and Mark, who wanted to build a table so they could cook and sit down to eat. I asked if she knew of anyone with a cabin to rent or to sell cheaply. Unfortunately, she knew of nothing available.

Mark and Tony were glad to see she had a garden and volunteered to help her weed it. She started most of her plants in her cabin before the snow melted, so then vegetables would have a good start when the ground finally thawed enough for planting.

Walt and Leonard again started around town, looking for work and a place for our tents. We decided any space available for two tents would be fine. It might be crowded, but it was preferable to staying on the scows.

Malinda and I sorted and straightened out the remaining things. We worked silently for some time, really missing those who had gone. There would be plenty of room on the scows to stay for a while, but we hoped it would not be for long.

When we finished, we walked down Front Street to see the city. We went north on Front Street as far as we could, stopping to look at the slide on the hill. It was pretty large, and very little grew on the displaced dirt. I wondered what had caused it, and how long ago it happened. There were a number of tents and even some log cabins below the area, so I guess they thought it was fairly safe there.

But something else caught our attention. Along the base of the hills we could see what looked like steam rising. Not knowing what it was, we went to have a look. It turned out to be a swamp! The heat of the day was making steam rise from the standing water all over. Even here tents were set up very close to it without actually being in it. The mosquitoes were everywhere in great numbers, and I wondered how they could tolerate such hordes of biting pests.

Somewhere in the Bible, in Revelation I believe, it says that in heaven there shall be no darkness at all. Well, there is very little if any real darkness now in

Dawson City, but it certainly isn't heaven with the mosquitoes around. And by the swamp, it must be like "hell." (I later looked up the Bible verse and found it to be Revelation 21:25.)

We turned back toward the main area of town, always looking for tent space but found nothing. I could not even guess at the number of people and tents here in Dawson City, and since the area was actually smaller than Lake Bennett City, everything was crowded much closer together.

One man we spoke to estimated there are over fifteen thousand men here now, quickly corrected himself, adding women, too. Unfortunately, he couldn't give us any help finding a place except to say some men had already left for the creeks, having found work washing the gold from the large piles of dirt dug during this past winter.

Malinda came up with a good term for the situation here. She said the area seemed like there was an "unorganized order" to everything. Cabins and tents were just helter-skelter everywhere, yet there was a Post Office where you could mail letters and even get letters from home if you didn't mind the hours it took to sort through the stacks of mail. The business district was all in one area, and the Mounties kept order everywhere though somehow they turned a blind eye to the "red light district" right behind Front Street. Another prostitute area was on the south side of the Klondike River, called Lousetown.

In the business area, we noticed the saloons were crowded and quite noisy. Even though other places were open and busy, it was the saloons which were the busiest, and it was only the middle of the day. We had heard them last night, but fortunately didn't hear any shootings or big fights resulting from all the liquor. One particular place caught my eye. It was named THE RED FEATHER SALOON. Malinda and I wondered about the name. Black or white feathers, maybe, as those are the colors of the eagle feathers. I'm certain there must be some red feathered birds around, but Malinda thought it was probably from the red feather boas the dancing ladies drape around their shoulders.

Thinking the men might have returned to the scows, we headed in that direction. About a block or two further, we literally bumped into Leonard. He was very excited and talking so fast we could hardly understand him.

Following Leonard who was almost running, he told us they might have a cabin for us! *Might!* We went toward the hills for a block or two and then toward the Klondike River. I didn't have any idea where we were going.

Winded and out of breath, Leonard stopped by a small log cabin. Out front two men were hastily packing pots, pans, bedrolls, boxes of food, and everything else onto a rickety looking cart. They were obviously leaving, but that didn't mean we could use their cabin. They may have already promised it or even sold it to someone else.

Quickly, Leonard went up to them, dragging me along. The men stopped working for a few minutes, and Leonard introduced me.

"Fellows, I'd like you to meet my wife, Freddie. As I said earlier, we've just arrived and are looking for a place to live, now that we think Freddie is expecting our first child. She simply can't live in a tent this coming Winter with a new baby."

"I'm glad to meet you. My name is actually Winifred, but everyone calls me Freddie, and I hope you will, too." Trying to be friendly and cordial, I even shook hands with them. My, but their hands were dirty and callused.

"Well, glad to meet you. Neither of you young ladies are dressed like the nice ladies around here, and not like them other 'ladies' either, if you get my drift."

I certainly did get his "drift" as he put it, and quickly told him my story of falling in the mud at Dyea so long ago. "I found wearing trousers tucked into my boots was a lot warmer, so I just kept on wearing them."

Malinda also told her story of being with the wrong group of "ladies" as he had put it, and of her escape to join with us at Deep Lake.

"You two have certainly had your share of excitement. If you don't mind me giving you some advice, I say keep wearing them trousers. It'll keep the mosquitoes off you."

Finally, the other man spoke. John was a short man with black hair, brown eyes and a full beard of curly red hair. His eyes twinkled in his smiling face. I saw his beard move up and down but couldn't see his lips because his mustache covered his upper lip and almost the bottom one, too.

"Well, as we told your menfolk, we wanted to meet the little ladies first. We wanted to make sure you would like our little cabin, which we built ourselves when we first got here last Summer. Our claim's out near Grand Forks, a ways from here. We did manage to come back several times during the Winter. Now the work of washing gold from the dirt is going on, and we really need to be on the claim. The men working with us have built another cabin there, so we're off to stay there."

"Well, come on in and see what you think, ladies." The taller man, whose name was David, indicated for us to go inside. "Now you must remember, we're bachelors, and probably not very good housekeepers, but the cabin is nice and tight against the cold of Winter, and that's saying a lot. Course in Summer, it does get mighty hot."

David was right. They were not much on housekeeping, and though it didn't seem to be as big as the family kitchen at home, but to me it was grand.

"Oh, this is wonderful. You men have done a pretty good job of making it work." I wanted to let them know it would be fine.

John spoke up. "Well, we try. But we're out on the claim so much, I'm afraid it'll need a good cleaning before you ladies will say it's clean."

"As I told your men here, we could sell it for a good price and sell it quickly, but when they came around looking for a place and telling us about the baby, well, John and I talked between ourselves, and told them that if we liked you ladies, you could have it for $100. Now that ain't much, but you could legally register the sale, and you'd have proof that it is rightfully yours. It'll be crowded with four of you, but you can manage. I'm not sure what you will do when the baby comes. Any idea when that'll be?"

"No idea yet. We just got in, and I want to talk with a doctor first. After that I'll know more." I didn't want to admit that I really didn't know if I was pregnant.

So while the men talked further about going to register the sale at the Police Post, I once again thanked God for helping us find this place, though small and dirty as it was. It would soon be our home. How nice that sounded!

"Say, does this place have a street name or anything like that? We would like to tell the others who came with us how to find us." I was thinking mainly of Tony and Mark, though I would certainly post a notice in the Post Office telling Ian and Liam where we would be when they came back into town.

"The street here is Fifth Avenue and down that way is Front Street. Dawson City is trying to get organized, but so far it hasn't gotten all the streets named." John answered pointing in the direction of the streets he was talking about.

David was a tall man, almost as tall as Leonard, but he was really thin, and looked like he could use a good meal, probably two or three. His long brown hair was a tangle of knots, probably because he never washed or combed it. But it was his eyes that drew my attention. They were blue, just like Walt's, though there was a terrible difference. One eye looked blind, and there was a very large scar running from that eye down his cheek, parting his beard into two sections. I guess he noticed me staring at him, and he held his head up straight and stood tall, saying, "Yes, I'm blind in my right eye. It happened when we first staked our claim. We went into town to register our claim after we had stepped it off all legal like, and planted our posts on each corner giving our names and the date. After filing the claim, we stayed in town for the day since it was the first time in town for almost a month. When we returned with our claim papers, we found two other men had ripped out our posts and were starting to dig on our claim. Well, that's called claim jumping, and it ain't legal no way.

"Well, a big fight gets started, and soon men from other claims come over to break it up, but before they could, one of those men had drawn a knife and cut me up pretty bad. I ended up lying in the dirt bleeding all over. But our neighbors weren't about ready to let those claim jumpers get away with anything. They tackled them to the ground and tied their hands behind their backs.

"Then, four of them started hauling the claim jumpers back to town. John, he takes off his shirt and presses it to my face, and with another man we start for Dawson City. It took us all day to get here. Other men stayed to protect our interests, and to replace the claim stakes for us.

"The Mounties put the claim jumpers in jail and then called in Mrs. Morgan. She's kind of like a nurse, but she didn't go to school or nothin'. She just knows what to do. She cleaned me up as best as she could and with a needle and thread stitched me back together. But she thought the eye was too badly damaged. And it was." David spoke as if the scar was his badge of courage, and indeed it was.

John filled in the rest of the story. Mrs. Morgan insisted David stay with her so she could change the dressing and clean the wound. John and the others returned to the claim site and found their stakes in the right places, and men everywhere asking about David. It took almost a month before he felt like going back out to the claim site, and during that time, John worked the claim, finding a good amount of gold.

Even then it took a long time for David to feel strong enough to work full days, but he took over the job of cooking for the two of them and for a number of other men who had helped them out at the time.

What a tale of courage! I could understand why he wanted to stand tall and tell his story. It was certainly one of determination in the face of a terrible wrong done to him.

Well, I got out money from the belt which Mom and I had made so long ago, and handed him $100. John and David immediately stopped packing the cart, and with Leonard and Walt went to register the sale of the cabin. Malinda and I went in again to look around. Oh my, it really did need a good housecleaning, but that could wait.

Before nightfall it would be ours, but I knew we would not be able to move in for several days. There was just too much to do. Now Leonard and Walt could put their minds to finding work. We needed income in order to live here with the high prices, but I had faith they would find work soon.

For the time being, though, we owned a little bit of Dawson City. Just a little bit of the City of Gold. Now, it was going to be up to us to find or earn the necessary gold to take home. First, I wanted to talk to a doctor, or maybe I could find Mrs. Morgan, who had helped David so much. Surely, she would be able help me. I must remember to ask him where I might find her.

The men returned with the papers signed. We were so grateful for our good fortune and thanked John and David very much. They told us their claim was just off Eldorado Creek near Grand Forks, asking us to stop by if we were ever in the area. They did add, however, that with so much work to do, there was little time for visiting. Visiting and calling on folks happened during the Winter, and even then there was lots of work to do. Walt and Leonard helped load their things on the cart which was piled high.

As they were about to leave, I asked about a key to the cabin. The men looked at me, and I wondered what I had said wrong. With all the gold in the cabins and tents around here as well as the businesses, I would have thought keys would be a necessity.

David finally spoke. "Freddie, there are no keys. It's the Code of the North, so to speak. No cabins, hotels, or businesses have keys. No one steals gold or anything. Why you can leave it out in jars on the table and no one will take it. The Mounties would run anyone out of town who tried such a thing. Besides come Winter, it might be a matter of life and death if someone needed to get in out of the cold and found a cabin locked. However, there is an unwritten rule. If someone needs to get in from the cold and uses your place, then he must leave enough wood cut and inside for you or maybe the next person to use. It's so cold in Winter, and if someone was really freezing, it would take him much too long to find kindling and start a fire. By that time, he could freeze to death.

"The second part of the Code is if someone uses your food, he should leave an appropriate amount of gold or money to cover what he ate. Why even John and I have had to use a cabin once or twice while coming in from our claim during the Winter. We were mighty thankful for them, too."

I apologized for asking about a key, and assured him I understood the importance of what he said. I promised to have wood inside for anyone to use and food in a cupboard. We bid them farewell and went into the cabin. It was now our home!

We found an old, worn broom in the kitchen corner and spent all day Friday cleaning. We swept everything, and when we were finished, we did it again. Leonard and Walt took apart the two narrow slat beds, saving the lumber. Malinda washed our windows, after walking to the Klondike River, several blocks away, for water. One of the first things we needed was a water barrel.

Saturday night would be our last night on the scows. We celebrated in a simple way. Malinda and I went to the store for something different for supper. When we asked about fresh fruit or even cookies, we were told to go down Front Street to a cabin with a green door. The lady there often baked cookies for the men in town, but he wasn't sure if she would have any left, as the hour was late. He added that Apple Johnny had sold all his fresh fruit, but when the next boat came into town, he would have some.

We left and found the cabin with the green door about three blocks away. Mrs. Greenly, we thought the door an appropriate color for her cabin, had several kinds of cookies costing $1 each. I thought it very high, but this was a celebration, so we bought four, two oatmeal and two sugar cookies. We told her we were celebrating as we had just bought a cabin from David and John. She knew who they were and welcomed us to Dawson City. She was glad some ladies were here, though she did look at the trousers we wore. We explained briefly why we wore them, and she thought we were smart.

Back at the scows, Walt and Leonard were cooking potatoes, beef from a tin, and even some tinned beans. Coffee was already made. It was truly a celebration meal. We were now residents of Dawson City!

# 27

## A HOME AND JOBS

June 19 - We Have a Home!

Our log cabin measures about 14 feet by 16 feet with a split wood floor. The peeled log walls are smooth inside and chinked with moss. The door is between two small windows about 14 inches square and two other windows about 20 inches square are on the longer side, but none of the windows open. They are real glass, however, not like some cabins which have bottle glass windows. Those windows are made by filling the window opening with clear glass bottles laid on the side with the neck of the bottle pointed into the cabin. Moss is used to chink between the bottles to make them as air tight as possible.

A big metal barrel, turned on its side with a small hinged door cut in one end, is used to heat the cabin. It is toward the front part of the floor space. Beneath the stove are several pieces of sheet metal to catch sparks. Some wood is stacked to the left of the door under a window. Suspended from the ceiling and above the stove is a wooden frame with heavy chicken wire stretched across it. The stove pipe goes through this heavy chicken wire and vents out through the roof.

I stood looking at the wire rack for a minute or two, wondering what it was used for when Malinda said, "That's a great place for drying clothes in Winter, above the stove but out of the way." That answered that question.

A small cast iron cook stove is to the right of the door. A tin can hung on a nail above the stove with a note inside which read:

"Use this for your sourdough starter.
It's the right place for it."

Beneath one front window is a very narrow board counter with a hole cut in which holds a small battered dish pan. A bent bucket under the hole is used for the dirty dish water. Walt thought the whole counter needed to be replaced.

On a shelf under the other front window we found two very dirty kerosene lamps. The glass chimneys were not broken, though they will need lots of scrubbing before they will give out much light.

While Malinda and I cleaned the cabin, the men were busy moving our things from the scows. I'm glad we cleaned first, because we couldn't have done it nearly as well later.

Sunday was move in day! I looked at all the boxes and crates thinking of the many times they have been moved. We sorted the boxes by content, filling just about every inch of space left inside.

Monday afternoon we went to the scows to gather the remaining small items, when three men stopped to ask if we'd like to sell one of our scows.

Leonard wanted to use the wood from the larger scow to build some furniture but said he'd sell the smaller one. The other men wanted to row it up the Klondike River where they would take it apart to use the wood. They offered to pay us in gold since they didn't have much real money. In fact they commented there was very little coin money in Dawson City. Gold was used for almost all transactions. When Leonard and Walt stepped to the side to talk, one of the men pulled out a small leather bag, called a gold poke. He poured several nuggets into his hand offering it as payment.

"Here gold is weighed and priced at $16 an ounce. I don't have a gold scale, but this should be about $100, which seems fair to us."

"That's just fine with us. Come on, we'll help you push some of these others boats out of the way so you can get the scow into the Klondike River." Walt was already shoving boats aside with his hands.

Walt and Leonard spent the day taking apart the boat they had worked so hard to build. Sky followed the men from the scow to the cabin as they brought the wood back to dry. The nails were straightened out to be used later. While the men built a new counter, Malinda and I went to find the mercantile to buy a new dishpan and bucket.

Our first stop was the Canadian Bank of Commerce. A man there politely weighed the gold, saying we had a little over seven Troy ounces, which at $16 an ounce was over $100. I asked what a Troy ounce was, and he explained that gold was weighed on a different scale. Troy weight is 12 ounces to a pound, not the 16 ounces we use for such things as weighing meat or cheese.

When the teller noticed the big smile on my face, I told him how we had gotten it. He explained that when paying for something in gold, folks usually handed their gold poke to the merchant for him to weight the gold. Many even turned away as it was weighed showing the merchant they trusted him. Merchants used gold scales, and seldom cheated anyone. The saloons sometimes went a bit heavy on the gold dust, but when they got caught, they quickly lost customers.

We thanked him, and asked where there was a mercantile store. He directed us down Front Street a couple blocks. We found the limited groceries quite expensive. For example, eggs were $14 a dozen, tomatoes $5 a pound, bread $2.50 a loaf, lettuce $1.25 for a small head, and other vegetables equally high. Fresh meat, such as chicken or beef, looked old and was too expensive anyway. Everyone here must hunt for their meat. I did get a tin dish pan but decided the bucket we had on the raft was fine.

While at the mercantile, I asked for directions to Mrs. Morgan's house. She's the lady who had helped David when he was hurt. Her cabin was on Fourth Avenue, about a block and a half back in the other direction, with beautiful flower boxes under her two front windows. Without house numbers, it helped to have a description of some sort.

We left and turned toward Fourth Street and took another look at the slide on the hill. It's called the Moosehide Slide and was supposed to look like the hide of a moose stretched out to dry, but I couldn't see the image.

We could hear the rasping noise from the Ladue Sawmill as we walked along. Mr. Ladue was gone now, but his sawmill was one of the first businesses established here after the gold was discovered almost two years ago. The mill cut wood, not only for buildings and houses in town, but also for flumes, sluice boxes, and rockers for the miners.

We found Mrs. Morgan's house quite easily. She was a pleasant lady, about 45 to 50 years old, with almost snow white hair pulled back in a bun at the back of her neck. Her eyes were light brown and her smile quite genuine. She wore a simple blue checked house dress, reaching almost to the floor, with a white apron over it.

She motioned for us to sit down and asked how she could help. I told her I thought I might be pregnant. She asked a number of questions, what feelings I have been having, and I answered, adding that I thought the upset stomach and crying were from the stress of the trail and the river. I added that my stomach seemed to be fluttering a good bit of the time, like I'd eaten something that didn't agree with me.

She smiled, saying this was called "quickening," meaning I was feeling the baby move. After more questions, she paused, and using her fingers, tipping her head, and even closing one eye as if that might help her figure something out, she smiled.

"Well, if you're right about what is happening now, I think you'll probably be a mother after the snows come, by mid-November." She added I should just keep on doing what I've been doing, and all would be fine.

At this point, Malinda and I both laughed. "Mrs. Morgan, I'm so sorry we laughed, but since we've spent almost four months crossing the Chilkoot Pass and coming down the river, I don't think we will do those things again."

I tried to pay her, but she shook her head saying, "Freddie, I believe you said that was your name, I'm so glad you came to me. Few babies are born here, only some Indian babies, and it would be a privilege to bring a new, little life into this rugged community. When the baby is here, why then if you and the Mr. want to say 'Thank You' some way, it will be entirely up to you. I will be pleased just to hold a little one again. My three children are grown. My daughter is in Vancouver teaching school, and my two sons are working our claim at Grand Forks with their father. Do come any time, if you have questions."

I wanted to tell Leonard as soon as we got home, but we were greeted with "Come see what we've done." The men were so pleased with what they had made I just couldn't interrupt them. Inside we found three bed frames along the back wall. The men had even put our bedrolls on the beds. A table was made from boards, with crates for chairs, so now we could actually sit down at a table. In the kitchen area, crates of a uniform size had been emptied, nailed up on the walls, and the contents put back in. I had shelves and cupboards without doors! Other shelves were built under the windows. The men even covered the floor, small though it was, with the canvas sails.

Our cabin looked like a real home. Malinda grabbed the bucket saying, "Freddie, we need to go to the river for water so we can wash those lamps."

"Don't need to do that. We found a water barrel with a lid by the woodpile and cleaned it up good. It's outside by the door. Just put the lid back on so animals and birds don't get into it." Walt actually looked rather smug about their surprise water supply. "Oh, and we hung a dipper inside, too." With the lamps cleaned to everyone's satisfaction, Leonard said that they looked really good, but with the long days, he doubted if we'd need them for several months at least.

It was very nice to fix supper standing up instead of stooping over a fire on the ground. Leonard and Walt had been given some moose meat by our neighbor, Mr. Jonathan, when he stopped by to help with their construction projects. They invited him for supper, which he graciously accepted, and we had a most pleasant evening. Mr. Jonathan will be leaving to go Outside at the end of the Summer, but he says he'll come back when the ice breaks next Spring. He's got a good claim but misses his family too much to stay another Winter. He's been gone for over a year.

Later I told Leonard about my visit with Mrs. Morgan. He was very glad we were now settled in a comfortable cabin and not on that terrible trail over the Pass. Now he had a good reason to find work soon.

Yesterday was spent unpacking more boxes, putting clothes on shelves, and even hanging things on the nails Leonard had put in the walls. By late afternoon, we had finished with as much as we could do. We had run out of shelves and cupboards, and Leonard would have to build more. It's a good thing we still have lumber left.

Walt and Malinda went for a walk down toward the Moosehide slide while Leonard and I turned toward the Yukon River. We stood for a while watching more boats pull in at the river bank. How well we remembered coming around the bend ten days ago and knowing our journey was over. So much has happened since then. I wondered how Tony and Mark were doing and told Leonard we should find them and ask them for supper soon.

We ate delicious moose stew for supper. Later, I sat on the bed writing a list of the new words used up here. It's a language all by itself.

Flume - a trough made of wood, used to carry water to the gold claims when there is no water source nearby

Sluice Box - a long wooden box with crosspieces of wood, called riffles, to catch the gold when the water from the flume washes over the mud and gravel

Rocker - another type of box used to separate gold from sand and gravel

"Lay" - a man, who does the mining for an owner of a gold claim, takes a "lay", meaning he takes a chance on what gold may or may not be found. He can get maybe as much as 50% of the gold recovered

Fraction - a small portion of land between two claims left when an official survey of sites is made

Pay-dirt - dirt, gravel, and sand dug from the rivers or mines which will be washed to extract the gold

Washed - running water over the dirt in a sluice box to catch the gold in the riffles

Clean-up - the process of finally recovering the gold

Dump – where pay-dirt is stacked in Winter when the rivers are frozen and water can't be used to clean the gold

Tailings - dirt and gravel left after the gold has been recovered

Cheechako - an outsider or tenderfoot to the country

Sourdough - one who has lived up here, experienced the river freezing in the Fall, the dark of Winter, and is still around to witness the ice break in Spring

It is now Sunday afternoon. We went to the Methodist Church this morning for services. There were mostly women there since the men were on the claims doing the gold clean-up. After church, Leonard and Walt went to talk with a man about work. Malinda and I stayed sitting outside in the sun. There are some mosquitoes, but I couldn't stay inside. I had bread dough rising in the kitchen to bake later. Maybe I'll even make some cookies. I just finished writing the folks describing our little cabin, and telling them they are going to be grandparents again! How I would like to tell them in person, just to see their faces. Later, the men returned, both discouraged. The jobs had been given to someone else. Wages in town are about $10 a day, if you can find work. Work continues out on the creeks, and they plan to go there soon. The men are not afraid of hard work; they just want to get some work anywhere. I know they must be discouraged and pray they will find work.

## July 5 - Two Big Celebrations

On June 21st, there was a big celebration here - the longest day of the year with twenty-two hours of daylight and two hours of twilight. The saloons and dance halls did a roaring business. The music played all day, dance hall girls sang, and men, in from the creeks, wandered from dance hall to saloon and back again. Some people hiked up to the top of the Moosehide Slide to enjoy the view of the river and city, but the men wanted to finished work in the cabin before they left to look for work on the creeks.

On Monday, June 27th, Walt came back from the creeks with news he had a job helping with clean-up out on Adam's Gulch, just off Bonanza Creek. He'll continue working through the Summer repairing flumes and sluice boxes. The claim is a good paying claim, and he will be paid $15 a day, but he'll have to move out to Bonanza Creek, because it is too far for him to live here and work there.

With that in mind, Walt and Malinda got married on June 29th in a small ceremony at the Methodist Church. Rev. Walters officiated, and Leonard and I stood up with them. Mr. Jonathan, Tony, and Mark were there, too. We wished Ian and Liam could have shared this occasion also. Mrs. Morgan came and so did Mrs. Greenly.

Before the wedding, Malinda had been so excited she even told two police officers and a Mountie about the wedding. So, these three also came. The police officers looked rather striking in their blue and gold uniforms, and the Mountie looked quite smart in his scarlet red uniform jacket and black trousers.

Malinda wore a lovely light violet dress with a cream colored crocheted collar. She was glad the dress was floor length, as her feet hurt so much in shoes she had to wear her boots. We laughed about it saying she should write her parents telling them "the bride wore boots." I told her it sounded like the title of a book, and maybe she should take up the pen and start writing.

I wore the blue dress I wore last Christmas Eve in Wisconsin and my Indian boots, and I felt rather finely dressed. The men wore clean trousers and the one good shirt each had brought, not knowing it would be worn to a wedding.

Rev. Walters and his wife insisted we gather at their Third Avenue home after the ceremony. Mrs. Walters served salted nuts, sherbet, and fruit punch, and Mrs. Greenly had baked a wedding cake. The table was beautifully set with a linen table cloth and napkins and her nice china.

We gave Walt and Malinda the larger tent and the Yukon stove to take with them to Adam's Gulch. They bought some pans and such from men leaving to go Outside, and Tony and Mark gave them tinned foods, flour, sugar, and canned milk bought from others leaving. We added other items, such as soap, matches, candles, coffee and tea.

The hardest part was saying good-bye. I cried and so did Malinda. I would miss her, but she and Walt were so happy, we knew things would be fine. As we hugged good-bye, she assured me she would come by when they came back for supplies.

Then they left. Mr. Jonathan had given them the push cart he used when he took supplies to his claim, and it was piled high with everything. Leonard stood with his arm around me, and try though I might, I couldn't do anything but cry. My friend was leaving, and I didn't know when she would be back. Malinda and Walt kneeled down to say good-bye to our little four-legged friend, who gave them wet puppy kisses and happy tail wags. As they walked toward the Klondike River and started to turn upriver, they stopped and waved. What a story they would someday be able to tell their children. They met on a frozen trail 4000 miles from Wisconsin, in the far north of Canada, where they went looking for gold.

I had also given her a tablet of paper and two pencils so she could start a journal of their lives together. Maybe no one else would ever read it, but she and Walt would always be able to remember the start of their lives together as they re-read the pages. I am so thankful Mom gave me the tablets of blank paper so I could write our story. Someday, maybe our baby would read them and know how we started the first part of our lives together here in the frozen Yukon Valley of Canada.

Later in the evening, Leonard and I wandered down to the river. The Yukon seemed like a magnet, drawing us down to its banks. I can't explain it, but to us there was something so calming about the river. We sat quietly watching the anchored boats rock gently as the water swept over rocks near the shore. The Yukon River just went on its way to the ocean, still over 1500 miles away. It has carried the stampeders here, and, without even a pause continues its journey to the ocean.

This really is a city looking for fortune and fame, and when a rich claim comes in, the saloons and dance halls are the first to reap the rewards. More gold is exchanged through those two types of establishments than anywhere else. The business owners are really the ones "mining" the gold. The prospectors do all the hard work, and the business proprietors exchange it for food, clothing, and supplies, and of course, for good times and drinks for anyone in the saloons.

Dawson City is about a mile and a half long and maybe a half mile wide. The mountain called Midnight Dome, with its Moosehide Slide, forms the northern boundary, and goes all the way to the river, ending in a rather high cliff. The Yukon River is the western edge of town, and the mountains to the east rise about 800 feet high, effectively marking the eastern boundary and the Klondike River is the southern edge of town. Beyond that river is Klondike City, or Lousetown as it is also called, another red-light district.

At one time, the hills behind Dawson City were covered with a dense growth of trees. Most were gone now, cut and milled by one of the sawmills here, for lumber to build sluice boxes and flumes. There are a number of very colorful Indians in town, dressed in skin clothes, adorned with delicate bead-work designs. Some shirts have the tails of small animals hanging down as decorations. Instead of boots, they wear soft leather moccasins. I've often wondered what they thought of the thousands who have come here looking for the yellow metal, and I wondered if they used the gold for any purpose.

Before we returned home, we went by Mrs. Morgan's house. We found her in the garden outside, tending her flowers. I introduced Leonard, and she was happy to meet him. She then showed us her lovely garden. While her flowers were big and colorful, it was her vegetables that got our attention. She had peas, cauliflower, celery, lettuce, beans of all kinds, cabbage, carrots, and tomatoes tucked in anywhere she could find some space. The vegetables were growing very well. She said the long Summer days made them grow fast and to enormous sizes, too. They were big now, but she said I should come back later in the Summer to see them then.

We left and silently continued our walk home. It would be so quiet in the cabin tonight without Walt and Malinda. Indeed, the cabin looked quite large and very empty. I guess neither of us really realized what a joyful presence they were to us and to the happiness found within the cabin.

We were just standing inside, looking around and feeling the emptiness in our hearts when Mr. Jonathan stuck his head in the door. He invited us to share supper with him on the condition that we stop calling him Mr. Jonathan and call him Henry. He must have realized we would be rather lonesome tonight.

He had made a big caribou stew. As we ate apple cobbler for dessert, he and Leonard talked about the gold mines around here, and the many claims men have not even worked, though they had filed them legally. Henry said some men were afraid to dig shafts to look for gold, fearing they wouldn't find any. It seemed one claim could have good pay-dirt and the one next to it could have no gold at all. As long as there was no proof gold didn't exist, the owner might sell his claim for a nice profit. Sometimes the claim proved to be worthless, but other times thousands of dollars in gold had been mined from a single test hole. He warned Leonard to check carefully before he bought a claim.

Later, while drinking coffee, Henry finally got around to what I think he was hinting at during supper. He offered Leonard a job as the gold overseer on his claim. Henry has a good-paying claim out on Eldorado Creek, but he doesn't like to handle the job of taking the recovered gold to the bank, nor does he want the job of weighing out the portions of gold his hired men are paid each month. He commented that his biggest thrill was just seeing the gold caught by the grooves, riffles, and cross pieces. He was a farmer back home in Missouri and really liked the feel of the dirt, though not the work involved with keeping accounts and paying his men.

Needless to say, Leonard was very happy to be offered the job and quickly assured Henry he would handle the gold honestly, and give a full accounting of all transactions. They talked business for some time, but already I could see a big change in Leonard's attitude. He had a job, earning a whopping 20% of the total gold recovered, and I knew he would give all his attention to keeping the books and records accurately.

He would have to be out on the claim site five days each week, collecting the gold as it was washed through the sluice boxes. One day each week he would come back to town, take the gold to the Canadian Bank of Commerce where the bank kept the deposits of gold from Henry's mining operation, and then he could have some time with me.

When we finally got up from the table, Henry told us about the two important days coming up - Dominion Day, July 1st and the 4th of July. The first was a Canadian celebration, and the second, we knew was an American celebration. Since Dawson City is really quite an American city on Canadian soil, both days were celebrated, and while the Canadians wouldn't admit it, the bigger of the two would probably be the 4th of July. Already, we had heard rumors the 4th of July would not be celebrated, but Henry assured us there were enough Americans here to make sure it would be.

I can attest that Dominion Day was really quite noisy. Music played in every establishment all day and night. The Mounties and the police officers kept fights to a minimum and hauled the drunks off to jail. Banners and Union Jacks were draped from every roof and flown from any flagpole. The celebrating went on day and night for three days.

Then came the 4th of July. Suddenly, as if from nowhere, American banners and flags replaced the Union Jack, and the celebrations took on a genuine American theme, much to the chagrin of many Canadians. There were all kinds of games, races, and even an impromptu parade down Front Street. There was no stopping the Americans, and they outnumbered the Canadians by many hundreds.

I must admit I felt a deep sense of pride being an American, but I also felt a good deal of pride for the Canadians. This new land has been good to us, and now with a job for Leonard and an income in real gold to take home, I knew we would fulfill our dreams of getting the gold. (Note: I did not say "find" our gold, as we will earn it.)

This morning, July 5th, Leonard left with Henry for the claim. Henry told me to help myself to the caribou meat he kept it in a wooden box, in a pit dug beneath the floor in the kitchen. There was a trap door, which could be lifted up to get to it. He said it was the permafrost in the ground below the cabin which kept foods very cold or frozen. Now I have another word to add to my list:

Permafrost – ground that is frozen permanently beneath a thin layer of soil, otherwise known as a Yukon ice box

I bid them good-bye and promised to take care of myself. As they left, Sky sat beside me looking a bit sad and perplexed as to why everyone but me was leaving her. We sat outside for a long time, and she kept watch down the road as if she wanted to be the first to see them come back. But they didn't come back, and sometime later, we went inside, quietly closing the door to the now very large and quite empty log cabin. I felt so small inside. I buried my face in my hands, threw myself on the bed, and just sobbed. Except for Sky, I was truly alone. I woke later to find Sky curled up at my feet. She is a good companion to a rather lonely young wife, far from home, yet really at home here in the Yukon Valley.

I lay in the twilight night in "my Yukon home" thinking about those out on the creeks. Walt and

Malinda were just beginning their life together in a tent, very small when compared to my cabin, where conditions on the creeks were terrible, sanitation even worse, and where typhoid and scurvy were rampant.

Leonard was out there, too, though Henry said they would be staying in a clapboard house with another man who was the claim boss. This man kept track of the men working and saw to it that no gold "accidentally" got pocketed by them. He also kept track of the time they worked

I lay quietly scratching Sky's chin, knowing I had five days before Leonard would be home. I thought there must be some way I, too, could earn some gold. I went to sleep without thinking of a way, but deep in my heart I knew there had to be something those here in Dawson City need or want. All I had to do was decide just what that "something" was. Sooner or later, I knew I would find the answer.

# **<u>28</u>**

## WORK AND NEW FRIENDS

### July 12 - Leonard Comes Home

The day after Leonard left, I went to see if Tony and Mark could come for supper sometime, but I couldn't find them. Their tent was there, so I knew they were still in town. Sky has appointed herself my guardian and keeper, staying by my side without a leash. More boats arrived, and the men arriving wandered Front Street looking haggard and lost. I was quite lonesome, and the walk didn't improve my outlook.

Returning home, I unpacked the last of our things, keeping each crate. We had originally talked about returning home by Fall, but those plans have changed. We were staying for the Winter, and I had letters to write, not only to the family but also to Mrs. Palmerston in Seattle, who was keeping our trunk. I thought of the clothes packed away in that trunk, but I knew they were not appropriate here in this climate. I must tell her of our change in plans and offer to pay her for storing our trunk.

Hearing the whistle of a steamboat arriving, I gathered my money belt and headed for Front Street. Down the gangplank came men who had started for the Yukon last Fall. They had come by the all water route around the western edge of Alaska to St. Michael and then started up the Yukon. Winter comes early up here, and the steamboat got iced in about a hundred miles from where the Yukon River empties into the ocean. There they spent the long Winter and were just now arriving in Dawson City. Other steamboats had arrived in June, bringing men who had been caught by the early Winter though they were further up the Yukon before freeze-up.

Crates of supplies for Dawson City were wheeled off the steamboat. People stood around to see what arrived. I wanted some fruit - an apple, orange, or maybe even a banana. "Apple Johnny" was at his fruit stand, opening crates, and selling apples and oranges for $1 each. The supply was limited, but I bought four apples and three oranges and thought myself fortunate to get that many. By the time the last crates were unloaded on Front Street, all the fruit had been sold. The town would await the next whistle, signaling the arrival of another steamboat and more fruit for "Apple Johnny" to sell.

The town was especially busy when a steamboat came in. Store owners displayed their wares out front as well as inside. Within a few hours, the city had well stocked stores selling everything from rubber boots to gold rings, from books of Shakespeare to ruffled curtains, from Bibles to canned oysters, bacon, coffee, tea, sausage, rice, flour, sugar, fairly fresh vegetables, and even fresh eggs (though they had been on board the steamboat for over nine months!) I learned of a man, Mr. Miller, who some time ago had floated down river with a cow, and Dawsonites could buy fresh milk from him. The arrival of the steamboats meant food prices were coming down. Bacon and flour cost only fifty cents a pound, and now would be the time to buy extra staples for Winter.

With more people and craftsmen arriving on the steamboats, the city was changing fast. There was a gaiety to the town when a steamboat came in, and I enjoyed the difference it makes. A few fashionable stores for ladies have opened, even a jewelry craftsman who displayed some beautiful gold rings and pins.

Later, while sweeping the kitchen, I noticed some floor boards were cut in a straight line, and realized this could be a trap door like Henry's. Leonard had stacked crates on one end, and they were heavy to move. Opening the trap door, I saw the large, very cold pit lined with split logs containing several covered pots filled with meats, potatoes, carrots, and even eggs! John and David had forgotten to tell us about it. I scrambled eggs for supper and while they tasted different, the eggs were good. The vegetables were crisp, and the meat smelled fine.

On Tuesday I went to the Post Office to mail my letters, and again found men looking for mail, but instead of the disorganized frenzy of several weeks ago, I found relative order. Mail had been put into small boxes by number or sorted alphabetically in bins. I asked for a box number and quickly added a return address to the back of the letters. How good it would be to get a letter from home. A notice posted on the walls said mail came in on the 15th of each month and outgoing mail went out the same day.

This morning I bought just two tomatoes, which were almost worth their weight in gold! Leonard would be home later today, and I planned to make the stew using items from my ice box. Sliced tomatoes would be a refreshing salad.

About a half block from home, Sky ran ahead and pranced around waiting for me to open the door. Inside Tony and Mark were playing cards at the table. Oh, it was so good to see both of them. I didn't realize just how lonely I was until I saw these two wonderful men. I put the tomatoes in the kitchen and sat down to catch up on their news. I asked them both to stay for supper, and of course, they agreed. They were still cutting wood, but they had also helped build two cabins on 8th Avenue, just below the hills. I told them about Leonard's job with Mr. Jonathan, knowing they would be interested in where he was and what he was doing.

As I prepared supper, we talked about Walt and Malinda and Leonard's new job. With little other work in town, Tony and Mark would leave soon for the creeks hoping to find some work there. I suggested they talk with Leonard tonight as he might know of something available in the area near where he worked.

Tony asked if there was anything I needed done in the cabin. I said I wished a window could be opened. Both men got up to see how the windows were installed. I'd found our mosquito netting which could be used to cover the opening. Finally, with hammers in hand, Mark began pulling nails from the inside of the window glass while Tony worked outside. Soon they had the glass out and laid on the table. The glass had been framed much like a picture so it was easily removed.

As Mark nailed small strips of wood around the window on the outside, Tony went to the hardware store, returning with two hinges. Mark nailed mosquito netting on the outside, and Tony mounted the hinges on the window glass frame. Then with Mark holding the window in place, Tony screwed the other half of the hinges to the top of the window frame. He shaved a little wood from the bottom of the window so it would fit snugly but not too tight.

Mark attached a wire to the rafters long enough to reach just above the window, making a loop in the end. He put a hook on the window frame which fitted into the loop holding the window open. Tony pried a board from one of the crates, cutting it about eight inches long. With this braced between the window opening and the glass frame, the window could be opened just part of the way. It was delightful to have fresh air in the cabin!

Leonard wouldn't be home until late in the afternoon. He had to take the recovered gold to the bank and wait until the proper papers were given to him before he could come home. I knew he would be glad to see Tony and Mark.

As I started cooking, I thought the men were probably as tired of soup and stew as I was. Then I remembered the fold-over meat and vegetable pies Auntie Pete used to make. These were individual pies made by cutting a circle of dough about ten inches across, filling half with whatever fruit might be in season or meat and vegetables, then folding the other half over and sealing it by pressing a fork around the curved side.

As I worked, Tony and Mark sat at the table now covered with the oilcloths I'd gotten in Seattle. Sky was stretched out under the table, thoroughly enjoying the occasional ear scratching she got from the men. Tony talked about their experiences, once again dragging logs down to their tent area before they split them into firewood. They'd been doing this for several days when a neighbor lady offered them the use of a cart her husband had. As a gesture of thanks, they had cut several carts of wood for her.

Suddenly, Sky got up and walked to the door. It was then I heard the familiar whistle we had heard so many times on the trail. Leonard was just a short distance away, and Sky had sensed it before I heard the whistle.

Leonard was happy to see Tony and Mark, and while the three of them admired the work on the window, I finished making supper. The men were delighted with the fold-over pies. We spent a most pleasant evening together, and when Tony and Mark left, I knew our friends would soon join Leonard working for Henry at the claim.

It was good to have Leonard home, if only for the night. He had to leave very early for the long hike back to the claim. Then he would take charge of the gold recovered during the time he had been gone. While he trusted everyone working for Henry, he wanted to do his job in the very best manner. His job also entailed doing a great amount of paperwork so that the account he recorded agreed with the account at the bank.

With Leonard now working and gone for almost a week, our little cabin in this northern city is home for the Winter. I thanked God for all our blessings, for my wonderful husband, and caring friends. I knew in time I would find a way to earn extra money. I was used to hard work on the farm, and knew I was not too proud to do most any kind of honorable work. This way I would stay busy and not be so lonely when Leonard wasn't home, and I would do my part to add to our small but growing savings of gold nuggets.

August 22 - Fall Comes Early Here

More than a month has passed since I last wrote in my journal though I did jot down some notes. So tonight, before going to bed, I put pencil to paper. Leonard, Tony, and Mark left about mid-morning July 13th for Henry's claim. They had liked the fold-over meat pies I had made for supper so I made more the next morning for them to take with them. I also gave them several loaves of bread to take to share with the men at the claim.

After they left, I heated water for laundry. Leonard and Mark had strung up a clothesline by the side of the cabin, and with the weather still nice, I hung clothes outside. Somehow, doing laundry on the scows in dirty river water didn't do a proper job.

Sometime later, there was a knock at the door. I couldn't imagine who it might be, and I must admit I was very surprised when I opened the door to see a rather big man standing there. He must have been at least as tall as Leonard but built heavier. He had dark brown hair, a heavy beard and mustache, and dark brown eyes that looked directly at me as he talked.

"Don't mean to frighten you, young lady, but I couldn't help noticing your laundry hanging on the line." He held his hat in his hands in front of his rather ample middle. "I've come to see if you take in laundry. I got a good paying claim on El Dorado Creek, but when I get to town, I want clean clothes to wear. I wouldn't be asking you to do all my things, as my Mother, God rest her soul, taught me while I was still a young lad how to wash clothes." He spoke rather slowly and drew out his words, taking a long time to finish each sentence.

I asked him in since the mosquitoes were really bad. He took a seat, and I offered him a cup of coffee. He introduced himself as Alex Bowman and asked if I would wash his white shirts and have them ready when he came to town. He said he'd pay me well especially if I could iron them, too. To myself, I admitted the shirt he was wearing was rather dingy looking.

I said I could certainly do the washing, but I had not brought my flat irons with me from Wisconsin. The mention of the state must have sparked memories. He had been born in northern Illinois, but his family moved to Milwaukee when he was quite young. He left home when he finished tenth grade, but he fondly remembered the beautiful Wisconsin countryside.

We talked, actually he talked for a while, and my thoughts of the farm came flooding back to mind. I refilled his coffee cup, then asked if he was hungry and would like a meat pie. He accepted the offer and continued talking about his family back in Milwaukee. When he got up to leave, he thanked me for the meat pie and coffee and the time he'd shared with someone from "his country," meaning Wisconsin and Illinois.

330

He said he would return the next day with some white shirts and then would be back in a couple weeks. Later he would be staying in town until freeze up when he would go out to the claim again. He explained that pit mining was done mainly once the ground was frozen. The pay-dirt was dug from the mine and piled in dumps to be washed once the rivers and creeks were running again the next Spring. In Summer the deep pit mines might be too wet for mining. That's when miners cleaned the gold and repaired flumes and sluice boxes preparing for the coming Winter of mining. The cycle just went on and on that way.

Then he pressed a gold nugget in my hand saying he really enjoyed the meat pies, coffee and conversation. Just before he left he suggested I make the pies to sell. He was sure there were many in town who would gladly pay for such a big meat pie. When the berries were ripe, he was sure I could sell fruit pies, too. I thanked him for the suggestion.

When he returned the next day with six white shirts plus two pair of overalls and four work shirts, I was a bit overwhelmed. He explained he hadn't planned to bring so much, but he would be most grateful if I could wash it all.

I told him his laundry would be ready when he returned and sent him off with a couple of freshly baked meat pies. As he left, he gave me several nuggets, saying he was glad he'd seen my clothes on the line.

He again encouraged me to bake the meat pies to sell, even suggesting I put a notice in the Post Office and maybe one near the bank, offering meat pies for $2 each.

He knew men would also appreciate someone to wash their overalls and shirts, too.

I thought about it the rest of the day as I washed his clothes, finally deciding this was something I could certainly do to add to our growing jar of nuggets.

So it was that doing laundry and making fold-over pies would become my work. It took several days to purchase the needed supplies, then write and tack up notices. I also remembered Leonard said he had opened an account for us at the Canadian Bank of Commerce, the same bank where Henry had his account. Leonard thought Mr. Nells, one of the bank officers, was a good man, and he would take care of any needs I might have.

I went to see Mr. Nells that afternoon and was very pleased with his help. I added the few nuggets I had received to our account, keeping only a modest amount for my purchases. I told him of my plans, and he thought they might just work out very well.

Well, my plans did work out fine. The meat pies usually sold in about an hour. I had put on the notice that I would only make about two dozen a day, and they would be baked by late morning each day except Sunday.

My notice about doing laundry was equally well received. Some days I washed clothes all day. Since I had bought several pieces of material at a church sale, I devised a system using pins with strips of colored cloth to keep one man's laundry separate from others. My days were busy, but I was happy. Before Leonard returned later that week, I had quite a collection of nuggets and even a few coins.

The weeks passed quickly. Some days I was not as busy as others but mornings were spent baking the pies. Laundry was finished by mid-afternoon, and then I took a nap as I tire quite often these days.

One event sparked memories of Skagway. I had been to the mercantile store and was on my way home, when I saw a man sitting on the board walkway reading the newspaper, *The Klondyke Nugget*. The paper was published weekly, and it was posted somewhere for all to read, but I had been too busy to do more than just glance at the headlines. I asked the man if I might read the paper when he was finished. He said I could as long as I stayed right near him, because he wanted to sell it to a friend out on the creeks when he was finished. I quickly took out a quarter, the smallest coin used here, and offered it to him. He pocketed the quarter and gave me the front page which he had already read.

I quickly glanced over it, looking only at the headlines before deciding which story to read first. But it was a short story with a small heading that caught my attention. As I read it, my thoughts went back to Skagway, to Soapy Smith and his gang of hoodlums, and to the brief conversation Walt and I had had with Frank Reid. Here was an article so typical of the misdeeds of Soapy Smith but with a very different ending.

The article reported that a prospector named J. D. Stewart, returning over the Pass to Skagway from Dawson City with his newly mined fortune in gold, was robbed by Soapy Smith's gang. This type of robbery had been done before, but this time the citizens had had enough of Soapy Smith's gang and had been incensed enough to take action.

The town's people went to a judge with a complaint, and the judge ordered the stolen gold returned immediately. Then, the citizens formed a vigilante committee to get the gold back. This angered Soapy Smith, who tried to blame someone else and bluff his way out of the accusation. Later the vigilantes were holding a meeting on one of the docks, and Frank Reid was guarding the meeting place to keep Soapy Smith and his gang from causing havoc. Soapy Smith came down to the dock and tried to bully his way past Reid, but Reid stepped forward, demanding the gold be returned and telling Smith to leave. Soapy would not return the gold and reached for his gun. As gunfire erupted between Reid and Smith, the vigilantes knew that one way or another the town of Skagway would never be the same again. Either Smith and his gang would be gone, or the citizens of Skagway would have to live with the evils of Soapy Smith and his notorious gang. When the smoke cleared, Soapy Smith lay dead in the street, shot through the heart. Frank Reid was mortally wounded by a shot in the groin.

The day was July 8, 1898. It took twelve agonizing days for Frank Reid to die of his wounds. There was nothing they could do to save him. With the death of Smith, the other members of his gang were quickly rounded up and jailed, or run out of town on the next ship south and told never to return.

Both Smith and Reid were buried in the local cemetery, just below a hill beyond town. The marker on Smith's grave was a wooden plank, but the citizens of Skagway, ever indebted to Frank Reid, were planning to have a marble marker for him.

I thought silently of our conversation with Mr. Reid so long ago, and how he planned to stay and make Skagway his home. Now, that dream was over, but the Town of Skagway would always remember his final act that saved the town.

After reading only this one article, I quietly put down the paper and stood to leave. The man looked up from his reading, asking why I was leaving so quickly. I told him of our meeting with Frank Reid, and now having just read of his death, the rest of the news wouldn't be interesting.

I picked up my purchases and slowly walked home. I knew Leonard, Walt, and the others would be interested in this news about Frank Reed, but it would be three days before Leonard would be home again. During that time, I realized just how much I have missed sharing stories or having a cup of coffee with someone.

One day while at the bank, Mr. Nell's casually remarked that his wife was not feeling well at the moment, and since he knew I lived on Fifth Avenue, he asked if I would mind just going a couple blocks further to check on his wife.

Of course I said I would be glad to stop by. They had one of the few nice houses in town on Seventh Avenue just two blocks further from us. There was a nice front porch, with a railing around it, on which pots of colorful flowers grew in profusion. I knocked and soon heard her ask whoever it was to come in. I went in and introduced myself saying her husband had asked if I would stop by to see if she needed anything.

She was a lovely young lady, about 25 years old, with shiny light brown hair hanging down around her shoulders. Behind her glasses I could see her eyes were a bright blue. She had on a lovely pink print dress, which reached down over her feet as she sat in a rocking chair. She was a small looking lady with fine features and a slim figure.

She introduced herself as Jane, apologizing for not coming to the door. I offered to make her some tea, which she thought a splendid idea, telling me where to find the tea. Over tea with some bread she already had beside her chair, we continued talking. I told her I would fix supper for them some evening, and also asked if she had seen a doctor. When she said she didn't know any, I suggested she might want to see Mrs. Morgan.

She seemed happy enough, even asking when my baby was due. I told her sometime in mid-November, and I had seen Mrs. Morgan myself. We talked a bit longer, then for some reason she buried her face in her hands and started to cry. Through tears she told of how, on their journey up the Yukon River from St. Michael late last Summer, she had lost a little boy three months before he was due. A doctor, who happened to be on board, had helped her when it happened but added she might never have another child. Now she thought she was pregnant again, and she was worried about losing another baby.

I offered to take her to Mrs. Morgan, and we made plans for me to come by the following Monday. As I stood to leave, she stood also and seemed in better spirits. I told her I would keep her in my prayers. She asked which church I went to and told me that she and Dan attended the Church of England.

A few days later, we talked with Mrs. Morgan, and she suggested Jane see a new doctor who had just arrived in town. Dr. Bowers confirmed Mrs. Morgan's diagnosis and told Jane to take care of herself and not overwork because of her unfortunate earlier experience. Dr. Bowers also noticed I was expecting, as my clothes were definitely not hiding my condition, and asked how I was feeling. I told him I was just fine.

By mid-Summer, Dawson City had an unofficial population of over 18,000 people. Each ship arriving brought more prospectors and left with those who had simply given up hope of finding gold. Some, who had found gold, boarded the ships heading down river.

Once again paths crossed in the land of men coming and going. One day, in town to mail letters home and buy some supplies, I was surprised to see Superintendent Sam Steele. He had been transferred here now that most of those on the river have arrived. It was good to see him again. I knew Leonard would be delighted he was here, knowing his firm hand would keep the peace in Dawson City.

Summer also brought telephone service to Dawson City. We were now connected to Canada and the United States. There was no denying Dawson City was really becoming a modern city. Some even called it the Paris of the North. While we had most everything any other city had such as telephones, telegraphs, mercantile stores which carried everything from feathered hats for women and top hats for men, not everyone in town had the means to take advantage of these finer things in life. Only a few of the townspeople enjoyed the high society life which one might associate with Paris.

Even though there is quite a lot of gold flowing through hands in Dawson City, there is very little crime. Gold can be left in unlocked cabins, and very little, if any, would be stolen. Law enforcement is so good there have been no murders, I was told, and very little serious crime. No one is allowed to carry a pistol or side arm in the city unless he gets a permit, and the Mounted Police issue very few permits.

Another interesting thing - there is no business done on Sundays. Dance halls, saloons, and such close at midnight Saturday and don't open again until early Monday morning. And the police enforce this law and even forbid cutting wood on Sunday.

I spent time with Jane when I could. We often went for walks, exercise being good for both of us. I invited her to tea one afternoon at my cabin, and she readily accepted. Of course, I didn't have the nice furniture she had, but I knew we were friends and finery didn't matter. She had met Leonard and knew he was working out on the creeks. In fact, just the week before, we had been invited to supper at their house. She mentioned that there was a lady in town leaving soon to go back home, and she was selling most of her things. So after tea we went by her place, and I bought some light green eyelet material which I thought would be just perfect for curtains.

The new curtains were finished and looked quite nice when Leonard came home on the 16th, just two years after the big discovery of gold. We spent what time we had together enjoying the Discovery Days celebrations going on in town. Some of the miners from the creeks, who had staked original claims, rode on a big wagon in a parade. Children, dressed as prospectors, walked behind the wagon. A few merchants formed a Band and did a pretty good job of playing. There was large town picnic that followed the parade, and everyone had a great time.

Leonard's time at home was all too short, but he said clean-up was quickly coming to an end on the creeks until Winter when the pit mining would begin again. Until then there was lots of work to do repairing flumes and rockers which separated the gold. With the top layer of soil now free of ice, many mines would be damp or even flooded. Then he and Henry would come home. He had seen Walt and Malinda once, and they probably would be coming back to town before long. I certainly hoped that was true. I have missed her even though I have kept busy with my baking and laundry work. Malinda has such a great way of making the day seem special just by her friendly conversation and her wonderful smile. And I missed Walt as well. I knew Leonard would enjoy having them around, too.

As I now finish bringing my journal up to date, it is raining outside. The cabin is nice and warm, and it feels good inside with a nice fire. The weather is getting colder. The days are quickly growing shorter, and there is definitely a night now. In fact, the nights are about eight hours long, just long enough for a good sleep.

A few days ago I noticed the date, August 19, 1898. It was one year ago today that Mom, Leonard, and I went to Clinton to get supplies. That was the day Leonard read about the gold discovery and set his mind to come up here. How well I remember that ride home, with him so excited, until Mom finally put an end to it. But, of course, the dream did not stop, and at supper that night he told everyone of his dream to come north with me to look for gold.

It didn't seem that long ago, in some ways, and yet when I think of everything we have been through and what we have done, it seemed a very long time ago. I wished I had remembered the date before Leonard left, but I will remind him when he comes home again. We will continue to dream our dreams. Our dream of coming here is completed, and we are certainly working hard to earn our gold. In many ways, I think that is the better way anyway.

I end my journal entry with joyful thanks for all we have achieved and for good health and safety for friends, and pray we will be together again soon.

# 29

## GOING "OUTSIDE" — STAYING "INSIDE"

### Late August - A Noticeable Change in Seasons

Jane and I spend time together each week. Though I was continuing to bake pies and do laundry, I always made time to be with her. She was happy about being pregnant again though, at the same time, she was frightened.

We took walks, picked berries, and when Leonard was home, we even shared meals together. It was a good friendship. One day in late August, I went to see her, even though it was raining. We sat around her warm stove, catching up on local gossip and listening to the rain outside. The weather was not really cold, though getting wet certainly chilled one to the bone.

Soon we realized the rain had stopped, and we walked down to the river. The river is always the same, yet ever changing. I know that's really hard to understand, but it's true. In late August, there was no sign of ice, but the river just "felt" different, as though it were in a different mood.

We plodded through the muddy streets, laughing like children out playing after a rainstorm. We stood watching the river for a while seeing some men packing a boat making ready to go down river to reach the coast at St. Michaels before freeze up. There they could get a ship back south.

As we walked along Front Street, we saw a most glorious rainbow stretching from the other side of the River to the top of the mountains on the east of the city. Its colors ranged from blues and lavenders to gold, yellows, and reds. We stood there awe-struck by its beauty, for it certainly framed the city perfectly within its arch. It was as though we were living at the foot of a rainbow. Maybe we were. We were all searching for that proverbial pot of gold, and where better to look than at the foot of a rainbow?

September Came in Color -

Late August and early September were beautiful times. The bright red high bush cranberries were ripe for picking, as were the blueberries. I even mixed the two together, making pies, and they were delicious. Raspberries, blackberries, and currants filled buckets, too. The fruits were so sweet, and I marveled at the quantity I always found. I picked bucket after bucket, using some for pies and storing most in jars in my Yukon ice box. There they would freeze, and we would have berries during the Winter.

The hillsides across the river rang with the sound of axes and saws as men cut the few remaining trees for their Winter wood supplies. Many cords of wood would be needed to keep cabins warm during the dark, extremely cold days of 50 degrees below zero. I heard that if a man was arrested for any crime, he had a choice of punishments. He could cut wood for the woodpile at the RCMP headquarters, or he could have the traditional "Blue ticket" out of town.

Leonard spent a good part of each time home cutting wood. Using a wheel barrow Henry had, he brought many loads and stacked it in long neat piles by the cabin. The pile continued to grow, but he kept cutting wood.

One warm afternoon, Jane and I walked along the banks of the Klondike River, looking for blueberries and watching out for bears, when we walked further than usual. We saw a sight both fascinating and awful at the same time. In the creeks, struggling against the current were hundreds of fish. They were salmon, headed upriver to spawn. The females were battered with big white blotches on their sides. They fought the current to get to the same place their instincts told them was where they had hatched. There they would deposit their eggs. The males were equally battered, but their heads were now bright red with a large hooked beak-like protrusion on the upper jaw. They wiggled, splashed, and slammed their bodies up river, ready to fertilize the eggs of next year's salmon. To me, it was nature at its best and yet also at its worst. It was beautiful to see, but in a way frightening to see such a change in the fish. This was also feeding time for bears, needing to put on the fat for the coming Winter, but we saw none, nor did we hear any.

We did see something that surprised us both though. Across the river some of the ladies from Klondike City were standing in the bushes, also looking at the salmon swimming up river. They were acting like school girls, laughing and giggling.

Imagine our surprise when we saw them in fancy lace chemises, sleeveless and with necklines cut rather low. Their waists were cinched in tightly. I looked at my ever enlarging mid-section, and I wondered if I would ever be able to cinch myself up like that again. Some girls wore ruffled bloomers, quite short, reaching only to the knees or even slightly above. They seemed to be enjoying themselves, out in the beautiful sunshine.

I hadn't expected to see them so casual in their dress and so friendly with each other. I suppose I expected there would be a sort of rivalry or competition among them. Both Jane and I admitted we felt ashamed of ourselves for looking at the darker side of the life around town, but we had not gone in search of them, having come upon them only by accident.

Through the bushes we could see some little cabins lining the street. I suppose each had her own place. Above the doors we could see signs, though from the distance we couldn't read what they said. I had always made it a point not to walk down Paradise Alley, just behind Front Street, so I had never really seen the "ladies" before.

Now, not wanting to be seen, we quickly left the area. I think we both grew up that day, realizing how fortunate we were not to have to resort to such a lifestyle as a way to earn money. I thought of Malinda and the group of ladies with whom she had started out. Some of them may very well be in Klondike City.

Jane and I thought the dance hall girls were not the same as the painted ladies. The dance hall girls, while beautiful and dressed in ruffles and lacy pantaloons, were more of an entertainment than a "service." I suppose that is as good a word as any to describe the work provided by the Klondike City ladies

Dance halls were popular places for men around Dawson City, with the Floradora being one of the largest on Front Street. One of the dance hall girls, Diamond Tooth Gertie, was sought out for her beauty and company. The Mounties, and certainly Superintendent Steele, would not have allowed the dance halls to operate in the same way as the girls on Paradise Alley or in Klondike City. Prostitutes were not allowed to do business outside of Paradise Alley, though I suppose some certainly did.

Leonard, Henry, Walt, and Malinda came home just before August 23rd. Walt and Malinda had stopped by Henry's claim, staying and helping out until work was done. Tony and Mark stayed on the claim to finish getting the cabins and houses made ready for Winter. Walt and Malinda stayed with us while Henry made his plans to go home to Missouri. After he left, they would stay in his cabin until Henry returned in Spring.

Our first frost came in late August. Though we don't get frost every night, it was often enough for me to unpack all our heavy Winter coats, boots, hats, and gloves. What memories those clothes brought racing back to mind! Days and weeks spent moving outfits from one relay point to another along a trail that never seemed to end, bundled up so much I could hardly move. Now, here we were, ready for Winter again, but this time we would be inside and much warmer.

After the first few frosty nights, the entire country burned with the brilliant, flaming colors of Fall.

All the gold of the Yukon Valley was not found in the ground. A lot of it dressed the country side. On the hills beyond the river, bushes were flames of red. It was a beautiful sight, though each day more and more leaves fell until finally the colors were gone, leaving only bare branches outlined against the Fall skies.

Overhead, flocks of geese split the cool, crisp Fall air, heading south in their ragged "V" formations, often changing leads. We had seen them come north while we were at Lake Bennett. Now, with the short Summer over, they were returning back south to warmer climates.

Leonard and I celebrated our first anniversary, a bit late, having supper with Walt, Malinda, and Henry. She fixed a nice caribou stew and lots of fresh baked bread to go with it. For dessert she had made an apple cobbler. She used some dried apples, and it turned out quite nicely. It was a wonderful way to celebrate with very dear friends.

September brought some unusually warm weather, days so beautiful they were certainly a gift from God. Yet, daily the temperatures slid lower and lower. Ice formed on the barrel of water we kept outside by the door. Leonard brought a smaller barrel inside, which we could later fill with snow melt water. With the colder temperatures, fog formed in the valley, closing in on the city, wrapping it in a blanket. Smoke from cabin fires rose straight up to hang in the air. It was as if the days were talking to us, saying "Winter's coming. It's cold! Prepare! Prepare! Winter here is nine months long!"

Henry has hired both Leonard and Walt to supervise the Winter mining work. He knew both were hard workers, and he knew I wanted Leonard home more now that my time was getting closer. He set up a two week work schedule since it was much too cold to travel such a distance each week. Henry also made arrangements for the bank to pay each man $500 a month. When the gold was washed next Spring, they would receive more if the amount of gold recovered was as much as it was this year.

Henry and Leonard spent most of one day at the bank, settling the accounts there. Henry's claim paid out very well. This year over $80,000 in gold had been recovered! He wanted to pay Leonard a full 20%, but Leonard argued that he had come after the clean-up was already underway. Henry finally paid Leonard $14,000! Leonard said I added over $2000 from my baking and laundry, and that, I admit, made me feel good.

It was so good to have Malinda back. She, Jane, and I got along well, spending afternoons enjoying what was left of our nice Fall weather. I would not bake meat or fruit pies much longer, and we both kept busy preparing fresh vegetables and fruit to store for the Winter. I'd already bought the staples I needed. I still do laundry, but only for Alex, the man who first came by. The last time I washed his shirts, I told him I would only do his laundry until the end of October.

About a week before Henry was set to leave, he, Leonard, and Walt all went hunting. They hoped to bring home a moose and maybe even a caribou. The first day out they managed to get a moose, and while they sighted a herd of caribou, they were too far away. Several days later they got a caribou. Then, as they were coming back, they managed to get three rabbits. Now we will have plenty of meat to keep us through the Winter.

Henry took the skins to an Indian he knew, who will use the hides to make clothing for his family. Two days before Henry was to leave, off they went again. They got two more caribou, giving the skins to the Indian friend along with most of the meat. In return the Indian's wife would use these hides and other fur to make parkas for Leonard and Walt.

Henry left on September 16th, headed down river to St. Michael and then south to Seattle. He would have a long train trip across the country to Missouri, but he could hardly wait to see his family. He assured us he would return by early Spring, to be here for the next gold clean up, leaving Leonard to start that process before he returned.

It was quite exciting the day he left. I had seen other steamboats come and go, all with a great deal of fanfare, but this time a friend would be leaving. He carried a good amount of gold with him, though Leonard said most of his gold was exchanged for bank drafts.

I think most of Dawson City turned out every time a steamboat left, especially in the Fall. So many men would leave, always saying they would return come Spring, but few ever did. Just before the boat was ready to pull in the gangplank, the last of the men rushed to board. In that crowd we sadly saw Tony and Mark leaving. We had a few minutes together before they had to get on board, just barely enough time to hear their story. Both had worked hard during the late Summer months and had done pretty well. Though they didn't say how much they earned, they did say they had enough to buy some land in southern California. Mark held a letter in his hand from his girlfriend, Marie, which he had just picked up at the Post Office. He had written earlier asking her to marry him when he returned, and by reply she had said she would await his return before giving him an answer. He was most anxious to get home to see her. Tony had not heard from his family, but he wanted to go back home, too.

They had stopped by our cabin on their way from the Post Office, but not finding us home, Mark said they had left something for us on our table, just a little something to say thank you for all the times and all the adventures we had shared.

With big hugs and equally big tears, we said good-bye. For so long we had been together, through many trials, over such terrible trails, and finally reaching the gold country together. Now, it seemed as if part of our family was leaving. It was a very difficult time for me, and I think for them also.

We stood on the shore of the river, which had been our home for weeks, waving as men slipped the ropes from the tie-downs and the big steamboat caught the current, rushing down river. We didn't leave until the last horn blasted, as they rounded the bend below Dawson City. Tony and Mark had come, following their dream, and now they were returning home, having fulfilled their hopes and expectations. I would miss them dearly, even though I had not seen them since they left to go to the creeks several months ago. Yet, somehow knowing they were still in the country was comforting.

Walt and Malinda quietly turned toward Henry's cabin. Leonard and I stayed there for a long while. He had his arm around me, holding me close as I cried for departing friends. Silently, I promised to write them, and with God's help, I will do just that.

Finally, returning home, we found five nice sized nuggets with a note saying one was for each of us, and the fifth and largest one was for "Our baby." I guess this child of mine will have several men to call "uncle."

Late September and October - Winter is on the way

By the latter part of September the river temperature was dropping daily. It would not be long before the river would freeze. It would also not be very long before the last boat left for the outside. Then, those left in town would be here for the long Winter. I wondered who else might be leaving, though I really didn't expect I would know any others.

However, I was mistaken. Jane and Dan Nells came over on October 4th, joining us for supper. It was always a pleasure to have them over, as the conversation was lively and the friendship genuine. It was especially nice to have them come this time since Walt and Malinda also joined us.

During the evening, we talked about friends who had gone outside. It was then Dan told us he had been transferred to Vancouver, British Columbia. I knew it was a good transfer for Dan as it meant a promotion, and I also knew Jane had been quite concerned about having a baby up here. It didn't make their leaving any easier though. They would leave on the next steamboat, arriving here in a few days. The four of us helped them pack. It turned out that they were only renting their house, which was furnished, so they didn't have much to pack. We bid them farewell, and though I wished she could have stayed, I understood her reason for leaving. I was very happy Malinda and Walt would be around.

As their boat steamed out of sight, I knew this was probably the last boat out. Already the ground was white with the first snow of Winter with temperatures dropping daily. We watched the river until the boat was out of sight, knowing we were here in Dawson City for the Winter, all nine months of it.

When we returned home, I found a wonderful gift from Jane. She and Dan had given us their iron bed, springs, and mattress. She left a note saying it was the only furniture they had bought in Dawson City, and since it would be much too costly to ship to Vancouver, they wanted us to have it. Leonard and Walt had known about the gift, keeping it at Henry's place until the Nells left. Then, while Leonard and I stayed at the river, Malinda and Walt had brought it to the cabin. Such a special gift from dear friends.

Before long the men would start two week shifts at Henry's claim, supervising the miners, making sure they had the right tools, comfortable and warm living quarters, and plenty of good, hot food. Malinda and I were glad we lived beside each other, as the long dark nights of Winter would be lonely with one or both of the men gone.

October 14th was a date we will remember always with fear and trepidation. Leonard and Walt had stayed up late, filling in shift times on a calendar, knowing one would leave shortly for the first of the two weeks at the mine. Suddenly, planning was interrupted by bells ringing and shouts of "FIRE!" Dawson City was on fire! Some said the fire occurred almost one year after another fire destroyed a good portion of the town in 1897. Now, history repeated itself as the fire ripped through town. This one was started by the same dance hall girl who had started the first fire a year ago. Apparently, that time she had left a candle burning when she went out.

Expensive hotels like the Green Tree and the Worden, and even the Post Office, were burned to the ground. Flames shot skyward with sparks torching other buildings as the fire raced up and down the street and back toward the hills behind town. The fire swept along Paradise Alley, from one small crib (a small dwelling for each lady where she could "entertain" her clients), to the next one until all were reduced to embers. Cabins, tents, and shops were not spared, as the flames raced through the wooden buildings. Men worked in front of the flames tearing down cabins and buildings, trying to stop the spread of the flames. Others chopped holes in the ice on the river, and forming a bucket brigade, doing the best they could, but these few buckets of water did little to stop the fires. Leonard and Walt joined the other men, doing what they could to keep nearby buildings wet, hoping to stop the flames.

Malinda and I kept watch from the windows in the cabin, but all we could see was flames and sparks shooting skyward. The fires raged all night and day, and by the time the men came home, exhausted and covered in smoke and ashes, they reported the worst was over.

Now, other men would stand watch, alert for any spot which might rekindle. Both needed to rest a while, get something to eat, and then go relieve those on the fire lines to take their turn on watch.

The fire had been ugly, leaping from room to room in the hotels, breaking windows, showering glass down on everyone. Walt just shook his head in disbelief at the intensity of the flames. Then he looked at the stack of wood in our cabin and moved it further away from the stove, keeping it out of reach of a stray spark from the stove. I was grateful for the lanterns we had found in our cabin, since we don't have to use candles with open flames, and I will be much more careful when I light the lanterns.

The fire equipment, not yet paid for, could not be used. The next day the equipment was paid for by the town folk and insurance papers drawn up. The city now had the newest fire equipment available, and a number of firemen were hired to work for wages, ready in case another fire ever broke out.

October 20 - Life Certainly Has Changed

Already the city is being rebuilt. The burned buildings are gone and new ones are going up. Men work hard trying to rebuild before the real cold of Winter sets in. Even now the creeks and rivers are freezing, though travel on the Yukon by dog sled is still weeks away. Right now we are cut off from the rest of the world until the Yukon is frozen deep enough for travel by dog sled. Then, the way out is south to Lake Bennett and then over the Pass or north to Fortymile and other communities. We are here in Dawson City, but it is our choice to stay. The temperature is near freezing during the day and much lower at night. Days are considerably shorter, with only about eight hours of daylight, and a lot of the time it is foggy and overcast.

The cabin is cozy and warm, for that I am most grateful. I had better add two other words to my list of words unique to this part of the world.

Outside – anywhere south of Dawson City and the frozen North. Usually used by saying such things as "I'm going Outside for the Winter"
Inside – the opposite, meaning to stay in the frozen North for the Winter.

Tonight, as snow falls silently closing in the land, and shutting off the sounds from outside, I finish writing in my journal. I pray for those who lost their businesses, homes, and all their possessions in the terrible fire. I think of our friends both here and ones somewhere on their way home. As I close, my thoughts turn to the baby within me. I pray for a healthy baby knowing he or she will be loved by us here and by those who will hear the news in letters I write. One day, we hope to visit these friends, not only to share our blessings but to meet their families and share their blessings.

# <u>30</u>

## A NEW LIFE AND A YEAR ENDS

### October 31 - The Men Leave for the Claim

Walt left on October 21$^{st,}$ taking the first two week shift at Henry's claim. The three of us remaining here will share supper together. This will help me since I am so uncomfortable and tire out quickly.

Before Walt left, he and Leonard took apart our wooden bed and made a much needed settee. It is just a bench with a back, but it is certainly more comfortable than the chairs the men had made from packing crates. I bought four cushions at a church sale someone had once used on chairs. Probably the frames were burned for heat before the owners left to go Outside. The fabric was worn, but I covered them with a blanket. Now, we have a comfortable place to sit though getting up is difficult for me.

Leonard also made a baby bed about the same height as our bed. He said as the baby grows, he will cut the legs shorter so it won't tip over when the baby learns to stand. Malinda made a mattress for it by folding an old blanket and covering it with a sheet she had gotten at the same sale.

I think I have the things I will need for the baby, and I know I am big enough to want this baby born.

Mrs. Morgan thought it would be several weeks yet, though I tried to convince her otherwise. She just smiled and said, "The baby will come when he is ready, not when you are."

Malinda and I had already bought more food supplies when the last steamboat came in, and I really think we have sufficient food supplies for the Winter. Store owners are thankful this Winter won't be like the "starvation Winter" of last year.

One day, while baking bread, Malinda and I reminisced about our attempts to bake bread on the trail and even when we were at Lake Bennett. On the trail, the weather had been too cold for the dough to rise, so I made fried biscuits instead. We tried at the lake in the warmer weather and managed to make a proper loaf though the bread did not bake evenly in the Yukon stove. So far I have not noticed any drafts in our cabin, and I'm sure we will be able to bake bread this Winter just fine. I told Malinda about our last morning in the big farm kitchen in Wisconsin with the aroma of the baking bread and what special memories it always brought to mind - memories of home, family, and anticipation of what lay ahead for us. Now I savor that special aroma in this little cabin.

One of the things everyone likes to do is to bundle up and go out to watch the aurora borealis. The skies are so dark now, and the blue, green, yellow and scarlet lights, fluttering across the sky, are a special sight. The bands of color dance and swirl across the sky, making me think of ladies' dresses at fancy dances, whirling around, always moving across the sky. We first saw the lights here in late August, but the skies were not as dark so they didn't show up as well.

The city is very peaceful and lovely after a snowfall. It is quite cold now, and the snow gets deeper and deeper, though it is a dry snow, not at all suitable for making snowmen or for snowball fights. Leonard does his best to make snowballs but ends up just throwing snow at Malinda and me when we are outside.

This morning I cut up two flannel sheets Mrs. Morgan just gave me to make diapers. I had made some from dish towels, being careful not to use the towel Ian and Liam had used so much on the trail, the one with all the spots from the meals they had cooked. That one I wanted to save always.

I wish I knew where those two dear men were now. We haven't seen nor heard from them since they left shortly after we arrived here in June. I suppose they are busy, but I would sure like to open the door one day to see them standing there. Then again, I doubt they even know where we live.

November 4 – Leonard Leaves for His Two Week Shift

I also made two wool baby blankets from one of the wool blankets we used on the trail. There was even enough left to make a throw to cover my shoulders when I'm reading or writing. Malinda borrowed knitting needles from Mrs. Morgan and knitted a rose colored baby blanket using yarn from a sweater she had bought at a sale and unraveled. I must ask Malinda to teach me how to knit. She did such a beautiful job, and I would. like to be able to make sweaters for Leonard and me.

Leonard kept plenty of firewood inside and made sure the small water barrel inside was filled with fresh snow. He has helped out in so many ways these last few weeks. Malinda and I do the cooking, but Leonard had been washing dishes. He still remarks every once in a while how clean his hands are – reminding us of those comments from the men whenever they helped wash dishes on the trail or the river while coming here.

Last night as Malinda helped cook supper, there was a knock at the door. When Leonard opened it, in walked Henry's Indian friend, handing Leonard a very nice caribou parka. Leonard tried it on and thought it would fit Walt better. He thanked the Indian and praised his wife's workmanship. The parka was made with the fur inside for warmth, and the hood was trimmed in beaver fur for added warmth around the face. The Indian, his name was George, though I suppose that was a white man's name for him, said his wife would make the second one a little longer to better fit Leonard. He will wear this parka when he leaves to relieve Walt, though he will take his wool coat, too.

After Leonard left this morning, Malinda and I made cookies and baked a blueberry pie. It's Walt's favorite, and she wanted to surprise him when he gets home tonight and joined us for supper which we will eat here. We both know the men eat well at the work site, but it is such a treat to have either one of them home that we try to make something special for them. I get tired easily now and find it harder to stand by the stove and cook and so Malinda is now doing most of the cooking.

She really enjoys cooking, and I am happy to let her do it.

November 7 - The Day Arrives

This is me, Malinda, writing now. Freddie woke very early this morning, knowing something was happening, saying she was in a great deal of pain and could hardly move. As she was trying to dress to come get me, Walt came in with a big load of wood. Before he could say anything, she told him to get me immediately. In just a few minutes I was here, and Walt was going after Mrs. Morgan.

Just before 9 AM today, November 7, 1898, Sylvia Mae Stanton was born. Mrs. Morgan had been here only a very short time when she was born.

Sylvia is very small. She was quiet until Mrs. Morgan gave her a good swat on her little bottom, and then she let out a scream! At least we knew she had a good set of lungs! She has dark brown eyes, just like Leonard's, and what little hair she has is a medium brown with little waves. She tries to open her eyes but is not too good at keeping them open. She continued to scream until Mrs. Morgan wrapped her in a flannel blanket, giving her to Freddie. Freddie looked very tired, but through tears streaming down her face, she kissed her little daughter for the first time. I know she wished Leonard were here.

As soon as Walt knew Freddie and Sylvia were fine, he left for the claim. He would make sure Leonard got home as quickly as possible. He kissed Freddie on the forehead saying he wanted to let Leonard be the first man to kiss his little daughter.

Mrs. Morgan stayed for several hours, caring for Freddie and making sure little Sylvia was doing OK. She was concerned because Sylvia was so small and said she was going to ask Dr. Bowers to come by to check on her. As she left she said she would come by later tonight to see how both were doing.

Freddie slept a lot during the day, waking only to nurse Sylvia. There is no doubt when the baby is awake. She has a lusty cry. Sky kept watch from a distance but spent most of the day curled up on the bed at Freddie's feet.

I wrote a note to her family and will add Leonard's comments about Sylvia before I mail it. Oh, yes. The baby is named Sylvia after Freddie's grandmother on her mother's side. The middle name, Mae, is Leonard's grandmother's name on his father's side. Freddie knew Grandma Mae would be delighted to have a great granddaughter named after her. I think Freddie said Grandma Mae was in her late seventies now. I think Sylvia Mae Stanton is such a beautiful name. And she is a beautiful little girl. What a story this tiny child will be able to tell later about being born during the Klondike Gold Rush in this northern land in the cold Winter of 1898.

November 9 - Dr. Bowers Pays a Visit

Leonard came home late yesterday morning. Both Freddie and I were surprised he had gotten home so quickly as he certainly couldn't have run in this cold weather. His lungs would have frozen from the cold air. Once he had kissed Freddie and held his little daughter for a few minutes, he sat down to drink a cup of tea. I gave him a bowl of the hot soup I had made earlier for Freddie and me.

I asked Leonard how he got back here so quickly. Well, Walt had gotten a ride on a dog sled when the driver had seen him running on the trail. The driver was taking supplies to a mining claim, and when he heard Walt's story, he gave him a ride to Henry's claim. Then, he told Leonard to wait a couple of hours, and when he returned with an empty sled, Leonard could ride down with the dog team.

I made more tea for them, and made sure they had whatever they might need, and then I left for the night. I came this morning to find Leonard holding Sylvia, her head cradled in one hand. He sure looked like one proud father. Dr. Bowers came by late yesterday to see Freddie and Sylvia. He said Freddie was doing fine, but she might welcome my help for a few days. Mrs. Morgan was here at the same time. Dr. Bowers declared Sylvia in good health. He looked through the shelves in the kitchen until he found a five pound tin of lard. Then with the lard in one hand and Sylvia in the other, he guessed she weighed about five pounds. He told Mrs. Morgan she had done a fine job, but the baby really needed to be bathed more thoroughly to remove the rest of the birth fluid from her hair and body. He cautioned her not to put Sylvia in a basin, but just wash her off, making sure to keep her warm at all times.

So when the water was nice and warm, with Freddie watching, Mrs. Morgan and I both got busy giving Sylvia a bath. I thought it quite amusing to see three grown women giving suggestions on how to wash her, and all the while Sylvia was giving us her opinion of the bath. I dare say the opinion was not good as she screamed the entire time. Once dry, wrapped in a blanket and fed, she went right to sleep. Leonard just quietly watched.

I'll write more in the journal later. I added a few notes to the family letter asking them to tell Walt's parents also. After all, Walt calls Sylvia his "little girl," too.

December 31 – The Last Day of a Really
Incredible Year

Tonight as I bring my journal up to date, I realize what an incredible year this has been, filled with hopes and dreams, hardships and victories, old endings and new beginnings. Someday Leonard and I will share this journal with little Sylvia.

The first two weeks after Sylvia was born the cabin was filled with sleepless nights and days when visitors came to share the joy of our little girl. Malinda has been a great help preparing meals, keeping a record of gifts received, and caring for Sylvia so I could write thank you notes to each person, which Leonard then delivered personally.

News spread quickly about the arrival of Dawson City's newest citizen, and one of the first visitors was the wife of the Dawson City Commissioner.

She stayed only a few minutes, but gave me a beautiful baby dress, which she had bought in Vancouver just before her husband was posted here, knowing it would be nice for the Commissioner's wife to present a gift to any child born in Dawson City. Apparently she had bought a number of baby outfits for both girls and boys.

Rev. and Mrs. Walters stopped by one afternoon, with a chicken and dumpling hot dish and a lovely baby sweater and cap she had knitted. They have been good friends, and I remember so well the graciousness with which they hosted a reception for Walt and Malinda following their wedding.

Mrs. Morgan came by a number of times, checking on Sylvia and me. One day she brought a very nice, warm flannel gown for me. My only gown was getting a lot of use and a second one was most appreciated.

A most unusual gift came from Constable Stanley and his wife, Carol. The Constable had been one of the two police officers at Malinda's wedding. Constable Stanley and Carol loaned me the use of a rocking chair for as long as I needed it. How nice it has been to rock Sylvia to sleep, or to feed her while slowly rocking. With a wool shawl over my shoulders and a blanket over my legs, we're both warm and comfortable.

Other gifts of prepared meals, a baby blanket, and baby gowns came from neighbors near us. I couldn't thank everyone enough for such their thoughtfulness. Even two neighbor men, who are card dealers at the Bodega Saloon, stopped by. Both miss their families back home and have sort of adopted Sylvia. One brought some fresh eggs from the chickens he kept in a room attached to his cabin. He said he had to put lanterns in the room during part of the day in Winter so the hens would lay eggs. In Summer he had to cover the windows part of the day. It's a lot of work to get hens to lay eggs up here. The other man brought two freshly killed and cleaned ptarmigan. It made me remember the ptarmigan we had while building our boats at Lake Bennett so long ago.

Then, a week before Thanksgiving, there was a knock at the door, and in walked Alex. I hadn't seen him since I stopped doing his laundry before Sylvia was born. He stood with his hat in his hands, turning it round and round by the brim and shyly asked if he could see the baby. Such a big man to act so shy, but I knew he was a gentle man who loved people, especially children. I had seen him talking with the children around here during the Summer after picking up his clean shirts.

Sylvia was asleep in her bed, but I picked her up and handed her to Alex, who fumbled, dropping his hat before taking her. He smiled at her until suddenly she let out one of her incredibly loud screams. Alex looked at me as if to say "What did I do? She's screaming so!" I assured him she was fine, she just screamed loudly whenever she woke up. Alex breathed a very loud sigh of relief, and then very softly talked to her. Well, Sylvia quieted down as quick as you please, and he looked quite satisfied with himself.

He sat down on the settee, and I offered him a cup of coffee. We talked for a short while then he stood to leave, handing Sylvia back to me. As he put on his parka, he asked if I would launder his shirts again. He hadn't found anyone who got them as clean as I did, and he would willingly pay me even more than $1 a shirt to wash them. I told him I'd gladly wash them though I couldn't promise I would have them done as quickly as before. Then he opened the door, retrieved a bundle from beside the step, and handed it to me. It was his shirts! He is such a kind man it would have been hard to turn him down.

Malinda was a tremendous help in so many way during these weeks. When Leonard was home he filled the water barrel with snow daily so I had plenty of water inside for laundry which dried quickly on the suspended drying rack above the stove. When he was gone, Malinda kept the cabin well supplied. We took turns writing letters home telling the folks about the men's work and keeping them up to date on news about Sylvia. Dr. Bowers came again before Thanksgiving and pronounced Sylvia quite healthy.

When one of our neighbors was going out to his claim, I asked him to take a message to Walt telling him to come home for Thanksgiving. Leonard would go to the claim after Thanksgiving, giving Walt two weeks at home. After all, Walt had relieved Leonard when Sylvia was born, and now it was time for Leonard to do the claim work.

We had Thanksgiving dinner about mid-afternoon at Henry's cabin. It was truly a time to give thanks. We thought about those who had lost so much in the fire in October and were most thankful no one was seriously hurt. Most of all we gave thanks to God for our daughter. We thought of friends we have made, some of whom have gone Outside - Tony, Mark, Dan, and Jane - and wished Ian and Liam were with us sharing this wonderful and very special time.

Our delicious meal consisted of roast moose with vegetables and piping hot bread. Soon we pushed back from the table to enjoy coffee and blueberry pie. When there was a knock at the door, Walt opened it, ushering in George, the Indian from the village of Moosehide who made the parka, and his wife whom he called "Jo." He said someone called her a "good Jo" for all her fine hand work, so Jo became her white man's name.

In the same quiet manner of the Indian who became part of our lives on the trail, George gave Leonard the second parka Henry had asked his wife to make. The parka, like the one made for Walt, had fox fur around the hood. Leonard tried it on, and it fit very nicely. Then Jo handed me a little rabbit fur blanket for the baby. She indicated the fur should be next to the baby for extra warmth.

Tears came to my eyes as I thanked them for such a fine gift. Jo stood quietly by the bed where Sylvia slept, just looking at the baby girl. Even though I usually didn't wake Sylvia when she was asleep, I made an exception and handed her to Jo, who softly rubbed her hand over Sylvia's fine brown hair. Sylvia just looked at her, squinting her little eyes which were still heavy with sleep, and for once she didn't cry.

After the Indians left, and I remarked that in a way, our Thanksgiving was like the very first Thanksgiving many years ago. At that time, the new settlers in our country had shared a feast with the Indians of the New World, and now here we were, miles away and in another country on a different side of the continent, sharing a portion of the day with Indians here. It was almost like history was repeating itself, but in a different way.

December brought dramatic changes. Early in the month, the sun was gone, leaving only twilight for a few hours. Now, lanterns were needed all the time. Temperatures dropped steadily each day to 40 degrees below zero or more and little moved in town when it got that cold. The horses of the Mounties had to be in the stables. It was too cold to be outside unless protected by thick coats and blankets.

The cabin was warm with a fire always roaring in the stove, but we noticed the nails Leonard had put in the wall to hang clothes on were frosted over. When Leonard came home in mid-December, he put crushed paper against the windows and covered them inside with wood to keep out any drafts. Now the cabin was even darker. I hadn't realized how much light came in the windows, even in the Winter twilight. When we first arrived, one of the store keepers had told me that Dawson City had only two seasons - Winter and Summer - and Winter was nine months long. Now I understood what he meant.

Periodically, when the cold subsided, it was a thrill to get all bundled up and step outside for a few minutes to watch the Northern Lights. The colors, brilliant bright reds, greens, yellow gold's, and blue's, floated across the sky like lace curtains blowing in the windows of the world. It was always a thrill to see them, and now that it is dark all the time, they were visible most of the time.

Winter is really the social season for the finer Dawson City ladies, and Malinda and I were thrilled to be invited to tea at Mrs. Morgan's home. It was a very cold afternoon, and Walt volunteered to take care of Sylvia. So we dressed up in our finest clothes, which I knew were not nearly as fancy as those the other ladies wore.

Tea was served from shining silver tea pots. Porcelain tea cups and saucers looked almost too fragile for use. The table, with its lace cloth, was spread with such delicacies as salted nuts, fudge, assorted tea cookies and orange sherbet. The centerpiece was a large basket of purple asters, pink peonies, and lovely greens. I found out later there was a man in town who grew flowers in his house just for such occasions! If he didn't have fresh flowers, he used some lovely silk flowers, and this particular tea was one time he needed to use his silk flowers as none others were in bloom. I didn't realize they were silk until Malinda told me, and even then I had to touch them to make sure.

The ladies were dressed in their finest. Hats trailed long ribbons down the back or net folded over the brims. Some had added flowers around the crown. Dresses, with satin and silk trim, swirled around the floor at ankle length. Dress shoes, with bright gold or silver buckles and little heels, peeked from beneath the dress hems. Dress bodices were cinched so tightly I wondered how the ladies breathed. Some necklines were cut low and trimmed in lace, others were high and adorned with a gold or precious stone brooch.

The conversations centered around the upcoming theater performance, who had which box seats reserved at the theater, and who was going to share the box with them. Now I understood why Dawson City was sometimes called the Paris of the North.

When Leonard came home on December 20[th,] he went to the bank to do some claim business and seemed to be gone a much longer time than usual. When he returned, he had a small Christmas tree he had cut from a valley near town. He had seen it on his way from the claim and hoped no one would cut it down before he could. We put it in a corner, far from the heat of the stove, and we spent the day making paper ornaments. Malinda joined us, wishing Walt could have been here, too. We began making plans for our Christmas celebration, planning to eat at two in the afternoon. Malinda wanted to make a special dessert, but she wouldn't say what it would be. Leonard had shot several wild geese in late Fall, and we saved one in our Yukon ice box for Christmas. I would roast it with a cornbread dressing made with chopped fruit and nuts, as Mom did last Christmas. We'd also have rolls and vegetables.

Leonard and I had already put small gifts under the tree for each other, Sylvia, Walt, and Malinda. With some crayons, we decorated butcher paper with Christmas trees and Santa Claus men for our wrapping paper. Our little northern home looked bright and festive for the occasion.

Late the afternoon before Christmas, Sky got up from where she lay near Sylvia and went to the door, just sitting there wagging her tail and tilting her head first to one side and then the other. Then she stood up quickly and put her nose right against the door. Leonard noticed it and said he bet we were about to have visitors. As if on cue, there was a knock at the door, Sky barked happily, and in walked Ian and Liam!

Sky greeted her friends as we hugged each other warmly, a greeting genuinely felt by all. Sylvia woke up with a husky cry, as if to say, "I want to meet these friends." Ian and Liam stopped immediately, took off their heavy parkas, and reached out to hold their little "granddaughter." Both these men, hardened by work at the mines, were the gentlest men I have ever known. Large, callused hands caressed Sylvia's head and held her little hands. Each kissed her tenderly on the forehead then looked at Leonard and me. Both had tears welling up in their smiling eyes. These men, who had meant so much to us in the many months it took to get here, were holding a little child so precious to them and to us.

Liam spoke first, "My! She's a lovely little lassie, such a tiny little girl." With her tiny hand curled around his finger, he spoke as he looked down at her, "Little Sylvia, we knew ya was a comin' way long ago. Now ya's here, and we love ya every bit as much as ya Mom and Dad."

Ian broke in saying, "Ya sure is mighty pretty, too. Must get ya good looks from ya Mother, but I bet ya will talk with a Scottish brogue if we stick around here. And we's sure gonna come visit often."

Leonard stood with his arm around my shoulder, finally admitting that he had made a special trip to find them during his last time on the claim site in order to invite them for Christmas and to tell them about Sylvia. What a special gift to share this time of the year with two of the dearest men I have ever known. Now, Christmas would be extra special.

Just then, Walt and Malinda came over. Walt had just returned from the claim, having told all the workers to take several days off to share Christmas with family and friends in town. Once more our little group was together. Ian and Liam already knew Tony and Mark had gone outside, but we wished they could have been here to share this Christmas time as part of our special family.

Quickly, Liam opened a large box they had brought in, sharing the contents with us. We stood around amazed at the plethora of goodies they unpacked. There was a large ham, a tin of nuts, jars of jelly, cheeses of several kinds, coffee, tea, and cocoa. They even had a box of chocolates for Malinda and me. What a feast we would share!

I sliced some of the cold ham and put out other treats while Malinda sliced some warm bread she had just finished baking. Christmas Eve supper was a time to reflect and give thanks for good friends. We talked until late in the evening when Walt and Malinda invited Ian and Liam to sleep at their place. Even they knew the men were coming and had prepared the bunk beds in Henry's cabin for them.

Needless to say, Christmas Day was extra special. Everyone joined us in our snug little cabin, and while the men talked mining and gold, Malinda and I cooked our Christmas feast. Leonard even fed Sylvia her bottle when she cried. He did well, but he gave her back to me when she needed her diaper changed.

I dressed Sylvia in the pair of little overalls Ian and Liam had given me before we got to Dawson City. With a long-sleeve cotton shirt, she looked so cute. Even though the overalls were small, they were still a bit too big for a seven week old little girl, but I had to let Ian and Liam see her in them. I'm glad I remembered the overalls and knew where they were. The men were quite pleased I had made the effort to dress her in them, though I don't think Sylvia cared what she was wearing. She had been passed around so much the night before, she simply fell asleep.

Finally, with food on the table, Leonard offered a Christmas prayer, and it was time to eat. Since the table was not large enough to seat six, we each filled our plates and sat around the room. We were blessed with a bounty of delicious foods, beautifully arranged on the table. Our meal was certainly more than we ever shared on the trail or the river but had it been the beans or hotcakes we ate so often, we still would have been blessed and rich with our friends!

So I will always remember the feast we celebrated with our wonderful friends, here are the items on the Christmas table.

| | |
|---|---|
| Roast goose | Ham |
| Dressing | Potatoes |
| Gravy | Carrots |
| Squash | Hot rolls |
| Cheese | Jelly |
| Ice Cream | Blueberry pie |
| Coffee | Tea |

I was certain even the socially elite of Dawson City could not have enjoyed a better meal.

And yes, we did have ice cream! Malinda had made custard of eggs, sugar, condensed milk, and cocoa. When it had set almost firm she whipped in some snow to make it fluffy, she said, and then set it outside to freeze. It was really quite tasty.

A mound of gifts surrounded the tree. Leonard gave me a bracelet of small gold nuggets, and Walt gave Malinda the same. I gave Leonard and Walt wool shirts, and Malinda gave them new wool socks, which they really needed. Leonard and I gave Sylvia a small gold necklace, from which hung the gold nugget Tony and Mark had left for her.

I really felt bad that I had nothing for Ian and Liam, as I had not known they were coming. In fact I had heard nothing about them or from them since they left us in June. Instead, I gave them my love and promised always to write them with details of Sylvia as she grew up.

Our Scotsmen gave Leonard and Walt heavy, fur-lined, waterproof gum boots for work at the mines. Malinda and I received beautiful sweaters, and Sylvia got a gold poke with several nice nuggets. They even gave Sky a gift. I'm not sure she will like it, but she might since she is part sled dog. They gave her a small sleigh and a lovely leather harness with bells. Now, she could pull Sylvia around outside when it gets a little warmer.

Sylvia was passed from person to person, and Sky went to whoever would scratch her behind her ears. The whole day was quite wonderful and so very special.

I doubt there was any place else on earth with as much love to share as we shared that day. We were blessed indeed.

Now, it is the last day of the year. Ian and Liam stayed for a couple more days, leaving on the 28th to go back to their mines. Leonard will leave tomorrow, while Walt will stay here until mid-January. It is nice to have either Leonard or Walt around to help with bringing in some wood. Though Malinda has done it on numerous occasions, we both appreciate their help. Besides, we really enjoy having their company. We especially like to hear how things are going at the mine, though I have to admit some of the words they use are unfamiliar to me.

Right now, Leonard and Sylvia are asleep. I sit in the rocker, closing out the year by completing my journal. It has been a year like none other I have ever had. Last year we were home in Clinton with the family, including Grandpa Leon and Grandma Mae, Pop's parents. We knew then we were going to the Yukon, but our plans called for us to be home in late Fall, and nowhere in the plans was there mention of a daughter.

We have been places and survived trials we could have never imagined. We have met and learned to love dearly our wonderful friends. We have witnessed friendships destroyed over small disagreements, vowing never to let such differences come between us. And even when such an incident had threatened to divide us, it was the long-term friendship which brought us beyond the difference, thus keeping us together. Walt certainly didn't expect to meet and marry such a wonderful young lady, and Leonard and I never planned to be parents before returning home.

Through it all we have thanked God for His constant and abiding love and His guidance when we were exhausted beyond words or were at a loss for what to do.

I looked at the clock and realized the time had changed while I was writing this last little bit. The year is now 1899. What this New Year will bring, we don't know, but I do know that with faith and courage, we will return home to our families, richer in spirit and more faithful to the teachings of our God.

Thank you 1898 for giving us dreams to dream and friends to share those dreams. I look forward to whatever 1899 has in store for us, for we still have dreams and hopes, a wonderful family, and an abundance of love to share with friends.

# 31

## LIVING IN A DEEP FREEZE

**Friday, March 10 - The Weather Warms Up!**

Shortly after Christmas we got our first letter from Mom and Pops. It was so good to hear from them, and they and the Jackson eagerly await our return this Summer so all can meet both little Sylvia and Malinda. Now I must write them more often with news from this frozen northland.

Leonard left for work at Henry's claim on January 1st, and it was cold that day! He wore his heavy skin parka, a wool scarf tied around his face with only his eyes showing, his snow goggles, and fur lined gloves. Beneath his wool trousers, he wore long woolen underwear and another pair of wool trousers. He had on two pair of wool socks and his new fur lined boots. He looked fat, but it was the only way to keep warm.

Malinda and Walt found that drafts came through the cracks in a number of places in Henry's cabin. With blankets nailed over many spots, it was still quite cold. Walt heard it was -40 degrees outside, and he quickly added it was not much warmer inside!

After two very cold weeks, Leonard came home just about the time the sun began to peek out above the mountains. It was just a sliver of light, but it was there, and, believe me, it was good to see it again. It wasn't any warmer, but I began to think that the worst of the weather was behind us.

Each day a little more of the sunlight crowned the hills across the river, painting them in shades of gold, pink, and salmon red. We could see our shadows in the snow again, and it was a joyous feeling. We even played the game we did so often as young children - trying to step on each other's shadow.

Still, the fog hung above the city. The colder it got, the thicker the fog seemed to be. Mixed with the fog was the smoke of all the cabin fires. Now the snow had a gray tint to it, and Walt dug deep to get the cleanest possible snow for the water barrels.

Having experienced a cold Klondike Winter, we are considered "Sourdoughs". Of course, there is another way someone can become a "Sourdough" according to the stories around town. Leonard said he could never qualify with this second way, namely -

To become a "real sourdough" a man had to shoot a bear and sleep with a squaw.

Some said they would rather do it the other way.

Walt left on January 15th for his two week shift, taking with him some supplies needed at the site. I thought about the weight the men carried day after day climbing the Pass, and I couldn't imagine this could be worse until Walt reminded me the lowest temperatures on the Pass were only -10 degrees!

Some nights Malinda stayed with us, sleeping on the settee when Walt was gone. Henry's cabin was too drafty to keep warm, and our woodpiles seemed to be dwindling too fast. Each day Leonard would put just enough wood in Henry's stove to keep the place from becoming so cold as to be unusable even for the short times Malinda went there to get something she needed. There would be no more wood chopping until Spring, since all the trees were frozen.

January 17th was a night we will never forget. Just after midnight there was a terrible banging at the door. Sky barked loudly, and I was really surprised she had not heard someone coming. Sylvia woke up screaming at the noise. Leonard rushed to the door, letting in a man, covered in frost and out of breath.

"Come to tell ya, I jest took Walt to the hospital. I'm working a claim near ya, and last night one of your men come in saying Walt was doubled over in pain."

Malinda began sobbing almost hysterically. I tried to comfort her at the same time trying to quiet Sylvia's crying, and I didn't seem to be doing a good job of either.

Leonard grabbed the man by the shoulders, and gruffly asked, "Tell me, what's the problem? How long did it take to get him to town? Anything, man, anything!"

The man caught his breath and swallowed before he continued. "Well, it was about supper time, maybe a little later, when one of ya men, Stewart, comes running up asking if I could hitch up the dogs and get Walt to the hospital immediately. Of course, I could. Any man will help another in trouble.

"Well, I thought he'd been hurt or burned as so many are, but Stewart said he had not felt good earlier and now was doubled over, clutching his belly. Well, I get the dogs hooked up and run to get him. I wanted to give him a slug of whiskey to ease the pain, but you can't drink up here when it's so cold cause you can die from it. One of your other men, don't know his name, but he's the older fellow, with the white streak in his beard, said it looked like appendicitis to him. Told me I better hurry, too, 'cause if his appendix burst, he'd die fer sure then."

"Look, I'm sorry I yelled at you, but tell me, what did the doctor say? And what's your name?" Leonard pointed to a chair so the man could finally sit down.

"My name's Michael. Michael Sawyer. I didn't see no doctor, but a nurse said he would be called immediately. Walt was very quiet on the ride in, and we went like the wind. My dogs must've sensed the urgency, 'cause they run the whole way. Walt was covered in blankets, and when we got to the hospital, he said he was really warm the whole way. The nurse said he had a fever so that may have been why he felt warm. Then I followed his directions and came right here to tell ya."

By now, Sylvia was quiet, Sky was sniffing the man's legs, obviously smelling his dogs on his trousers, and I had put on water for coffee.

"Look, thanks so much for your help. My wife, Freddie, will fix you something hot to eat and drink. Stay as long as you want. What can we get for your dogs besides our usual dog food? Anything special?" Leonard tried to calm everyone down, and finally realized nothing would calm Malinda until she could get to the hospital.

"Please stay a while to rest and warm up before you go back. And excuse us, but Malinda, Walt's wife, and I need to get dressed and get to the hospital right away."

"Thanks for the offer of something to eat, but if you've just got some bread for me, that'll be fine. I got to get the dogs back to the mine. They help haul the buckets from the pits, and so we gotta leave real soon. The dogs will be fine. They'll get their usual food once we get back." Mr. Sawyer spoke as he stroked Sky's ears, knowing just where a dog liked to be scratched.

Leonard and Malinda immediately went to the hospital, just a few blocks away. Mr. Sawyer had two cups of coffee and soon left quickly. I cleaned up the few dishes, nursed Sylvia, and had a cup of coffee myself. I even made the beds, knowing there would be no more sleep that night. Thankfully, Sylvia went right back to sleep. Oh, to have the innocent mind of a child and be able to sleep even when something like this happens. I kissed her and tucked a blanket around her, letting her dream her baby dreams.

Leonard returned later saying it was indeed appendicitis, but the operation had gone well. The appendix had not burst, though Walt was very weak and quite restless. He would need to be in the hospital for a week or more, as there was always the possibility of complications or infection. He added that Malinda would stay with him for a while. She would come back later, but she would stay with Walt for several days caring for him. I got Leonard something to eat, and within the hour, he was gone back to the claim.

Malinda stayed with Walt in his room for four nights, sleeping in a chair. She came home a short time each day to eat something, but she was very worried because Walt was still running a fever. She said there were many miners in the hospital suffering from terrible frostbite or scurvy. She told of going to visit a few while Walt slept, and how her heart ached for those with no one to visit them.

Dr. Bower said this was his first appendix operation. He had only watched another doctor remove an appendix once. Finally, after four days the doctor felt Walt was out of danger, but he needed to stay until he was stronger and the stitches could be removed. On January 30, almost two weeks after he was rushed to the hospital, Walt came home. He was noticeably thinner, his face drawn and pale. He was weak and couldn't stand for more than a few minutes. He slept in our bed, and we checked on him during the night, getting what sleep we could on the settee or in the rocking chair.

During the days that followed, Sylvia was a perfect little girl. She cried when she was hungry, but most of the time she simply smiled at anyone who paid attention to her. As the days went by and Walt got stronger and stronger, I let Sylvia sleep beside him as he was awake a good bit of the time now. It was a real joy to see him smile and talk to her.

And speaking of attention, Sky spent a lot of her time sleeping on the bed near Walt. She was almost full grown, weighing about 60 pounds according to Leonard's guess, and we needed to break her of being our foot warmer.

Malinda and I carried on with the daily duties, bringing in wood when needed and getting snow for the water barrel. It took effort to do even these few things outside, as we had to dress quite warmly even for the few minutes we were outside. I am thankful for our plentiful food supplies, as we didn't need anything, and we managed just fine.

Leonard came home on February 2nd and was relieved to see Walt up and about. He stayed home only two days, but he had been concerned about Walt and made the special trip to town. During that time, the cabin was as crowded as the tent was so long ago. Walt and Malinda took the bed, I slept on the settee, and Leonard dragged out all the blankets we had, plus some from Henry's place, and slept on the floor. At least we were warm in the cabin, and we laughed when I said, "Here we are. Cozy again."

Malinda and I knew Walt was getting much better when he and Leonard began talking about the mining. Malinda and I were interested to hear how it was done since neither of us has been up to the claims, and we have no plans to go there during the cold Winter.

Since most or all of the surface gold which was found in the stream beds or close to the surface of the ground, had been mined during the first few months of the gold rush, the only way to get to the gold now is by digging down to the bedrock. Sometimes the bedrock is twenty to forty feet beneath the surface. With the ground frozen solid by the permafrost, a pit is dug and each night a fire is built in the bottom to thaw the ground. The next day, the men get down in the pits and shovel the thawed mud and muck into buckets which are winched to the surface by a windless, where it is dumped on the ever growing dump pile. The dumps get bigger and bigger throughout the Winter.

This work is extremely hard on the men. All day they take shifts in the pit, shoveling mud in buckets. The ground around the pit is frozen, so in addition to being hard work, it is very cold at the bottom. The work goes on all Winter, until the Spring thaws soften the top few feet of ground. Then it could become too wet and dangerous to be so deep. Also the melting snow flows into the pit, and water collects in the bottom.

No one knows if there is gold in the muck or if all the Winter work is for naught. Only when water again runs in the flumes can the job of washing the gold be done. Then and only then, will miners know if they are rich, or simply out of luck.

Leonard and Walt both felt that Henry's claim would continue to pay for some time. During the Winter, when they have needed supplies, they've taken a bucket of the muck from the dump and washed out the gold in a big tub used for laundry and occasionally for baths. They indicated they didn't work long to recover the gold they needed.

I guess that is one reason Henry wanted both men to supervise the work. He trusted both of them, and while he felt his men were honest, temptation might be hard to resist when gold is so close at hand.

Walt got stronger and stronger as the days went by, and on February 12th, he said it was time for him to go back to work. Neither of us could convince him to stay a few more days. Reluctantly we sent him off with several meat pies to eat while on the trail. Malinda urged him to rest along the way, as he still didn't have all his strength back yet. Of course, we both knew he would probably walk all the way without stopping, but maybe he would walk more slowly.

Leonard got home a couple of days after Walt left us. He stayed an extra day at the claim to make sure Walt was strong enough, and he even made him promise to stop the work earlier each day.

On February 15th, I reminded Leonard that it was one year ago that we had left Clinton with the Jacksons, to go to Sharon and start our trip to the Klondike, yet it didn't seem that long ago. What a year this has been!

The latter part of February proved to be the coldest we have had so far. I hoped and prayed it would not get any colder. Leonard said it was probably lower than -50 degrees. The heavy fog grew thicker and thicker. Nothing stirred outside unless absolutely necessary.

We spent his two weeks at home, enjoying our daughter. She was now three months old and getting bigger and cuter every day. She has been sleeping through the nights for some time, and it sure felt good to know we, too, can get a good night's sleep. Occasionally, she will wake, but usually just rubbing her back puts her back to sleep.

She smiles and actually laughs when I put her on a blanket on the floor. She pulls at Sky's fur, and her little arms fling out, often hitting Sky, but the dog never growls or nips at her. When Sky has finally had enough, she simply gets up and walks away.

Mrs. Morgan thought I could feed Sylvia some thin oatmeal cereal, mashed potatoes, or mashed vegetables. Meat should wait as she might choke on even a small piece. At first, Sky ate most of the food since Sylvia spit it on me and the floor. Gradually she began to eat more. She's really fun to watch, and her personality is coming into its' own. Leonard washed her face one day, and such a sight. I'm not sure who smiled more as he made a game of it. He's a good man, and I'm blessed indeed.

At the end of February the weather was still very cold though I thought it was getting somewhat warmer. Walt came home on the 24th, saying he never felt better. Work had gone well on the claim, and he was certainly glad to be back at work. Leonard said he would go back to the claim on Sunday, but he had a surprise for us on Saturday afternoon. He wouldn't give us any hint of what it might be. The only thing he said was that we would enjoy it.

Saturday afternoon Leonard told us to dress very warm. He said Sky could come, too. I put a warm sweater and cap on Sylvia and wrapped her in the rabbit fur blanket. At 2 o'clock two dog sleds pulled up out front. We were going for a dog sled ride!

Our drivers were Indians from Moosehide who worked on the claim. Leonard had given all the men several days off because the weather was getting better, and some men needed to go hunting. Then, he had arranged for the Indians to take us for a ride.

Walt and Malinda climbed on one sled, and we climbed on the other. After getting settled, the Indians covered us with bear skin robes. Colorful wool Indian blankets were put behind our backs and around our shoulders. Sky, tied with a rope, ran beside the sled as the Indians didn't want her getting too close to the sled dogs fearing a fight would break out.

The sled dogs wore bells across their massive shoulders, which rang delightfully as we raced along. The sleds were decorated with brightly colored pompoms and flowing ribbons of bright yarn. Those dogs loved to run, and their shoulders seemed to flow rather than move. We stopped to rest far up the Klondike River, and Leonard said we weren't too far from the claim site. When the sleds stopped, the Indians put down a metal stake, deep in the snow, to keep the dog from taking off again. But the dogs stayed quiet. Some lay down in the snow, curled up with their noses covered by their bushy tails, while others just sat down, looked around as if to ask why they couldn't keep running. Their big white teeth gleamed in the little sunlight we had, and long tongues hung from the sides of their mouths. If I hadn't seen how much they enjoyed running, I would have thought the dogs had been worked too hard. All too soon the anchor stake was pulled up, we were off again, racing back to town.

What a wonderful afternoon! Sky ran alongside the sled but never close to the dogs. Someday we will tell Sylvia about the dog sled ride she was on, though she slept the entire time. Then again, she was only four months old!

By the middle of March, with about 10 or 11 hours of daylight, we hoped Spring would be here soon. When the temperature reached a balmy 20 degrees, people all over town were out enjoying the warm weather. To those living Outside, 20 degrees would be cold, but to us who wintered here, this was now good weather.

Each day we hoped to get a letter from Henry telling us when he would return. Yet, I knew he would not return until the Yukon River breaks the bonds of ice that hold everything in check. I wonder just when that will be? I remember our time of waiting last Summer. When would the ice break? When could we leave for Dawson City? Now we are here waiting for the ice to break to bring Henry and his family here.

June 8 - The River Runs and the Clean Up Begins

Now in early March it is warmer and the daylight hours are getting longer. An ice film still covered the outside water barrel each morning. On Front Street there are wooden sidewalks, but the streets have turned to mud ankle deep. I sure am glad we still have our rubber boots.

The sun was warm and delightful. I took the covers off the windows and washed them, letting the sunlight into the house, raising my spirits. I could understand why people here got cabin fever from the long, dark Winter when it was too cold to go outside unless absolutely necessary.

Leonard came home March 13th, and the first thing we did was to return the rocking chair to Constable Stanley and Carol. I appreciated its use, but after four and a half months, it was time to return it. I baked a blueberry-cranberry pie as a thank-you gift for their kindness in loaning it to me.

Sylvia loves to go outside, especially when she is in her sled with Sky pulling her. And she is growing so fast! She is sitting up by herself and even attempting to crawl. Actually, all she does is fall over from her sitting position and wiggle forward a bit until she gets frustrated, and then she cries. Leonard had to cut the legs shorter on the baby bed, when we saw Sylvia pulling herself up and leaning over the side.

Then April brought good and bad - forty degree weather and bears. With hibernation over, bears were roaming the hillsides, looking for food. Squirrels, voles, and rabbits must be a very small meal for such big bears. I haven't seen bears in town, but people say bears sometimes come to dig in the trash heaps people have yet to clean up after the Winter.

One day, Malinda came running over, saying Walt heard caribou were migrating near Dawson City. He hadn't seen them, but we rushed to the Yukon, hoping to catch a glimpse of the herds. Some described over one thousand animals heading to their far north calving grounds. The old timers here say that when the ice is gone, caribou swim across the river. Oh, how I hoped they would cross where we could see them. It must be a spectacular sight, but alas, we saw none.

With the snow melting fast, we've been talking about when to leave this Summer. We know we can't take much with us, just our clothes and the sled. It will be perfect for other sled-rides back home, with Sky pulling Sylvia across the farm fields.

Last year the ice broke here in Dawson City on May 8th, sometime in the early evening. I wondered when it would melt, or break-up as it is usually called, this year. Mrs. Morgan said towards the latter part of April, someone will start a betting sheet, where people can guess the day and time the ice will break. A year ago in late April, we were at Lake Bennett, cutting trees and sawing logs, building the scows, and getting ready to come down the river. Now, once again we wait for the ice to break. Will it be late April or early May this year?

Old timers say the sights and sounds of break-up are something never to be forgotten. Large chunks of ice, sometimes more than four feet thick, creak and grind against the ice mass. The noise is likened to two freight trains roaring through town, crashing into each other. Blocks of ice often can be seen being tossed into the air, some landing on the river banks along Front Street. When it starts to move, everyone in town runs to the river to watch the spectacle. It must be exciting, and I admit I anxiously await the experience.

Spring also brings the wild flowers. Some of the first are the wild crocus poking their heads through the melting snow adding lovely shades of lilac and pink to the now dirty snow. Birds have arrived and must be building nests nearby. I hope cats will not get them, though I don't remember seeing any cats in Dawson City. I suppose they must be indoor cats, because cats would be just the right size meal for eagles or bears.

When the river runs again, the town will await the arrival of the first steamboats coming up river. That will mean fresh foods and supplies for folks waiting to take that first bite of a crisp Washington apple. I wonder if more men will come in on the steamboats, or if the tide has turned?

Leonard talked more and more about when to leave. We will wait until the clean-up is nearly finished, but our thoughts have definitely turned toward the family and farm in Wisconsin. We heard little from Henry during the Winter, only two short letters, one at Christmas time and another in late February, asking how things were going. Leonard answered both, giving a good report of time spent at the mine and the good signs of gold he has seen when small amounts from the dump are washed.

Then April 26th came, a day that changed Dawson City forever! Walt had come home the night before, and we enjoyed a nice supper together. The weather was delightfully warm, and we eagerly awaited break-up. But nothing could have prepared the town for a disaster the magnitude of the one that occurred.

FIRE! Another fire! This one started in the Bodega Saloon though I don't recall anyone saying how it started. Flames shot into the air and the conflagration spread from building to building with lightning speed.

The river was frozen, just as it was during the October fire. After the other fire, the city had paid the balance owed on the trucks and had the equipment insured. All should have gone as anticipated, with trucks pumping water from the river to control the fire. But just last week, the firefighters, hired by the city, had walked off the job, demanding more money. The fires in the boilers, needed to keep the trucks operating, had been allowed to go out. Thus, when the fire began, the boiler fires had to be re-lit. It took time to get up the steam needed to run the boilers and water pumps.

There was no wind, and the flames went straight up, but as quickly as a building caught fire and collapsed, sparks shot onto other buildings and started them ablaze. Finally, with boilers operating and holes chopped in the river ice, the hoses were laid, but the water temperature was so cold it froze in the hoses before it could even get to the fires!

Men ran ahead of the fire, and using dynamite, they blasted buildings down to cut a firebreak. Paradise Alley was torched, as flames shot skyward. Some of the oldest buildings along Front Street were consumed quickly. Big saloons like the Pioneer and the Northern went up in smoke. The Aurora was blown up; the Opera House consumed by flames. Downtown Dawson City was gone.

The fires burned cabin after cabin, tent after tent, business after business. Even the Bank of British North America went the way of other buildings. And there was very little anyone could do to stop it. In all, some 120 businesses and homes were destroyed. Those buildings left standing were covered in frozen mud, as men again used buckets of water and wet blankets to beat out flames.

Leonard and Walt joined every other available man to help. Malinda and I watched from inside our cabin, ready to leave with Sylvia and Sky if we felt at all in danger. We watched all night, fearing to sleep lest we might be caught unawares.

By the next afternoon, it was over. But there was no joy in the city. No lives had been lost, and for that we all gave thanks, but the city was gone, its heart burned out. Men walked around in a daze, realizing how much had been destroyed. Some poked among the ruins looking for anything which might be salvaged.

I thought of the gold stored at the bank, wondering if it melted and how they would ever know how much each person had lost. Our money and gold was in another bank, but that did not stop us from thinking about the misfortunes of others.

Yet, within a day, saloons were back in business, operating in tents. I suppose the first saloons were also in tents. The citizens took hammers-in-hand and started re-building, but the quaint charm of the old town was gone. Even though the town was really only three years old, there had been a feeling of stability to it.

Soon a new Dawson City rose from the ashes. Now the city took the opportunity to install sewer pipes and surface the streets to cut down on the Summer dust and the mud in the Spring and Fall. Plans were made to build schools, construct substantial business establishments, and build homes instead of cabins and tents. Even though many realized the mad rush for the gold was over, the city would remain. Many claims have been bought by large companies, and these companies needed homes and schools for families, and businesses were needed to supply the needs of the permanent residents.

Leonard left to go back to the claim on May 1st. He was very concerned about the conditions down in the mining pits. Already, small waterfalls could be seen running down the hills behind the town. If it was warm enough for streams to run, then the ground ice also would be thawing. He didn't want anyone deep in the mines working in very cold run-off. He returned May 4th, saying their men were cleaning up the flumes, preparing for the big clean-up.

Shortly after his return, the Yukon River started grinding and creaking. Break up would not be long in coming. Somehow though, the city was too busy rebuilding to take much heed of the river, and Malinda and I were busy moving their things from Henry's cabin to ours. We had received a letter from Henry, saying he was at Lake Bennett and would come by the first steamboat down river.

We boxed up winter coats, parkas, gloves, hats, and boots. We sorted through clothes, packing only the essential ones knowing we could not take everything. I made sure the special towel used so often on the trail and the river was packed along with the little overalls. Furniture would not be taken. The freight was prohibitively expensive.

Leonard built a wooden box big enough for the sled, and inside it we packed as much as we could. The clothes we decided not to take were given to the church for sale. Over a year ago we packed pots and pans, bags and tins of food, and clothing we thought necessary for our trip here. Now, we planned to leave with only our clothes, a few other things, and the gold nuggets we wanted to keep. The majority of the gold would be exchanged for some cash and bank notes which were easier to carry and certainly the safest way to take money back home.

One day we realized the ice was gone! We had not heard the bells or horns which were supposed to sound when the river broke. We had missed it! I realized the city had more to do than watch the ice break. There was a new city being built, and everyone wanted the city ready when the steamboats arrived. No burned-out city would greet newcomers. Instead, a bigger and better city would await the arrival of the boats.

May 11th came, and with it memories of a wonderful surprise birthday at Lake Bennett. It also meant Sky was a year old. Leonard gave me a ring, made of Yukon gold nuggets, so I would always remember our time here. It was absolutely beautiful and certainly one of a kind, but in my heart I knew I would never ever forget neither the journey here nor all the months we've been living here in the heart of the Klondike gold rush.

By mid-May, the men were up on the claim, washing gold from the partially frozen dump. They worked in week-long shifts now, each bringing the recovered gold back to town when he returned. Leonard handled all the records and accounting at home. He wanted to make sure everything was up to date when Henry arrived. Malinda and I thoroughly cleaned Henry's place, even washed the windows. Walt and Leonard even chinked some walls of Henry's cabin with moss.

By June it was daylight over nineteen hours each day. The snow was gone completely, and the mosquitoes were making up for lost time, biting any skin not covered, even biting through long sleeve cotton shirts. I was still washing Alex's shirts, and now that Sylvia could entertain herself somewhat, I was able to do more of his laundry, adding gold to our ever-growing nugget pile. I had no idea how much we had, but we knew we had enough to buy some farm equipment and build us a house.

June came with a burst of wild flowers on the hillsides and with birds everywhere. Ducks and their ducklings swam in the Klondike River. The geese had long since flown north to their nesting grounds. Spring quickly turned to Summer as it does up here. There is really no Spring or Fall like we have in Wisconsin. Temperatures occasionally reached into the seventies, and it was light much of the time.

Now it was time to wait. When would Henry come? Surely he was on the river by now. Steamboats had come in from down river, but we anxiously awaited the first steamboat from Lake Bennett to the south.

Then early one morning, the whistles blew in town. The steamboat had arrived. Malinda and I rushed to Front Street, with Sylvia holding me tight around my neck with her little hands. I was sorry both Leonard and Walt were up on the claim. Leonard had left yesterday, and Walt was due back this afternoon.

Dawson City turned out for the steamboat's arrival. Soon it tied up to the shore with the gangplank in place. Men and women began to descend into a new Dawson City. We kept watching for Henry, but there were so many coming down the gangplank, we were afraid we might miss him. Then suddenly we saw him, and we waved and shouted. He saw us and came over, giving us a big hug. He introduced us to his wife, Lucile, and his son, Bill, ten years old, and his daughter, Ellen, a lovely seven-year-old. I introduced them to Sylvia. Leonard had written, in one of his letters to Henry, about Sylvia's arrival, and now they got to meet her in person.

While Henry and Bill waited for the bags and bundles, the rest of us went home. I invited them to share supper with us, but first we showed Lucile and Ellen the cabin, which would be their home until they went out in the Fall. I was glad Malinda had suggested we pick a bouquet of wild flowers for their table.

Walt returned in the late afternoon and was excited to see Henry again. Supper lasted a long time; or rather we sat at the table a long time, just talking. Walt wanted Leonard to go over all the accounts with Henry, so he declined to tell him anything other than to say things looked really good on the site.

The evening was really special, talking with Henry and Lucile while Bill played outside with Sky, and Ellen entertained Sylvia on the floor. Finally, though almost too soon, Henry and his family went back to their cabin. Malinda and I cleaned up the dishes while Walt straightened up the table and chairs. Very soon Henry would go to his claim, joining Leonard there.

Sylvia is now sleeping peacefully, and Malinda and Walt have gone for a walk. I am bringing my journal up to date, writing how glad I am Henry and his family can share time with us before we leave. I know Leonard and I and Walt and Malinda have been blessed beyond measure. Little Sylvia is a blessing and a miracle from God. Malinda and Walt are so happy together, and they know how fortunate they are, turning a bad future for Malinda into a beautiful marriage. I wish Leonard were here tonight. I look around our cabin knowing we will be leaving soon. I will miss the coziness of this log cabin in the North. Finally, I give Sky a goodnight scratch under her chin, kiss Sylvia goodnight, and go to bed.

# <u>32</u>

## GOING HOME

### July 6 - Time to Enjoy Dawson City Before We Leave

Leonard was to relieve Walt on June 22nd, but Walt came home with Henry on the 20th instead. Henry wanted to celebrate the Summer solstice with his family, so he had brought Walt along, too.

The next day, Malinda and I packed a picnic lunch of bread, butter, sliced moose roast, and some tomatoes for us and the Jonathans. Lucile made potato salad and brought bottles of punch to drink. I also made my blueberry-cranberry pie, using the last of our berries. With Sylvia tucked into a canvas sling I made for one of the old pack frames we had used on the trail, we set off.

We had never climbed to the top of the Midnight Dome, sometimes called the Moosehide Slide. With the sun up on the longest day of the year, almost twenty-two hours, it was a perfect time to make the climb. We were not the only ones climbing to the top. There must have been at least fifty who started up when we did.

As we climbed, Henry told us we were following a trail taken by miners when they went to cut timber. We passed the local cemetery, now blooming in beautiful wild blue lupine with long spikes of blooms waving above the wild grasses. Yellow arnica and reddish-purple fireweed added to the tapestry of colors carpeting the hillside.

It was a beautiful day to be outside. The weather was warm, and as we climbed, Sky scampered ahead, occasionally sitting down on the trail, waiting for us as if to say, "Hurry up! I want to see what's around the next bend!" I looked ahead at Leonard with little Sylvia on his back. As always, his back was straight and his shoulders squared to the world. Ellen was right behind him, showing a flower to Sylvia, who tried to grab it and couldn't, but laughed instead. Henry led the way with Bill right behind him. What a joy it is for Henry to have his family here for the Summer season. Lucile and Malinda were right behind me, with Walt last. Lucile is a delightful person and is glad Henry insisted the family come, though she has said she didn't think she could ever survive the cold Winters.

What a view awaited us when we reached the top! We looked far across the Yukon River to the Alaska Range beyond. We could see miles up the Yukon River. There were hundreds of islands in the river, and how well I remember the men straining at the oars, keeping the scows to the right bank as we approached Dawson City last June. In the vast wilderness of the river basin beyond Dawson City, I saw not one single column of smoke from a chimney, not a single boat on the river, indeed not a single thing to indicate people were out there.

Below, the city was bustling, doing the everyday business in the saloons, hotels, banks, and mercantile stores. Yet only a few miles upriver, the land was silent and empty. A year ago, we had been on the river with thousands of others racing to Dawson City to get the gold. Now the race was over. As I stood there, quietly absorbed in my own thoughts, I realized the river was not without boats. In the far distance I could see a steamboat coming to Dawson City. Soon others would arrive at the City of Gold.

Sitting on a big bed sheet Lucile had brought, we really enjoyed our picnic and the view. Henry said many folks climbed up, planning to be on top at midnight, usually arriving in time to see the sun slide behind the far mountains for its short night, only to reappear a little over two hours later.

It was a wonderful day, and a perfect way to celebrate the longest day of the year. As we started down, Henry suggested we stay up late to watch the midnight softball game, which usually started about 11 PM. The players, with energy to burn, played softball at midnight. Where else could they do that?

After supper, Walt and Leonard had their heads bent over a calendar. It was just a year and a half ago they sat at the table in the family kitchen at home, doing the very same thing. At that time, they were deciding when to begin our trip to the Klondike. Now, they were trying to decide when to go back home. That year and a half has encompassed experiences we will never forget, for they have changed us in so many ways.

The men wanted to stay until most of the clean-up was finished. Yet, they wanted to leave with plenty of time to take the trip upriver and back over the mountains to Skagway. They knew, from Henry, that it took about ten days to reach Skagway where we would board a steamship south.

We did go watch the softball game, knowing if we didn't go, we would later wish we had taken the time to do it. I'm not really sure anyone at home would understand why we did these things, but it was important to us.

Leonard left with Henry the next morning. Now I got busy packing so we could leave shortly after the Fourth of July. Henry had said the train being built over the White Pass was just about completed to Lake Bennett making it unnecessary to hike back over the trail. I was only too happy to hear that news as I didn't want to repeat that hike back over the trail.

Lucile came over asking if we slept well. She and the children were having a terrible time sleeping because of the constant daylight. Malinda told her we had had the same problem last Summer until we finally put canvas over the windows. During the day we simply pulled them up to let in the sunshine.

Leonard and Henry were to come home on June 30th to enjoy the two celebrations - Dominion Day and the 4th of July. The day before, I left Malinda with Sylvia sleeping quietly in her bed. I wanted to get some tomatoes from Mrs. Morgan, who was always most gracious about selling me a few. I wish I could have gotten some corn, but the growing season is just too short to grow certain vegetables.

We would celebrate both holidays this year since we plan to leave on or about July 6th. Walt had checked at the steamship office to see if a steamboat would be coming about that time. If the boat was on time, it would arrive on the 8th, and leave later that afternoon to go back upriver.

Malinda and I had packed most everything in several of the crates we had saved. These Walt labeled and took to the steamship office. He also purchased tickets for the four of us, since Sylvia would go free. He told them we were taking Sky, and the agent said a lot of people going Outside took at least one of their dogs, but Sky would have to be tied up on deck. We could not take her into the cabins he reserved for us.

When Henry and Leonard got home, they went to the bank to deposit the gold. The claim panned out much better than anyone anticipated. Leonard and Walt sat at the table, while Henry calculated what he owned them, and both were surprised to get more than $22,000 each! On Monday July 3rd, the three of them went to the bank, and Henry paid them what was owed plus a bonus for doing such a good job. Leonard converted most of the gold into bank notes, but we wanted to take home some gold nuggets to share with those who had helped us - family, church members, and Walt's aunt and uncle, Sheila and Lloyd Michaels who had given us the $300 at the beginning of our trip. We also wanted a special nugget for Mrs. Palmerston in Seattle. I had received a letter from her, saying she still had the trunk and looked forward to seeing us. She would even have our two rooms ready for us, and she was most anxious to meet Sylvia and Malinda.

Now, it was time to join the festivities once again. And like last year, the Union Jack flew from every hotel balcony and any flag pole. Music blared from the dance halls for three days. The saloons did a roaring business, and gambling and drinking went on all night. Policemen walked along Front Street keeping order, and arresting those who had too much to drink. And again as had happened last year, suddenly the flags were changed to the American red, white, and blue for the Fourth of July celebrations.

It was an unusual time for us, though. We wanted to celebrate, but at the same time, we were rather sad. In just a few days we would be leaving a place we had come to love. In many ways it was our home; certainly it was the place of Sylvia's birth. And by such birth, Sylvia was now a citizen of both Canada and America! Later, she could decide for herself if she wanted to keep the dual citizenship or declare only one country as her home. What an adventure she has had so far in her young life. Though she will not remember it, she has been a part of the living history of the Klondike Gold Rush.

July 8 - The Time Has Come to Leave

I write now after we have been underway up river for several hours. I simply couldn't write any sooner, and I am not sure I can write my feelings now, but I must try.

I got up very early this morning, wanting to bake bread to take with us. Malinda and I had prepared some food to take, though we knew meals were provided on the ship.

After breakfast, there was a knock at the door, and we greeted Al and Margaret Petersen from Montreal, Canada, who had bought our cabin. He had been transferred here a week ago to work in one of the government offices. They heard we were leaving and came by, hoping we would sell them our cabin. We sold it for the same $100 we had paid for it, and all papers were signed. They had come to see us off and to give us a box of chocolates. Somehow, even as much as I loved chocolate, I would have given the box back if we could have stayed longer, though I knew staying longer would only make leaving all the harder.

We shared time together, drinking one last cup of tea and thinking again of Ian and Liam. The bread was finished baking, and turned out nicely on the counter to cool. Then suddenly, I was flooded with memories of the day we left Clinton. Here again the aroma of the freshly-baked bread filled the room and brought back so many thoughts of that last day on the farm. I wanted to curl my feet under me and stay here. How often had baking bread brought back those memories of the wonderful kitchen on the farm? Most certainly here, but also along the way here, though it was usually fried biscuits on the trail and on the river. I don't think I will ever bake another loaf of bread without memories of this great adventure coming back to mind. I really believe that bread is the fundamental element of life and love.

Too soon, Henry and his family came to help us carry the few bags we had to the dock. Bill and Ellen shared the duty of keeping Sky on her leash. Poor Sky. She simply did not understand why now, all of a sudden, she had to be roped up.

Finally, it was time to board. Mrs. Morgan had come to see us off, and with tears in my eyes, I bid her farewell. She hugged Sylvia and even hugged Leonard, and that was quite a sight. Mrs. Morgan is about 5 feet 4 inches tall, and Leonard towered over her by at least a foot. Leonard tucked a small box into her hand and left before she could see what it was. We had had a local jeweler make her a gold brooch, depicting a gold pan with tiny nuggets in the bottom, a reminder of the gold discovery here in Dawson City.

As we started up the gangplank, someone called our names. We turned to see Ian and Liam running towards us and right behind them was Alex, the special man who insisted I did the best job ever washing his shirts.

We stepped aside to let others pass, and as tears of sorrow at parting filled my eyes, I hugged each one of them. Liam pressed a gold poke into my hands saying, "We're blessed beyond all measure from our El Dorado claims. We've also been so blessed to have had the joy of sharing yar family as ours." Ian told us to use the gold to build our dream house. How could I tell them our little cabin had been our dream house?

The whistle blew, and I knew it was time to board, but I didn't want to leave. The men all shook hands, and even hugs were exchanged. Then unable to stop crying, I hugged everyone and walked up and onto the boat deck. Again, the whistle sounded, and we waved good-bye from the ship's railing. Ropes were untied and tossed on board. The engines began to move us into the river, and we were off. Slowly we turned, heading back the way we had come so long ago.

We stood on the back deck, watching Dawson City slowly recede into the distance. We looked at the scar on the hill, which we had searched for last Summer. Now, we were going the other direction, back up river.

As we rounded the bend, the city and the scar disappeared. Leonard held me close while we waved one last good-bye to the place we had called home for over a year. We would never forget Dawson City. Once it gets in your heart, I don't think anyone could forget the wonderful little community and its friendly people. It was not the prettiest or cleanest of cities. The streets were muddy, the miners from the creeks were dirty, and it certainly didn't have many of the resources of a big city. But it was Dawson City, our city, and we loved it every bit as much as if it had been Paris, New York, Chicago, or even Clinton, Wisconsin. In our minds, we were really leaving home again as we had done over a year ago.

We had come for the gold. True, we did not actually mine the gold on our own claim. We earned it by hard, honest work. But we found within ourselves a wealth of strength to continue pursuing our dreams. Just getting to Dawson City over that treacherous trail of snow, across the Chilkoot Pass, and down to Lake Bennett had been a monumental task. Then we had to build boats and wait for the river of ice to break before running the 550 miles of lakes, rapids, and river. That was in itself the completion of a dream.

We also found richness beyond measure in new neighbors, friends, and a new church in a great land where beauty beyond measure or description can be found, if one only took the time to look around. We leave with a beautiful little girl, Sylvia Mae Stanton, a true daughter of the Klondike, born in the City of Gold.

We leave behind an incredible land laced with endless Summer light, or wrapped in the dark nights of Winter, when it is silent under a blanket of snow.

We have lived our dream and made it come true. Dawson City is in our blood, and we will not let it fade away even though we leave now. We will return, not for the metal gold, but for the gold found in the people of Dawson City and the beautiful mountains we saw every day. We have learned we can accomplish anything we set our minds to do. We vow to return one day with Sylvia, and maybe a little brother or sister, to show her and tell her of our great love for this place.

I leaned toward Leonard as he hugged me closer. Alex had slipped him a small poke, saying it was for Sylvia to come back to her home here in Dawson City someday. Tears streamed down my cheeks. I couldn't stop them even if I tried, and I really didn't try.

I looked at Malinda and Walt, knowing they felt the same as we did. They, too, had a gold poke from Ian and Liam, but I also shared a secret with Malinda. They were taking home something more precious than gold, and I wondered if she had told Walt yet. We smiled at each other knowing, that before the end of the year, there would be a little Jackson in the family. Some gold is more precious than the golden metal we came for.

Sky sat quietly at our feet, rubbing against my legs. She, too, would soon have her own little puppies. These we would share with Leonard's nieces, Mary Jane and Martha Anne, and hope they would like names like Tundra and Klondike.

Quietly, we watched the river and the islands slip by. We were going home, though at the same time we were leaving home. We have been blessed indeed and are rich beyond all measure. And for that we were most thankful.

I whispered a prayer of thanksgiving to God for giving us the blessings we have shared with some wonderful friends from California and especially to Sylvia's two "grandpas" from Scotland, knowing with all my heart He has been with us each and every step of the way. By His good grace, we have lived our dream and leave now to dream even more.

# Marte Franklin

Photo by Elaine Folsom

      Marte Franklin first enjoyed camping with her family as a child when they visited our National Parks. This enjoyment of the outdoors followed her as she began backpacking in the Grand Canyon in Arizona, the Sierra Nevada Mountains in California, and backcountry areas in Idaho and Alaska. River rafting added to her adventures as she rafted the Green River in Utah, the Middle Fork of the Salmon in Idaho, rivers in California, and the Colorado River through the Grand Canyon. It was after a kayak/raft trip down the Yukon River from Whitehorse to Dawson City in Yukon, Canada, that she developed an interest in the Klondike Gold Rush of 1898. This then became a passion as she returned to Alaska and Canada to begin her research on the Gold Rush.

      She has written numerous magazine articles for national and local city magazines in the United States and Canada. She has also written many poems on the wilderness country she has visited.